D1639473

90710 000 480 370

CULT
FOLLOWING

CULT
FOLLOWING

**MY ESCAPE AND RETURN TO
THE CHILDREN OF GOD**

BEXY CAMERON

MANILLA
PRESS

First published in the UK by Manilla Press
An imprint of Bonnier Books UK
The Plaza, 535 Kings Road, London, SW10 0SZ
Owned by Bonnier Books
Sveavägen 56, Stockholm, Sweden

Hardback – 9781-7-86580-92-4
Trade Paperback – 978-1-786580-93-1
Ebook – 978-1-786580-94-8

A CIP catalogue of this book is available from the British Library.

Typeset by IDSUK (Data Connection) Ltd

Bexy Cameron ... the author of this
work in a ... Act 1988.

Every reasonable effort has been made to trace copyright holders of material
reproduced in this book, but if any have been inadvertently overlooked the
publishers would be glad to hear from them.

This book is a work of non-fiction, based on the life, experiences and
recollections of Bexy Cameron. Certain details in this story, including names,
have been changed to protect identity and privacy.

Manilla Press is an imprint of Bonnier Books UK
www.bonnierbooks.co.uk

This book is dedicated to the kids I grew up with.

To the ones who've flourished, the ones still in trauma, the ones who have struggled, the ones who 'made it', and the beautiful souls that decided that this world, and that pain, was not for them anymore.

See you on the other side.

Contents

Tell Me Everything: 15 Years After

'Please, tell me everything.'

I have heard this in the pub, at 4am at house parties, at my desk at work. The person asking could be a friend, sometimes it's a complete stranger. It can come from a face filled with pity, one wet with excitement, from one that's serious, or even well meaning.

'Tell me everything' comes when people find out that I'm a 'Sex Cult Girl'.

And it's why I sit here now, in this truck, 15 years after I left the 'Children of God', parked under an Arizonan night full of stars. It's what drove me to this vast stretch of desert, why I'm surrounded by the ticking sounds of an engine cooling and the shallow night breaths of Sofi, my friend and fellow filmmaker, asleep behind me. It's what made me leave my home in London, my brothers and sisters, and my job, to re-join the world of religious communes and cults.

The words 'tell me everything' supercharge my brain in an instant, explosions of memories, while physically I become vacant, mute. Not because I'm afraid of sharing darkness, or my history, or even because this *might* be the moment where

I could completely change in your eyes. It's just that a chat in the pub, or in the witching hours at an afterparty, or over a cup of whatever at work doesn't provide the space, time or depth to tell someone 'everything'. What I was born into was as banal as it was unbelievable, as traumatic as it was *my* ordinary, as complex as it was controlled. And, *perhaps* I have just described 'growing up', perhaps our childhoods have more similarities than we know.

And even though I have achieved more than the 15-year-old me leaving the gates of a cult could ever have imagined, I still feel like an imposter. Maybe now more than ever. Sitting here, more than 5,000 miles from home, after joining yogic communes, Armageddonist tribes and cosmologists in Sedona, battling my demons and myself, four months into a journey that seems far from over.

So, to 'tell you everything', what *could* I give you in five minutes that might reveal what it was like being raised in a 'Sex Cult'?

Do you want to hear about a generation of kids, fuelled by the war in Vietnam, who genuinely believed that the world was coming to an end? Or the charismatic leader who gave them purpose, rescuing them from the families they didn't fit into, from drug addiction or maybe just the horror of being middle class and *normal*?

Or do you want to hear about my exorcism? About when the moms became glorified prostitutes for Jesus? About my parents going on every media channel in the UK and beyond to defend a group that abused thousands of children? Or would you prefer to hear about the summers I spent running like a feral child with my brothers in Africa? The hot, hot days napping on cold floors in India when I felt like I was in a normal family? Would it help to know that where we come from, my childhood is considered a 'lucky one', that my sisters and I talk about how fortunate we are because '*Dad isn't a paedophile*'?

Would any of this really give you an idea of who I am, or the world I grew up in? You would get fractions of it all, sure. But out-of-context splinters like these could pull you further away from both me and what a story like this could reveal about our basic human need for connection and purpose, about surviving our childhoods, about the gifts that trauma can bring, and maybe at some point, what we, actually . . . hopefully, what *I*, could learn about forgiveness.

But as my fingers stroke this very real dashboard, my frame to this very real adventure through America, I still can't quite wrap my head around how all of *that* brought me *here*. Of course, I know it's to try and understand my parents, to figure out my tangled history with a cult that did so much damage and to get a little closer to 'my truth' but still, it seems, sitting here, a pretty batshit idea.

I would love for you to think that I'm a warrior rising out of the ashes of a cult, or a hero righting the wrongs of the past, or a filmmaker with a master plan. I would even settle for you think-ing I'm an objective person, able to give unskewed versions of what I see, the secrets I reveal, or the things I experience. But the truth is, I really have no idea what I'm doing.

The ticking of the engine slows, the smell of petrol fades as my mind escapes from the front seat of the truck. I rise above myself, parked up in the desert, flying higher and higher until my Ford pickup becomes a tiny dot in a massive expanse of emptiness. The unknown. High above a truck that feels like it's taking me through time, space, faith, trauma and healing. A truck that is my wings on a road trip of meltdowns, breakdowns, meth cooks, monks and soap-making Armageddonists.

All in the hope that by the end of this journey, I can tell you *everything*.

CHAPTER 1

Prophets That Prey: 1968

He was a prophet.
He was a paedophile.
He was a dictator.
He was Grandpa.

David Berg, Dad. Father David, Moses David. The King . . . These are some of the names of the Leader of the Children of God, the cult I was born and raised in until the age of 15. I didn't even know what he looked like until I was a teenager. Us kids called him Grandpa. His identity was so secret that, instead of photos, we grew up with drawings of him. Cartoons. Like a dictatorship, surrounded and commanded by an overlord that you cannot touch or see. We read his new writings every single day. Everything he did was recorded. His dreams. His declarations. His bowel movements. Yes, they would write down how and when he would take a shit and we would read about it.

Looking back through adult eyes, I see him as a dogmatic, sexually motivated, gibberish-talking, narcissistic, corrupt, dangerous pervert. As a child, to me, he was all-powerful, confusing, but also boring in a way that a fish doesn't know it's in water: he was our ordinary, he was everywhere, but his unstable mind could change our lives within an instant. Understanding him is difficult. He was not a handsome Charles Manson, or even a David Koresh, he was a balding, grey-haired, sunken-eyed man born in 1919, who somehow managed to persuade thousands of people to forsake their lives and follow him. Including one woman from a tiny village in Derbyshire and a man from a seaside town in Kent. *My parents.* Without him, they would not have married. Without him, I wonder if I would have been born.

The history I *knew* about David Berg was fabricated by him, stories that he wrote about himself with a grandiose pen. I loathe giving him airtime when so much of my childhood was taken and polluted by this piece of shit. But in this dig around in my past, and then my parents' history, I have to go back to the source and that's him. To understand them, and then to understand me, I have to try to work out how a failed preacher with obvious deviancies managed to inspire a worldwide movement, which at one point had 25,000 members.

I suppose at the crux of it, I want to know how David Berg 'tricked' my parents.

* * *

This is where this journey – and story – starts, long before I was born, back in the 1960s and while this isn't my parents' story, and it absolutely isn't David Berg's, it is the beginning, whether I like it or not. As a child, I was taught this was our moment of creation: this was the point where our world began. The late 1960s were, unquestionably, a time of great change and this was a decade that gave birth to many cults.

A few years ago, I went to an exhibition in London titled *Revolution*. I wanted to see this decade from a fresh perspective. Immediately, I was sucked into a world of lyrics, movements, art and cultural shifts. The poetry of Bob Dylan, photographs of the race riots and the sound of 'Eve of Destruction' playing in my museum walk-about headphones were enough to stir something in my gut. Fuck the man. Abandon the conveyor belt. Rebel from the past. Even with my loaded history, I felt it. A film about Woodstock lit up every wall, media types and tourists lay around on beanbags, soaking up the revolutionary atmosphere – whether it was Jimi Hendrix centre stage, nude hippies off their chops, or Janis Joplin's pained performances – decades after the fact. Standing in the middle of this exhibition, I could feel the catalytic ripples of transformation.

Imagine actually being there. Imagine growing up in rural England, in a 2.5-child family, a member of a church, going to a girls' or boys' school amid the contrast of the revolution. Imagine being in Middle America – raised in the fifties – when advertising was at its apex of selling the family home ideal – it was *everything* and post-war, 'toe the line' attitudes were *everywhere*.

And then, suddenly ... Vietnam. Civil rights. Women's rights. The sexual revolution. Counterculture started to surge, spawning a generation whose minds were cracked open by injustice and fuelled by psychedelics. LSD factories were popping up in California, supplying kids who wanted to love their neighbours way more than they wanted to bomb other nations. Love and Peace were weaponised; Allen Ginsberg inspired a new type of riot, War for Peace; young people armed themselves with guerrilla theatre and flower bombs. A young Abbie Hoffman declared, 'The cry of Flower Power echoes through the land. We Shall not wilt.' The revolution budded, then bloomed.

This was a generation that demanded change. And in the case of my parents, that change was not coming quickly enough politically, globally or locally. So, when the change they were craving came to them, they not only accepted it, but would give up their lives, identities and emotional ties to receive it. There is a part of me, even retrospectively, knowing what came to pass later, that respects my parents during this time. The rebelliousness, the ideology, the piss and vinegar to 'drop out'. This spiritual awakening is where the leader of the Children of God emerges, birthed in the viscous rebellion, on the sands of Huntington Beach.

Huntington Beach was to Southern California what Haight-Ashbury was to San Francisco. The epicentre for counterculture; drugs, long hair, sun and free love, and it's where David Berg started to preach to the hippies and the birth of the Children of God began. *Our Creation. Our Big Bang.* As children, we were told about this moment in the same way that I imagine other kids are told about Santa. It was painted as, and seemed like, pure magic. Picture a man in his fifties, white hair, white beard, giving out peanut butter and jelly sandwiches on a beach. Sun-soaked, salty air and a side of Christ. Day after day, the hippies would come back and the congregation of long-haired, dropout misfits soon grew. The birthing of the Children of God is one of perspective, revisionism and PR. This is the story that I was told, growing up. The great vision of a great man, the organic tumbling of a movement, in a world that was ripe for change.

And this is certainly *a* version. But it's not the only one.

It's like your whole life, you've had a painting in front of you, you're familiar with every brush stroke, every line, every colour, and then you reach an age, or a moment, or a feeling where you start to scratch at it, because maybe something on it never felt right. You scratch a corner and it reveals something underneath. Some colours are the same, maybe a few lines cross over, but the picture is tainted. You keep scratching until the painting reveals itself. Sinister. Twisted. Scratching until you lose a nail. But it finally makes more sense.

Understanding why a movement starts, especially one as rebellious or potentially extreme as this one, is not just about the context of the situation. It's also about the context of the man; a mix of ingredients that make it so potent and powerful. What need did this group fill for people like my parents? And in the case of the Children of God, what need, craving or purpose for David Berg was *the group* serving?

* * *

David Brandt Berg was born in 1919 to travelling evangelists Hjalmer Emanuel Berg and Virginia Lee Brandt. But it's David Berg's mama who had the most influence on him. If I allow my mind to stray, I create a relationship between them like the mother and son in a Hitchcock film: over-doting (controlling) mother, Oedipus complex, creepy co-dependency, classic psychopath territory. But this story really doesn't need sprinkles (although one 'sprinkle' does come from the multiple stories we were read as kids, where Grandpa dreamed that he had a 'tender, but hot' sexual relationship with his mama).

Virginia was one of the first successful female travelling evangelists in the United States. I find this important, as it gives a role model for David Berg within this world. She always knew that David would be the one to follow in her footsteps. Out of her three kids, he was the extraordinary one to her. The *special* one. The *chosen* one. Virginia started her own tabernacle tent throwing huge 'revivals' for audiences ranging up to 7,000 people. Imagine being her son, watching her from the wooden makeshift pews with thousands of other followers, the awe of looking up at the face of this *woman*, among a sea of sweaty, pious men, the smell of sawdust and body odour thick in the air, Virginia's face pumping out the bright essence of God. How could you *not* look up to her and want to emulate her? How could you *not* want to emanate and imbibe the power of the Almighty?

And so, David Berg grew up with his mother on a pedestal, literally, a pulpit. And judging by his accounts, she had one for him too. He was her special boy, destined to live a life 'for the Lord' and in the spotlight. And she was right. In the late 1930s, David Berg, in his twenties, joined his mother in her work, as her chauffeur, song leader and general assistant. Then, in the 1950s, he went on to his own pastorate, in a church called Valley Farms. And here, again, are two versions of this.

In both versions, David Berg's pastorate was short-lived and ill-fated.

Version One: While at Valley Farms, David Berg invited Native Americans to worship with the all-white congregation. The Valley Farm flock freaked out, they didn't want them in church. David told them that they were 'a pack of racists' and then he left, disillusioned with the state of Christians and the immorality of the church system. This is where he says his rebellious attitude and seething distrust of the establishment began. And these feelings of rebellion and disillusionment were building in tandem with, and perhaps in preparation for, the wave of revolution that was just on the horizon. He was bang on track.

This version ties in beautifully with the idea that David Berg is a man of the people, a 'dropout' himself, full of conviction; enough conviction to leave the Church and *everything* that he had worked for and wanted in life. It makes a hero and role model for our hippies: if he can do it, they can too.

Version Two (one that is more accepted as truth by his family, who were there at the time): David Berg didn't leave in a fit of righteousness. It was nothing to do with race or rebellion. He was expelled from the Church for sexual misconduct with a church employee. And like finding a kitten's skeleton in the childhood garden of a psychopath, this for me is one of the early signs of what was to come. The predilection of a man who could rewrite history to fit his needs and who would put his sexual desires above the 'work of the Lord'. This for me shows his corruption before the group was founded, points to him being not just a man who let power desensitise him once he became a messianic leader, but a man who perhaps had this in his plan all along.

And so, I keep scratching.

* * *

By the time the 1960s rolled around, David Berg and his wife, Jane, had had several children and they'd started their own travelling band of Christians called 'Teens for Christ'. David was not a lone old man yelling on a beach, a selling Armageddon, handing out peanut butter sandwiches. He had hippies by his side. Good-looking ones. *His kids.* They opened a mission called 'the Light House' on Huntington Beach pier, where they talked sweetly about love, belonging, going to heaven and finding your purpose. At this point, David Berg starts to metamorphosise into Father David; he got rid of his suit, dressed like a hippy, grew his beard and his hair, and he gave his sermons an update, preaching about the establishment or 'The System', the catch-all phrase at the time for the evil power structure that oppresses the masses, controls the world's economies, and creates war.

I try to put myself on that beach in the sixties. Perhaps I haven't been to my childhood suburban home since that last fight about Nixon, maybe I'm just exhausted from the fuckery I have seen in the world on a daily basis. I take a bite of that sweet and salty sandwich, my teeth ache as they mash through the cheap white bread, while someone talks to me about *my* life, *my* purpose, with mothering tenderness. I imagine that kindness on an acid comedown (or even after a big night that leaves me feeling vulnerable). Perhaps just the day before I asked myself what the point of life, work – in fact, ANYTHING – is. And now, someone is offering me a new way.

Maybe a better way.

David Berg told the hippies at the mission that they were just like the true 12 apostles of Christ – the original dropouts and rejects. He gave their status meaning. In an age of defiance, he capitalised on it by redirecting the youths' desire to rebel and protest. He used and manipulated scripture to back up his ideas of following the Lord and so following *him*, 'And when they had brought their ships to land, they forsook all, and followed him.'

To create a movement this powerful, it is crucial to get your followers to prove that they will put it above *everything* else. The concept of leaving father, mother, job, home, land and any other social influence was essential for full-time membership and essential for David Berg's plan. After all, the Bible was really clear about this too: 'So likewise, whosoever he be of you that forsaketh not all that he hath, he cannot be my disciple.' On Huntington Beach, it was the challenge that David Berg and the Teens for Christ put out to the hippies: 'Come! Forsake all and follow Jesus.' In a sense, many had already done that, many of them had taken the first step. They had already left their families and homes and jobs. All that was required was a slight variation in the direction of their lives to get them to do it for Jesus' sake.

And when it comes to proving that you believe, that you are worthy and that you are all in the same club, is there anything more real or potent than giving up *everything*? To build a community, is there anything more intoxicating than knowing that each and every disciple paid the same initiation price?

And here we come to our Big Bang.

For David Berg, this moment has been described by his daughter Deborah, who was 22 at the time, as his 'big break'. In his words, 'The hand of the Lord was beginning to move!' He had been waiting for his entire life. Now 49, finally his purpose had come, now was his chance to prove that he was worth something. And his natural hatred for the Church, the government and the world that had both failed him and that he had failed in, meant that when he preached, he preached with a raw authenticity. Because the words came from a very, very real place. It was powerful and it was passionate. His bitterness towards the Church; his rejection of the social establishment, the capitalist system: his contempt for parental authority – all crystallised into a Gospel of Rebellion.

And it was enough to start his own revolution.

When David spoke of rebellion, he skilfully tied in the beliefs of the young with his own ideology: 'The parents want them to follow in their footsteps in a selfish dog-eat-dog economy in which they not only murder one another, but they conduct massive slaughters of whole nations ... The young people are sick and fed up with what really amounts to a pagan, cruel, whoremongering, false Christianity. They're trying to return to the peace-loving religions of old, including ancient Christianity, and the parents will have none of it. So, who are the rebels? If you mean rebels against the looks of the ancients and the economy of the ancients, then the parents are the rebels.'

*   *   *

As they grew from the Teens for Christ into their hundreds, they moved out of The Light House to a ranch in the country. Believing the end of the world was nigh, they prophesied daily and spoke in tongues. They wore sackcloth robes, covered their faces in black ash and shouted 'Woe' in the streets to warn the world that the end was coming. Imagine the smell of soot on your face, the itch and dust of sackcloth, the screams of woe from hundreds of raw voices full of fury. It was RADICAL. This was a time of unsettling violence and oppression, and the teachings of Allen Ginsberg and Abbie Hoffman were being used with a very real purpose.

The end of the world was coming!

The way that David Berg spoke about his followers was with fire and pride – 'This is the real, one and only, genuine revolution that'll ever survive, because this is the revolutionary Kingdom of God and Jesus Christ!' – cementing their status as End Time prophets. The group moved into vans to pollinate this gospel throughout the United States. David gave group structure, spotting the kids that had leadership qualities and training them himself (he called them his Archbishops). And a mere two years later, the group had picked up enough followers and momentum to move to the UK and ignite the 'Revolution for Jesus' movement there.

Which is where my parents' story starts.

* * *

In 1972, my parents joined the group and while they were brand-new recruits in a factory in Bromley, being trained to go and preach the word and do missions in Amsterdam, Paris and beyond, David Berg had already gone into hiding. This was just four years after the group had been founded in Huntington Beach. Again, we have two versions.

Version One: The Press started to kick up in the States about the Jesus Movement and the Children of God, parents saying their children had been brainwashed, kidnapped and hypnotised. David Berg was worried about the law following suit, so he kept a low profile in case the shit hit the fan.

The other version is that things really were not that bad *yet*, but David Berg, as he morphed and rebranded into Moses David, needed to distance himself from his followers. He started to shed the people who knew him before he proclaimed himself a prophet and had realised that elusiveness and mystery were key to maintaining the belief that he was one. Holding his followers at arm's length so that they could not see 'the man' was more likely to make them believe in 'the prophet'. Perhaps if my parents had met him, they would have realised he was a creep with a drinking problem (as his daughter has described him) rather than a messiah.

By then, he'd shed his first wife Jane (who had been rebranded to 'Mother Eve') and had taken a girl half his age called Karen Zerby (later known as 'Mama-Maria') as his concubine (although there was a painful five-year crossover between the two women). She would be instrumental to both him and the group until his death. In fact, she leads the Children of God to this day.

Whatever the reason, while my parents were being renamed and rebirthed in the Bromley factory, they never met Moses David, who was a mere two miles away, orchestrating the revolution from a small family home in a quiet cul-de-sac. I don't know how long he lived in the UK, but Moses David never again came out of hiding.

By 1972, the Children of God had over 10,000 members in 130 communes and I would like to believe that the vast majority of these people were *good* people, my parents included, trying to make positive change, or looking for real purpose. They didn't join a cult that said 'Become a Hooker for Jesus' or 'It's OK to abuse kids', they joined a revolution. But the slippage into some truly fucked-up teachings happened quicker than I even realised growing up. 'Flirty fishing' as a practice was introduced in 1973 in Berg's inner circle and for the group by 1974, just two years after my parents joined. It was a way that women would go out and recruit new disciples, show the Lord's love (through sex) and reap the rewards (through money). They were 'fishers of men' just as Jesus told his disciples to be.

More disturbingly, the concept of 'Child Bride' was released in 1977. So perhaps brainwashing is one of perspective: is two years a long time when it comes to conditioning and controlling women enough to become 'Whores for God'? Is four years a substantial amount of time to desensitise your followers to the idea of sexually abusing children and making them 'Child Brides'? When you think that my mom was converted in five hours, perhaps a few years in these environments can have the effect of decades. But what does seem clear to me when I look at David Berg is that he was rotten from the outset, perhaps just in secret. Even if it took time to desensitise his followers, he was already an abusive, controlling paedophile.

And then, we scratch through to another discovery, which runs through my bones like a razor. The year 1968 – the year all this started – was the year that David Berg's mother Virginia died. A turning point, because many, including his daughter, believe that his mother was the very last restraining force for morality in his life.

So, was it her death that triggered him into action? The catalyst? Was this the day he had been waiting for? Because after she died, he pulled out all the stops. After she died, he started to craft the group that would go on to do unspeakable things in his, and Jesus' name.

And this is ours, my family's, my commune's, my story's beginning.

CHAPTER 2

One Simple Question: 12 Years After

She wakes me up with a slap.

A jolt. A current convulses through my body. It's not gentle. I don't feel drowsy. I am wide awake.

Insomnia. That bitch! I never win the fight with her. Insomnia makes the bed itch, she makes every position irritating. Every noise of the night amplified; the radiator, the electrical static, the heating system.

Glowing red numbers mock me from my bedside table; 3:45am.

'Fucking *perfect*!'

It's pointless to try to sleep. I'll thrash around plagued by thoughts of unfinished work, a stupid thing I said last week will burrow in my mind, digging its way through my sanity, fears of being found out as the imposter that I am whisper, then murmur, then shout. All the things that I can keep quiet in the day when I am *oh so busy*. 'Cause keeping busy, keeps *this* quiet. Insomnia kicks the door down, she opens the gates and cruelly lets it all in.

'Fuck it!'

My reflection catches my eye as I get out of bed. The whole wall is mirrored – the one thing I haven't changed since

I bought this place, this two-bedroom former council house in east London. My home; the security I desperately craved that living in 30 communes over four continents by the time I was old enough to buy a packet of cigarettes hadn't given me. The girl in the mirror is a wild-haired, scrawny, 27-year-old who needs some sleep. And maybe a healthy meal. Give that girl some coconut water. A vitamin. Perhaps some vegetables. Maybe tell her to cool it on the work and partying, cut down those 80-hour weeks at work, perhaps calm down on the four (OK, six) nights a week on the booze and drugs.

Exactly how do you think you're going to look? Fresh?

It's 3:46am and I'm already having an existential crisis.

'Fucking PERFECT!'

Those mirrors have *got* to go.

* * *

I creep down the stairs, careful not to wake up my flatmate, Roxy. The house is in a quiet cul-de-sac of Bethnal Green, it's pretty silent at night. Unusual for London. In fact, the nuisance on this street is us. Most weekends (and some weekday nights), we've had the council round with noise complaints. We keep the official letters from them on the fridge as if they are a good school report, an honour. Perhaps hoping that visitors will ask about them. The last one says we'll get a £2,500 fine and they'll 'confiscate the sound system'. I 'borrowed' this system from my work; it's expensive, powerful and supposed to be for music festivals, so we're keeping it quiet for now. Are we a fearless rebellious generation? Brash, loud and unapologetic, or just a cliché of youth? Damaged, vapid and pathetic?

I'm proud of my work. I'm good at what I do. *I think*. Well, at least I put everything I have into it. I work as a creative in the music and film department of a big music website. Roxy does the same kind of thing. So, there are no grown-ups in the house telling us to be more 'moderate'. *Everyone* I know lives like this – it's normal, we'll sort it out later. When we become boring. Move to the suburbs. Talk about extensions and catchment areas. I spend most of my summer on the road: gigs, music festivals. Covered in mud, interviewing musicians, getting royally (horribly) trashed. And then the time in the office is long and hungover. I don't watch the clock, it's not that kind of job, just keep working until someone says, 'Everyone is in the pub.' Twelve- to fifteen-hour days are normal, sleeping in the merchandise closet is normal, as is buying clothes on the way into work because you pulled another all-nighter. At work, what we do is *so important*, operating with the urgency of people who are saving the world. Pushing ourselves into the arms of exhaustion. Then some prick will say, 'It's *only* a website' to lighten the mood. *Piss off, mate!* As if we don't know the only people who *should* be working this many hours are the ones *actually* saving lives.

And perhaps not even them.

I sit in my living room, itchy with awakeness, surrounded by the posters of the 'secret shows' we have put on at work. Artwork for the band 'The Gossip' is on the wall. I illustrated this gig poster; it features a woman's chest, ripped open to reveal a black heart made of tangled weeds. Black and thick, strangling each other. My artwork now unnerves me, my hand shoots to my heart as I feel it pinch.

You are disturbed, I whisper to myself.

My screen flicks on. The glow from my laptop illuminates the room. I'm tempted to start work now – 'get ahead of the day' – but I know it doesn't really work like that.

I open a folder on my computer called 'Night Writings' – it's the latest method I use to pass the time in the middle of the night, writing stories from my childhood. I want them to be dark, comedic, twisted: 'So much messed-up shit happened when we were kids,' I laugh and say to my friends. 'It would make a brilliant comedy series.' Occasionally, I chuck a short anecdote from my childhood into a night at the pub. Flippant, throwaway, LOLs. Nothing that delves into the darker stuff. Because when you are *over* something, you can laugh about it, see the funny side of the bleakness. Right?

If I'm honest, I pity the kids I grew up with, the ones who constantly bleat on about it. The sadness, the pain, the shit we went through. Yes, we went through it and it's over now. I pride myself on not being affected by it, scornful of the people I know who STILL haven't been able to pull themselves out of the cult quagmire.

Get. Over. It. You are out now, get a life.

I look at my files. I haven't finished a single one of these stories yet. I get stuck usually about a page in. But that's how writing works, isn't it?

Maybe the computer is the problem. Maybe these should be handwritten. I walk into the kitchen to get my notepad. The evidence of our lifestyle fills this galley kitchen, the recycling stuffed with booze bottles, ashtrays in the drying rack, painkillers displayed on the counter, how some people might have cookies. A packet of menthol cigarettes looks at me provocatively – 'Only babies smoke menthols,' Roxy says. I'm tempted to light one up.

Does a part of me like the idea of sitting in the dark of night, a cigarette dangling from my mouth, struggling to write?

'*So* tortured.' I shake my head.

I open my notepad to my list of ideas: 'Beverley – funny story about prostitution', 'Joel and Jeremiah – snot bubbles in devotions', 'Stealing neighbour's toys after they were killed by armed raiders' and then underneath that are the words, 'My Guardian'.

My Guardian. I have told this story a few times. I tell it in confidence to friends who know a bit more about my past – the *real* past where these stories come from.

My Guardian completely changed my life's trajectory when I was a child. Momentous, big deal stuff. For as long as I could remember, I'd idolised this man and how, with just one question, he had flipped my axis when I was ten years old. He showed me that my future might not be predestined. He lit me up, he gave me hope. He pointed a finger to the crack in the wall that I might one day escape through.

I pick up my pen and I start to write.

'The Guardian is coming.'

All the kids keep saying it. The Guardian *journalist is coming. We don't know who they are, we don't know what they look like, they could be anyone. But we do know this: this is very important. The adults have been preparing for weeks. We must make a good impression. There have been so many extra jobs – painting scrappy bits of the house, mowing lawns, packing anything away that isn't needed or wouldn't look good to outsiders. We take down the demerit charts and schedules, we clean for days. We must make everything perfect because 'The Guardian' is coming.*

We had a devotions where they explained that this was a 'big opportunity' and a 'trial to see if we can stop going underground and let our lights shine'. That this was a 'huge responsibility'.

We must, above all, take this 'extremely seriously'.

This is the first time we have had an outsider in our home. A Systemite staying and sleeping here. It's exciting, but it's dangerous too. So, an important part of the preparation is learning how to answer their questions. Because a few of us kids are actually going to get to talk to 'The Guardian'. Some of the kids have been selected. And I am one of them.

I rest my arms on a freshly painted window sill, breathing in the smell of emulsion, clean and chemically. This spot gives me a clear view of the driveway. A car drives slowly through the gates, my mom and dad wave eagerly. He steps out of his car, my parents shake his hand. I can only see their backs, but I know they will be smiling. 'The Guardian' smiles too. I'm surprised. He is old. Older than my parents, maybe as old as grandparents. He has pure white hair just past his ears. A kind face. He is tall and thin. He doesn't look like the adults here.

'Welcome!' I can just about hear them say.

I run through the house mirroring their path so I can keep watch through the windows. My dad's voice is loud as they do a tour of the outside.

'As you can see, there are no guards keeping anyone in, no Rottweilers or barbed wire,' my mom laughs. 'People are free to come and go as they please.'

This home is right in the middle of the countryside, with nothing for miles around. I wonder where we would be pleased to go.

We sit for lunch. It's a special lunch – sausages and mashed potatoes, the tables set out with knives and forks and there are jugs of juice on the table. Today, it's like we're kings and queens.

'Well, this is delicious,' he says. 'I was warned not to eat anything with you, as you might poison me and convince me to stay,' he adds with a wink and a chuckle. 'But how could I resist bangers and mash?'

'Bangers.' I feel myself mouthing the word so I remember it.

My dad laughs. 'I am sure you have heard many ridiculous things about us, which is why we were keen to have you come and experience our lives for yourself.'

While we eat, he tells us stories of his children – they love being outdoors but also watch too much TV. He tells us that he has travelled all over the world, talking to people about their lives. My parents tell him about our travels too.

'We have served the Lord in India, in Africa, in . . .' my dad makes a list on his fingers, his chest expanding with pride as he says, 'Our children have had very varied lives in many different cultures.'

He must be talking about the temperatures we've lived in – it's true, we have lived in many.

When 'The Guardian' speaks, he looks us in the eye. He really looks, like he's sure something interesting will come out of our mouths, almost as if we're as important as the adults. He smiles a lot, laughs and if he catches you staring at him, he winks to let you know that it's OK. I know this because he caught me.

'The Guardian' makes you feel like you can let out the breath you have been holding on to. But they, my parents, did warn us that he might make us feel like this; that we could relax, but we know that we shouldn't. Because 'The Guardian' could be trying to harm the group and our way of life. If we slip up, say the wrong thing, because we are relaxed, because of his smiles and his winks, he could write something bad about us and we could all be put in prison.

My mom comes to tell me that it's my turn to talk to him. The jumping starts in my stomach. I walk through the living-room door to see him sitting on the floral couch that I scrubbed just two days ago to get the stains out. Cleaning the embroidered petals for his arrival. Light streams through the window and hits his white hair. It glows like when you hold a dandelion up to the sun.

'Hello, Bexy.'

'Hi.'

'How are you today?'

'Very good, thank you.'

I settle into my seat.

'So, you know quite a bit about me, Bexy, from the last day or so, but I don't know much about you, do I?'

I shake my head.

'So, would you mind if I ask you some questions to find out a bit more about you?'

I nod – 'Yes.'

His eyes seem to reflect me back in them. There are folds of skin that crinkle round the sides of them when he smiles.

First, he asks me how old I am.

'Nearly 11,' I say.

He asks where I was born. He asks me about my brothers and sisters; to name them and give them ages. He says it must be nice to have a family that big.

I say, 'Yes, it is.'

He asks me if we have any favourite games. I tell him about one we used to play before we got to England, where you would hide a potato – we called it 'Potato! Potato!' He laughs and tells me that it sounds fun and he would like to try it.

'The good thing is, even if you don't have much else, you normally can find a potato,' I say and then feel silly for saying it.

He doesn't ask me the questions that they told me he might, about the Armageddon, about Moses David, about flirty fishing. He seems to mainly be interested in things that I never talk about, that I am never asked about. Then he asks me something, a question that feels like a knock on a door that I didn't know I could open.

'Bexy, what do you want to be when you grow up?'

The question stops my breath. I feel my eyes widening as it expands in my mind. It runs through my whole body – I can feel it supercharging my veins, I can feel it in my heartbeat.

The ceiling above him opens up, burning with the fires of the Armageddon, black clouds and brimstone. I can make out the Holy Spirit Jesus and God and Moses David standing in their glowing white robes, swords in their hands, and an army of angels – legions of them fill the violent sky.

The earth on fire, I see flashes of what is to come. I see myself as a teenager fighting the Antichrist's soldiers. I see my death, the death that we have all been preparing for. I see the many ways I could be killed; shot through the heart, hung from a tree, bleeding out naked on a cross, decapitated with my brothers and sisters in a square as we refuse to renounce Moses David.

His voice comes through the vision, the celling closes up. And it's just the two of us again.

Me and 'The Guardian'.

'Well, have you thought about it? What you would like to be when you grow up?'

I try to read the lie in his face, I search to find the dishonesty, maybe a joke, and I find none. It is a genuine, sincere and maybe a very normal question. So, maybe there is that chance. Maybe I will grow up?

And I say to him, because I can't think of anything else: 'I want to be a journalist, I want to be like you.'

My words bleed across the page like watercolours, blue letters blend into each other. I wipe my eyes before my tears do any more damage or erase this moment. The blue hour has just hit, flooding the room with its soft light. My eyes mist and I step inside my writing. It is from me, flooded out of me and has filled this house, this room, covering the home I fought so hard to get, the stuff I fill it with, the life I didn't dare think was possible. And I realise, as I sit among the blueness, inside this moment from the past that changed me and allowed the life I have now, that I need to find 'My Guardian' and thank him.

*   *   *

It's a week since I started looking for 'The Guardian'. My friends Jess and Selina are round for dinner.

'Creature! You cooked?' Jess says and she comes in, surprised. The girls renamed me 'Creature' a few years ago – '*You're like a tiny feral animal*' – I take it as a compliment.

'I *can* cook,' I say. 'I cooked all the time when I was a kid.'

'Yeah, but it sounded pretty rank, from what you've said.'

'Ah, shame! Cause I made you one of my cult classics . . .'

'Sacrificial Lamb of Christ?' Selina cuts in.

'Really?' Jess says.

'No. It's spicy rice noodles, you dumb dumb!'

I arrange some cushions on the floor around a coffee table, then I pop some wine for the girls.

'Very sophisticated,' Selina says.

'It's just for you two, you know I can't handle the stuff,' I say.

'You can handle three nights on the trot raving, but you still can't manage a finger of wine?' Selina says.

'Not even one finger,' I say, smiling.

'You'd make a crap Catholic! Can't eat wheat, can't handle wine,' Jess says.

'Straight to hell!' I laugh.

We slurp up the spicy, comforting food and get stuck into life. Jess has moved away, Selina is moving closer to me. Selina has started dating. Jess is the most adult friend I have – she got married last year.

'What work you got on at the moment? Any gigs lined up you want us to come to?'

'Yeah, we have actually . . . well, there's always gigs coming up.' Then I swiftly change tack. 'I've told you both about the *Guardian* journalist, right?'

Jess and Selina are two of the people who do know about my childhood. Not all of it, but enough to know what effect meeting the journalist and 'That question' had on me.

'Yeah, of course,' Selina says.

'Why? Has something happened?' Jess asks.

'I've decided I want to find him and thank him,' I say.

'Brilliant, brilliant, brilliant!' Selina clasps her hands together.

'How you gonna do it?' Jess asks.

'Well, I did some research and I've narrowed it down. I've found out who was working at the *Guardian* during that time period, but I can't find the article he wrote about us . . .'

'Bexy, you do know that Zach's dad and mom both wrote for the *Guardian*, right?' Jess says.

'No, I had no idea what Zach's parents do,' I say.

'Well, maybe we can ask them if they know who this guy is. They've been writing for years, they will be able to help, for sure,' Jess says.

Zach is a friend of ours. I've known him for years, we even dated for a brief minute.

'Well, that would be awesome,' I say, feeling like this might become real.

'What's the guy's name that you're looking into at the moment?' Jess says.

'Walter . . . Walter Schwartz,' I say.

'Fuck off!' Jess jumps up.

'What?'

'ARE YOU SHITTING ME?'

'Why?'

'Bexy, Walter Schwartz is Zach's dad!'

* * *

We drive through the countryside to Greenacres. Zach is at the wheel, his girlfriend Laura in the front seat, Selina in the back with me.

'I still can't wrap my head around this,' Zach says.

It seems so bizarre that someone I met in a nightclub would be the son of the journalist that changed my life. Zach had told me on our first date that he'd love to introduce me to his father. I thought that both weird and forward – I didn't know then that his father was a collector of strange stories and people. It makes more sense now.

'So, Walter met you when you were a kid? In the cult? That is bonkers!' Laura says.

'To think that we've known each other . . . I mean, it's bonkers,' Zach says.

'Bonkers!' Laura agrees.

It is bonkers, I think.

'I can't wait to see what it's like when you two first see each other,' Laura says. 'What are you gonna say to him?'

I start to feel nervous, the expectations are too high.

'We're not in a rom-com, I'll just say hello. Anyway, I wrote him an email with everything I wanted to say the other day so he knows how I feel, thank fuck! I don't know how I would say all of that in real life.'

I had written to him straight after the dinner with Selina and Jess.

Hi Walter

This is probably one of the strangest emails I've ever written. I was going to say that I don't really know what to write, but I've thought about it so much that I've got a million things to say, I just don't really know where to start.

Firstly, I'm not expecting you to remember me. I can imagine that you have done a million interviews during your life and I was just one of them, but maybe that's not really of any consequence because whether you do or you don't, meeting you had a massive impact on me as a child. And really, I just wanted you to know.

This might sound melodramatic, but the majority of my friends have heard the story about 'my Guardian journalist' and know that the day I spoke to you, things changed for me.

It's probably a good idea to give you a bit of background on me. My parents were Gideon and Rachel Scott, who were essentially the PR for 'the Family'. We were handpicked as a family because we were probably the most outwardly normal-looking/sounding family that the group had to offer.

I went on to have many, many interviews after the one I had with you, most of which blur into one big question and answer time, but the one with you was very different.

I am assuming that your knowledge of their doctrines are pretty extensive but growing up, we were told that we were living in the 'End Time' and that I was essentially born to be a martyr. That I wouldn't live past the age of fourteen. I'd never thought about my future and many children in the Family had a feeling of hopelessness, that our fate was predetermined. School was not necessary as why would we need an education if we were going to die before we got to use it? During our interview you asked, 'What do you want to be when you grow up?'

I felt like a door had been opened to another world, where I had the option to be something when I grew up.

I've wanted to say thank you since I was ten years old – I'm sorry it's taken me till now to find you.

Bexy

He responded an hour later with, 'Why don't you come up to Greenacres this weekend?'

Selina holds my hand. *Can she sense my nerves?* She smiles softly.

'Whatever happens, it will be pure magic,' she says.

We pull into the drive and immediately it feels like a scene from the rom-com I just insisted this wasn't: barking dogs run up to greet us, followed by a woman with masses of hair streaked with grey, wearing a colourful onesie, waving excitedly. She has an umbrella cockatoo perched on her shoulder that seems overjoyed to see us too.

'Hello, Mom!,' Zach says as we pull up.

Then I spot him, standing in the doorway, holding a mug. He's tall and thin, with a little less hair, but instantly recognisable.

My Guardian.

Dogs lick our hands and faces, hugs are handed out, squeals of delight on all sides. The cockatoo somehow ends up on my shoulder and Dot, Zach's mom, turns to me and says, 'Well, you better go and say hello to him then.'

I walk towards him and in a voice that I have heard in a thousand dreams since I was ten years old, he says, 'Hi Bexy. Welcome to Greenacres.'

At the kitchen table, mugs of tea are poured, conversations happen on top of each other, dogs hang around under the table, hoping for crumbs to fall into their mouths. I know I'm saying things – I can hear my voice, but I'm really not sure what the words are. I'm full of nervous energy, my whole body is buzzing; I feel like I've stepped into another world.

Their world.

Their world, with its rolling fields, wild horses, rescue parrots and Boston terriers. Beautiful and chaotic. I instantly feel like I can take off my shoes, make my own coffee and get stuck into any and every topic under the sun. Nothing is out of bounds here.

I meet every parrot that she has in her mini-sanctuary and hear their sad tales before coming here to be rescued and looked after by Dot. I fall hard for one called Lily, who dances when you sing 'Happy Birthday'. She hasn't got wings because some boys cut them off, but she's still a happy umbrella cockatoo, who seems unaware of what she's missing, albeit a little needy. She makes a home on my shoulder for the weekend.

Walter and Dot have had well-lived lives. Their photo albums are full of pictures of them living in nudist colonies, on farms in France and adventures across the world. On the table lies a book they wrote together about how to live sustainably. They are quirky. Weird. Thoughtful and open-minded. We take long walks and drink too much coffee, we lie around and watch TV. I feel at home.

Over dinner, Walter says, 'So what are you planning to do with it?'

'With what?' I ask.

'Your experience?' he says.

'How do you mean?' I say.

'Well, you have been through all this, seen things that perhaps some of us will never see, experienced a life that is outside of the "norm". What are you going to do with it?'

'She doesn't *have* to do anything with it,' Dot says.

'Well, I have started writing . . .' I say.

'Really?'

'Yeah . . . Dark comedy mainly, short stories, funny stuff.'

Walter looks at me, confused.

'My dear, from what I understand . . . well . . . it wasn't, it isn't that funny.'

Dot looks over and perhaps in a bid to save me, she says, 'What about your brothers and sisters? Are they all out?'

'Most.'

I wonder if the word betrays the sadness I feel as I say it.

'Ah,' she says.

'The ones that are still in are too young to leave yet. They're OK, they're not in the same group I was in – I mean, it's complicated – the group went through so many different versions of itself. Now, it's like a Christian commune, not like a cult.' I say this, hoping it's true. 'I mean, if they were in the same group I was in, as in the same style, I would kidnap them all.' I say this with a bravado that I don't quite pull off.

'You mustn't feel guilty,' she says, 'that you are out . . . You must feel proud and brave.'

I'm embarrassed.

'Goodnight,' Walter says, placing a hand on Dot's shoulder.

Maybe he feels embarrassed too, or maybe he is ashamed of me.

*   *   *

I head to bed, but I'm not asleep for long.

That familiar slap comes.

I look at my phone: 2:56am.

Awesome, I think.

I climb over Selina's warm sleeping body next to me and head for the living room.

God, I was embarrassed tonight. And probably embarrassing. Talking about all that stuff. Looking at it and discussing it and dissecting it, it all feels like just a big fucking wallow. Repulsive. Not very me. Icky, in fact. I don't need to go through all that *shit* again, do I? I am who I am in spite of the group, not because of it. And yet here I am again, in the night, with no defence and unable to hide. My brain rattling. I get my pen and I start to write:

I've been awake for some time, thinking about last night. A strange mixture of feelings ... Some are warm. We had a lovely evening with two insanely intelligent older people. But I'm also frustrated, I don't know, a little messed-up over it.

After Walter went to bed, the conversation turned to me for about two hours. For ages. Felt uncomfortable, weird and self-indulgent.

We got on the topic of leaving 'The Children of God', what I did next and the 'survivor's guilt' you feel when you get out. I know I suffer from this because as I sit and write, I am supressing a pain that so desperately wants to come out. I hold it in because I am afraid if it comes, I won't be able to stop it. It will flood me. And I will drown in it.

Big fucking baby.

Everyone had lovely things to say: 'You need to disassociate yourself from the group, or you'll never get over it', 'You had to cut ties to discover yourself', 'If you'd spent the whole time in contact, you would have destroyed yourself'. Part of me knows this is all true. Part of me feels that I lead a really fickle and frivolous life while my siblings are stuck in a religious group. I abate my guilt by telling myself they are in a watered-down version of what I grew up in. But while I was out here 'discovering' myself, I had sisters still in the group, still in the abuse, my brothers abandoned by my parents in a township. And my youngest brother neglected because he was unable to speak.

I've tried to disassociate myself, but they are still in it. And I am realising that somehow, so am I.

The thing about pushing down trauma, you *think* you can decide if or when you want to deal with it, but sometimes it will simply decide for you.

You have to deal with your shit . . . Before it deals with you.

*   *   *

By the time we leave Greenacres, I feel something stirring in me; the way I am connected to Walter is magical and bizarre. I am blown away not only by the charm of it, but also by how it makes me feel.

I keep hearing his voice in my head, over and over:

'What are you going to do with it?'
'What are you going to do with it?'
'What are you going to do with it?'

Flooded with a raw urge to do something with my past, I am filled with more questions than ever. I feel like I have no choice. Being here has shaken me awake.

I start to think about what I will be leaving behind. My job. My house, the one that gave me the security I'd always craved. My friends. My family. My whole world, the one that's taken all this time to build.

A fear and excitement hit me; that I am going to have to go back to places that I promised myself I would never return to. That I might have to look into myself in ways that scare me. That I might have to ask questions that I don't want to hear the answers to. That it might get daunting, heartbreaking, maybe even nasty at times.

And that I might, maybe, be on the verge of the scariest and greatest adventure of my life.

If I'm going to do this right, I need to go to the motherland of cults. Back to where all of this started. Back to the root of our group, the starting point as to why I was born into this world of communes, separation, Moses David and Armageddon.

America.

CHAPTER 3

Can't Breathe: 7 Years Before

'Get in the van. NOW!'

A hand on the back of my neck pushes me through the side door of the van.

'I SAID NOW!' Dad's voice is loud and shaky, full of adrenaline. My head is covered, I can't see. I feel the metal floor of the van on my knees as the engine starts with a jump. We slide backwards as my dad accelerates out into the streets of London.

'How do you think they found us?' I hear my mom ask.

'Shut up, Rachel, and let me *drive*.'

Car horns beep as the wheels grip and then tear off the road. The tangy smell of burnt rubber fills the floor of the van. I push the scarf off my face and I grab my big sister Kate's hand. She's crouched down with me. Moments ago, she was dragging our littlest brother and sister into the side of the van. She looks straight ahead, steely-eyed. If she's scared, she's not giving it away. Kate's 13 and there's nothing left of the child she once was.

I am eight years old and this is the second time we have fled in just a matter of months. This is the second time that one of our communes has been discovered. It can't be a coincidence, there must be a connection. Someone *must* have told them where we live.

As I look up at my sister's face, she bites her lip – I think it's more from trying to keep balanced as we sway about than from any kind of fear. The last time we fled was about four months ago, because of a boy Kate liked in the 'Teen Home', who had put us all in danger. The Teen Home was a big old house out in the middle of nowhere, full of teenagers who were getting 'retrained' to be stronger, more obedient followers of Moses David, better soldiers for the End Time. Seven years of battle, of being on the run, of martyrdom that we children have been chosen to fight, and die in, by God.

We hadn't been at the home for very long when it happened. I had walked in one afternoon to find Kate lying across our mom's bed, crying. She'd closed the curtains to shut the day out, which stopped me mid-step. I hadn't seen her like that in forever; I hadn't seen any real emotion in Kate since we left Africa. I didn't feel I could ask her why she was crying – it was the kind of deep upset that you give space to. And then I found out later that the boy she liked, Solomon, had run away. He had tried to cross the border using a photocopy of his passport. I can't imagine how he even made it that far, he was only 14 years old. I overheard the adults speaking in low, serious voices about it. If the police stopped a minor trying to travel illegally, it was only a matter of time before they ended up on our doorstep.

'If he's smart enough to get all the way to the border, we should assume he knows our address. So, let's just go now, let's not wait for it to happen.' My dad, decisive, authoritative, the provider. He always seems to know what to do, he always seems so confident. If any of us kids have any kind of confidence, it's mirrored from him, mirrored perhaps because it feels like an empty reflection rather than something learned. And so we fled in the middle of the night, our home disbanded into multiple vans with multiple destinations for safety. My dad's quick thinking is how we ended up in the Hendon Home, but somehow, *they* have found us again.

I look through the crack in the front seats at my dad hunched over, shoulders fully engaged, speeding through the streets. His hair is mid-length and not as curly as it once was. It's going brown, or maybe grey instead of the red it used to be. The signs of ageing on his hands are pronounced as he grips the wheel; I worry his veins might pop like grapes that have been stepped on. The nausea that started with the rubber smell starts to rise in my throat. As I pull the scarf from my head, I sit up straight, hold on, clench my jaw to try and steady myself – the stink of the van's engine is getting to me.

This time, the people who found us were trying to take photographs of us, which is why Dad told us to cover our faces as we ran to the van.

'Are you a hooker? Are you a Hooker for Jesus?' I heard one of them shout through the window at my mom.

But even though I feel sick, and a little bit scared, I am glad to be leaving the Hendon Home. The Hendon Home was a standard, strict, closed-off commune in north London: scheduled days, lots of chores, prayer, devotions and discipline. A big-style commune, worlds away from the small homes where we lived in Africa and India. But, the real, huge advantage is leaving 'Uncle' Jonathan behind – that relief is greater than any fear I feel now.

'Uncles' and 'Aunties' are what we have to call all of the adults in our homes. It's a sign of respect for our elders. When we first moved to the Hendon Home, our whole family was squeezed into one bedroom, all eight of us kids sleeping on the floor, my parents in a double bed in the middle. My oldest brother Chad (15), then Kris (14), then Kate (13), then Joel (12), then me and then the younger ones: Josh (6), Sam (5) and Baby V (6 months) in the double bed. My oldest sister, Ruth (17) isn't with us anymore – she left when she was 14 to go to a teen training camp in Thailand. That was years ago, we haven't seen her since.

Chad is super smart. He is lanky and fair and always in trouble for having some kind of book that he shouldn't have. I don't know where he gets them. Most recently, he got caught with a dictionary and was made an example of in front of the whole home.

'What kind of soldier for the Lord hides a dictionary? What will you need all those long words for when you are fighting the Antichrist?'

The mocking he experienced for this dictionary was ruthless, but he knew the risks in having something like that on him.

My brother Kris is the highest-energy person I have ever known – 'hyperactive' I heard Dad once say. He is kind, he looks out for me, and has rusty red hair and loads of freckles.

Kate is quiet now. She wasn't always this way. When she was younger, she had a fire in her and a temper that she unleashed – more than any of us – but that hasn't been around since we moved to the new homes. She and Kris and Chad were sent to India to be 'retrained'. She was 12, they were there for six months. Whatever happened out there really changed her.

She doesn't talk about it, but every day she fades further and further into the background. It's a smart way to be. A smart way to survive. I wish in some ways I could do it, but my big mouth makes it hard for me to avoid trouble.

Joel is the opposite. He's brash, loud and mischievous. Blondish-brown hair, foolish to veering on stupid, the kind of boy who never thinks about consequences. He is the one that my dad bullies the most.

Josh is cute, clever and odd. He didn't speak English for the first few years of his life, preferring to exist in a language of his own invention that sounded closer to Russian. He is the closest to me in age. We've tussled for attention since the moment he popped out. He has always been small for his age – maybe because I stole his breastmilk, maybe because he was just born that way. Sam is like Kris – he looks just like him, but with the frenetic energy dialled down. He climbed before he could walk. A dangerous pastime for a tiny, gentle adventurer. And Baby V is just a bundle of blonde ringlets and gurgles. She is too young to understand any of this, or that we are in any way different.

You only begin to understand *that* when you are a bit older.

With nine of us and a 17-year age gap between us, there will always be divisions. Who knows, maybe that's true of all brothers and sisters? The older ones have to look after the younger ones, there are divides of different experiences, of maybe being treated differently. The first five in our family are super smart and had more outside influences, like meeting our grandparents (my parents had contact with them before travelling to India when they needed to raise funds for the trip). I am number six and was born just before we moved to India. Some of what my grandparents tried to instil in the older ones will always trickle through to the rest of us: empathy, protection for each other, patience. The younger ones might not know the types of freedoms we had before we joined the 'real homes' but they're also not as aware of the discipline, regimes and practices you have to follow when you are in the older age bracket.

One thing's for certain in our family, even if there are divisions, it's always US vs THEM. We are the pack, they, the adults, are the enemy. We protect each other, we are the line of defence against our parents, the Uncles, the Aunties. The Leaders, The Shepherds – whatever names they come up with that categorise *them* – the adults. We don't play favourites, there are no favourites. We don't do rats, snitches or squealers. It's an unwritten law that you are born into: us vs them.

That's how to stay safe.

It's really the *only* way to stay safe.

But now, we're on the run again. It's just our family in this van, so I'm hoping that wherever we go, it will just be us. Which would be the best outcome for a raid *ever*. Joel always tells me that I'm too optimistic, that I'm a silly dreamer and that things never turn out how I imagine they will.

But this time, maybe they could.

It's never really been just us. We always lived in communes back in Africa and India and Mauritius. But it wasn't ever like this. Before we came here, we weren't this closed-off – we got out with our singing troupe to visit leper camps, old folks' homes and supermarkets. While we weren't part of the world, we saw it occasionally. We dipped in. We knew it was there. And we had time. Free time. Beautiful, wonderful, unscheduled time.

It seems like forever since we had that.

In Africa, when I was about four, we had a large garden and a forest at the end of it. And sometimes we had hours unattended to roam around. In the greens and browns of our forest, gangs formed between us. Alliances and wars would break out between the Antichrist's Soldiers and Jesus' Army – the acorn bullets of Satan's footmen hitting hard enough to bruise, sometimes even to break my skin. At one point, the bullets spraying in our garden were not acorns, but very real lead ones, out of very real guns; when our neighbours' entire family were murdered by a gang. The bullets came through our living-room windows while we hid under the bed. I remember as our little bodies pushed up the mattress looking around at my brothers' faces and their eyes reflecting the same excitement I was feeling. We were raised to expect these moments: we weren't afraid, we just thought the End Time had come ahead of schedule that day.

And even though my dad has always made our lives difficult – an aggressive, angry, violent, dismissive bully – he was nothing in comparison to being in a real home. Like the Hendon Home, or the one before that, or the one before that. He is just one man.

In the homes, *they* are a legion.

'Where do you think we should go?' I hear my mom's thin voice, braving a question. Dad doesn't like to be asked things, especially when he is driving. But we've been in the van for nearly an hour now and his driving has slowed down. I can't see out of the front window, but it feels like we are on more open roads, there are less turns and my sickness has subsided.

'We can't go to any "home". We have been compromised, that home is burned.'

'We don't really have anything with us,' she replies, passive.

'We'll have to make do. SHIT! I left "The Trunk" at the house.'

'The Trunk' had everything in it. We have taken it with us to every country we have ever lived in. It's large, made of metal and leather. Inside are our passports, our birth certificates, Moses David letters and books, and our photographs. Thousands of them. To open up this trunk is like opening a hatch into the visual history of our family. My dad had always been a keen photographer – he would make a dark room in a cupboard in most of the homes so he could develop his pictures himself.

When I hear him say we lost 'The Trunk', I immediately think of portraits of Josh and Sam. They are big, black and white. And beautiful. We'll never see them again, but I'll never forget them. I close my eyes and there they are: Sam is blowing a kiss at the camera and has long ringlets. 'You look like a girl!' Josh had giggled. He looks beautiful. Although Josh smiles goofily in his photo, his eyes still hold some sort of peculiar wisdom. I want to remember more, more of our memories we will never see again, so I keep my eyes closed and try to trace the outline of a photo of me as a four-year-old sitting outside our house in South Africa, wearing a bikini made of pale and bright pink flowers that my older sisters made for me. I remember the two of them sitting in the sun, stitching together pink flowers, as I watched in silence, not wanting to pierce the magic of the amount of attention both myself and my queen-like outfit were getting.

I close my eyes tighter still and smile at colours and outlines of a photo from when my grandparents tracked us down, travelling across the globe to see us in Mauritius. The colours are golds, greens and sepias. We are in front of an old car; I am about two and a half, I stand in front of my grandpa as my grandma holds baby Josh. Me and poor Josh were breastfeeding at the same time at this point.

Without The Trunk, we have lost all proof that we were even born, our identities and our past all in one go. I wouldn't know how much this loss of identity would mean to me until much later.

'We'll go to a campsite and lie low there,' Dad says.

'OK, sounds like a good plan.'

Mom rarely disagrees with him. Then she quietly asks, 'Where?'

'Wales,' he says.

Whales? I imagine a big, beautiful blue sea resort full of whales. Swimming, diving, jumping majestically. 'Whales' must be a spot that people come to from around the world to see the biggest creatures in the ocean, the ones big enough to give Jonah a home for three whole days! It will be beautiful, like a holiday.

I smile at Kate, hoping she can read my mind. She looks back at me strangely as I get carried further and further away with the images in my head. She must know more about whales than I do, but we know better than to talk in the back of the van. Even when we lived in Africa, this was something we never dared do; my dad would fling his arm around the car like a wrecking ball, looking for something to smash through, just hoping 'The Loud One' would be in the wake of his fist. 'Thick Ears', my dad would call them, or 'Knuckle Sandwiches'. A thick ear is a punch to the side of the head; it doesn't bruise but will stop you dead. The other is a really hard knuckle wrap to the top of the skull. Also doesn't bruise, but will leave a nasty lump and gets the job done.

Keep low, shut up and stay away from Sandwiches and Thick Ears.

Joel gets most of these – he just doesn't listen, doesn't care or has a high pain threshold. Maybe all three. Joel will get at least one Sandwich a day.

We have been driving for hours, day has turned to dusk and now it's dark. I love driving in the dark, I love the lights of the tunnels and the streetlights and the cat's eyes on the road. If you squint, it can feel like you are time travelling – you could end up anywhere. Even from down here on the floor of the van, when you can't see much in the day except for pieces of a cloudy sky, at night the lights come to you – they get inside the van and dance across the ceiling, changing shape as you drive into or away from them.

Growing, stretching, disappearing. Friendly fires across the metal roof.

Finally, the van slows down: we have arrived. Wherever we are, it's colder here. Even inside the van, I can see my breath.

I can hear my dad outside the van, talking to a man with a funny sing-song accent that I have never heard before. It sounds like a negotiation of some kind: 'This is where you hook up your water', 'This is where you get your electric'. Dad loudly rattles the door of the van open and even though I know it's coming, the noise shakes through me as the freezing air hits me in the face. I stare out of the van at the huge slice of the starry night sky open above us. Sing-Song Man has gone – Dad would have waited because people are always surprised when they see this many kids getting out of a vehicle at one time. Outsiders often snigger and say, 'Don't your parents have a TV?' indicating that my parents have nothing to entertain them other than having sex. I have heard the 'Don't-you-have-a-TV?' joke so many times but the joke is on them, because no, we don't have a TV.

They are the devil's work.

We get out one by one, banging the cramps, slapping the pins and punching the needles out of our legs. And then we see our new home: a bright yellow caravan on the edge of a field, it stands out like a beacon against the dark night sky. Yellow might not be the best colour for going underground but I think it must be at least four-berth, which is luxury – three more beds than we had in the Hendon Home.

Yes! I'll still be on the floor because I'm the fifth in line to a bed, but it means we will have some space. This is exciting.

Anything is better than the Hendon Home, Uncle Jonathan and his son, Cainan. Any day outside of the commune is a win.

We shuffle into our new yellow home. The lights are turned on to reveal the wooden cabin interior and the brown upholstery with ridges of embroidered flowers on it. They are almost 3D. Their brown leaves look dead, like they've been put on a burn pile and are waiting for the fire. Tired, old flowers. We haven't eaten anything all day but there's a box of food in the kitchen that must come with the caravan.

That's handy, I thought we would be skipping dinner tonight.

All eyes look hungrily at a box that says 'SMASH' on it.

'What's SMASH?' I ask.

Kate has the box in her hands and reads the instructions: 'It's powdered potatoes. It's mash, but powdered,' she says.

'Woah!' Joel responds.

We've had powdered milk for years, powdered eggs and now powdered potatoes? I wonder what else could be powdered.

Powdered stuff is perfect for the End Days as it never goes off.

My mom and dad have gone into the back of the caravan and have shut the brown flower curtains for privacy, turning that area into a 'bedroom'. But with just the dead leaf fabric to shield them, we can hear their conversation.

'I don't know, Rachel. I DON'T KNOW! We just have to wait it out. *Someone* is telling them where we are.' Dad is agitated, clearly under stress.

'All right, all right.' Mom soothes him in a quiet voice.

Kate boils a kettle and we wait for our dehydrated dinner. I look around at my seven siblings, some standing, some sitting on the floor, some on the seats around the table. All of us are scrawny, we always have been, but the last few months have taken their toll. Maybe it's because I'm used to seeing us stained by the sun, covered in freckles, red-cheeked from the African wind that comes down from the Karoo Desert. The wind that feels like God is blowing a giant hairdryer on the land: hot, wild and bone-dry.

If I close my eyes, I can almost feel the wind whip through my hair. If I open them, I see the contrast of us now: pale, pasty, skinny. Like old washed-out socks, grey and shrunken from overuse.

The Smash has been shared around the room. We wolf down the powdered potatoes that taste a bit like pencil shavings and glue mixed together. But the food is hot and will stop the stomach squawks that can sometimes get so loud, you can't sleep. It's not delicious, but still, everyone is grateful.

We all find our spot in the caravan to sleep. Everyone knows where they are in the pecking order and we don't fight it out. I get a spot between two beds at the back and while pleased with it, I also hope that no one steps on me in the night to get to the toilet.

What a day, I think as I snuggle into the blanket. *Didn't see any of that coming. Our whole lives have changed.*

And tomorrow, we might see some whales.

*   *   *

This is the soggiest place I have ever been to. Everything is deep green and sodden. The grass is like a mattress or a sponge that's been soaked through and wants to swallow your feet. Bouncy and drenched. We have been here for a week, and every morning we wake up to a low fog and an icy wrapper on our campsite that's normally gone by midday, leaving a glossy shine on everything.

I was wrong, there are no whales here. But there are sheep that have whooping cough or bronchitis. They live behind a fence right outside our caravan and they cough all night long. The first night, we thought it was a group of old men – Kris said it sounded like they had been smoking their whole lives. When we saw it was a flock of sheep, we found it hilarious. Kris suggested maybe the sheep liked to smoke too. But it's not funny anymore. The coughing seems to never stop, which means we never really sleep.

But the one thing I was right about is that this is a holiday camp. There is a sign that says so on the front of the camp- site. And there isn't really anyone else here except for us, which means we have the run of the place and the huge shower rooms to ourselves. I step into the freezing shower room, my small feet immediately in pain from the cold metal and concrete. I push the shower tap on; it goes for 15 seconds before I have to push it again. It takes many pushes to get the hot water to flow out of its metal head. I try to avoid the ice water shooting out next to me as my teeth try to jump out of my jaw.

This is my first winter. I have never experienced the cold before and once you have it in you, you can't shake it off. It's nothing like the heat. The cold gets inside your bones and makes a home and won't leave. The contrast to how we grew up, in blistering hot countries, shocks my body. I think about how hard it was to cool down in every place we lived in before. When I was two, I would sleep on a stone floor in India to keep my face cold – no blanket, no pillows, nothing. I would rest my cheek on the floor and when it would heat up, I would turn my face over, like flipping a piece of bacon. It seems like a different life, a lifetime ago. Everything was in technicolor, so hot it could crisp up my memories. Now it's wet and foggy and icy and cold – and we're 'on the run'.

'Owh, JOEL!'

The sharp sting of a wet towel rips through the top of my leg. That's going to bruise. He spins the towel round, preparing to take another crack at me. I scream and run out of the shower room.

'Stop it! Stop it!' I laugh as I run.

Joel never misses an opportunity to disobey. And to drag me into mischief with him. He chases me around the caravan site till I can't run any more and then lays another blow on my leg.

'You need another shower,' he says. 'Quick, do it before Dad sees!'

I am covered in mud and freezing.

'Do you prefer it here to the Hendon Home?' I ask Joel as we walk back to the shower room.

'Yeah, of course. The Hendon Home was horrible!' The way that came out amuses him. 'The H-endon H-ome was H-orrrible,' he repeats.

'I like it here too. Even though Dad's here as well, it's still better,' I say as we walk in to see Kate putting a towel around her head.

'You must be missing your boyfriend, Cainan,' Joel teases me.

'Ugh, no!' I say, upset that he would say something like that. But Joel never misses an opportunity to torment me either (and now he uses Cainan, Uncle Jonathan's son, to do it). 'He wasn't my boyfriend, he was gross,' I add quietly.

'Uncle Jonathan wanted him to be your boyfriend, he wanted you two to Make Loooooove,' Joel says, knowing that will upset me.

'UGH!' I say, but I know he's right – Uncle Jonathan had been trying to get me to do *that* with Cainan.

'I think there's something wrong with him,' Kate adds.

Kate would know, she knows about these things.

'Uncle Jonathan has lots wrong with him,' I say quietly.

I think back to the many ways he tried to humiliate us: whacks with the wooden spoon, the yelling, facing the corner silently, drinking the dishwater if you didn't do the dishes properly and the worst punishment of all – the one where you have to hold your hands behind your head and stay upright on your knees for hours at a time until it feels like your limbs are on fire. Burning all through your thighs and upper arms. If you dropped, the time started from the beginning.

'Yes, Uncle Jonathan does, but I am talking about Cainan,' Kate says.

I remember the pressure Jonathan put on me to do things I didn't want to do with Cainan, the time he put me and Cainan in the same bed and told me to take my clothes off as he watched. Someone had walked in the room and I ran through the door with my clothes bundled in my hand.

'He is NOT my boyfriend,' I say, stung by both the memory and Joel's suggestion.

Kate says kindly, 'I told you that he was a Watchout.'

'Watchouts' are what we kids secretly call the adults that you need to 'watch out' for. You can usually spot them right away. We had become attuned to their behaviours early on. (As an adult, I would later find out that the real name for a Watchout is a pervert, paedo or child molester.) To begin with, older siblings would let you know who they were, but before too long, you could spot them yourself. Watchouts have a couple of tells: they might look at you for a bit too long or take too much of an interest in disciplining you. Sometimes, and these were the most difficult Watchouts to spot, they were the ones that were kinder to you than other adults. But really, those Watchouts were rare.

You don't have to be kind to do what you want to do to the children in our homes.

Most homes would have at least one Watchout. If you lived with one, you knew to try not to be in a room alone with them, or get on the wrong side of them. Stay with your pack and stay off their radar. The kids most in danger from the Watchouts were the older children who didn't have brothers and sisters to teach them, or the kids who were from smaller families that didn't have a wolfpack to protect them. The ones that were in the worst situations, of course, were the ones whose own parents were Watchouts. There had been a time when Uncles were allowed to marry their own daughters and some actually did. We are lucky, we are a strong pack – we've always looked out for one another and kept each other safe.

So far.

There are no Watchouts here. We can relax, it's a holiday camp.

*   *   *

We ended staying in our bright yellow caravan for nearly two months. The last month at the campsite went by in a blur of cold and sickness. Now we're back on the floor of the van and we're on our way to start a new commune called 'The Birmingham Home'. It's only been a few hours, but already it's like the holiday home was a dream that's quickly fading. Maybe we never went to Wales, maybe we've been in the van this whole time, but I know in my bones that isn't true because I feel so weak. My limp limbs remind me of the gastric flu I got on the campsite. I haven't played in a while, I don't have the energy. And I feel the cold much more than I did two months ago. The flu meant I couldn't keep food down for a very long time. I bend my legs as I lie on the floor of the van. They are tiny, little sticks in baggy trousers – the same trousers I have worn almost every day since we went underground.

The Birmingham Home, The Birmingham Home . . . I mouth these words over a few times; they feel funny in my mouth.

'I wonder what the next house is going to be like?' I whisper to Kate.

'Sshhhhhhhh.' She shoots a gentle warning as she strokes my hair.

I had heard Mom and Dad talking about a 'farm' earlier. I imagine a warm fire, woolly blankets, a roasted chicken, singing and big comfy sofas to lie down on. Everything glows red and smells amazing. I hold Kate's hand and smile.

We have good things ahead, I can feel it.

*   *   *

'A UFO could have landed in here, it looks like the site of a space wreck,' Josh says as we all stand around the edges of the disaster that is supposed to be a living room. We can see straight through to the floor below.

'We come in peace,' Joel says, laughing.

Kate tries the light switch.

'No electricity,' she says, unsurprised.

We are at the farm. This doesn't feel like a home. It's a collection of barns that have been under attack, like bombs have ripped their way through the bones of the building. My dad can fix anything, but this feels too far gone. No heating, no electricity and giant holes in the rooms.

My mom walks into the shared disbelief of her children.

'We will all sleep in one room for warmth. We'll get the gas fire and put it in the middle and you can make a circle around it.' As she says this, the wind eerily changes tune as it whips through the holes in the house. 'This will be warm and safe in no time,' she adds weakly.

We nod in agreement. I look at Mom trying to make this OK for us. She is always *trying*. She is always pacifying Dad, soothing him, standing by his decisions. If any of us kids have the tendency to 'people please', it's an echo of her. She is the buffer between us and him. It's tough when it comes to Mom, hard to know just what to think or feel about her, it's confusing, but I have always wanted to protect her.

In a way, it almost feels like she is one of us, like she is being led around too, like she doesn't have much choice in this. She's always pregnant, always breastfeeding, always giving birth. Even when it seemed like there was a break between kids, those were the years she gave birth to stillborns. And she has spent *years* being really unwell. She lost most of her hair and got so thin. I remember watching her in bed too weak to rise, wanting to save her but not knowing how. Was it our fault? Did we, her many children, each take a piece of her when we were born? Maybe it's not just me, maybe we all feel a sense of protection and guilt when it comes to Mom.

*   *   *

It's the middle of the night and the room glows red from the gas fire. Everyone is asleep and there's a symphony of night sounds: breathing, squeaks, shuffles. I move very carefully towards the glow of the gas heater, moving my feet as close as I can. This close up, I get about three minutes of warmth through my socks before my feet start burning. I know the white heat is coming, but I need that warmth. *Bang!* When it comes, I rub my feet quickly and try not make a sound as the burn hits. As the pain subsides, there will be a good five minutes of warm feet.

Heaven.

The world outside looks like it's moving in slow motion. The wind has died down and the house itself has magically gone quiet. I see something through the window that's too slow to be rain and too big to be hail – it's *snow*. Josh and Sam prayed for snow this morning because we had never seen it and here it is. I move towards the window and touch the glass. Big chunks of the sky are floating down and settling on the ground, like manna from heaven.

It's so beautiful.

'Get back to bed!' My mom's voice cuts through the dark.

'It's a miracle,' I whisper. 'We prayed for snow and *look*!'

'Back to bed,' she says again gently.

The boys are going to be so pleased, I think, as I shuffle between two bodies to get some sleep. Their prayers must have been powerful ones, because when we wake up the next morning, there is over four feet of snow. Mom comes from the north of England, where it snows all the time, and even she says this is a lot. Josh and Sam are giddy, packing the snow together in their bare hands to turn it into weapons. Our cries of delight turn to shrieks of pain as the cold gets inside our fingertips like tiny icy knives under our skin. We don't last very long, but the snow does – it settles for weeks.

Every day, we make more progress on the house, patching up the floors, painting walls. We only have a limited amount of time to work each day because the winter sun is transitory. It seems to want to hurry to bed in the afternoon, maybe it feels the cold too.

'BexyBoots . . .'

It's Kate's sing-song voice as she shakes me through my bundle of blankets.

'Yes?' I say excitedly, sitting up.

'Happy Birthday,' she says, putting her hand on my shoulder.

I had nearly forgotten. Our group has never celebrated birthdays, but my brothers and sisters do. It's something they learned when they stayed with our grandparents all those years ago. For years, my parents haven't told our grandparents where we live. Any mail they send gets forwarded from other people's addresses for safety, all set up in case they send money. But this means that about six months after your birthday, you get a card from Grandma and Grandpa. They never forget. There is usually a cheerful cartoon on the front. Sometimes there's a big number on it and inside, in their handwriting, there's a message saying how special you are and that they love and miss you. At the top, it always says *here's five pounds for you* next to a piece of sticky tape torn away from the empty card.

They always remember us.

So now, Kate remembers everyone's birthday and always does something for each of us. And I know since it's just our family here, she will do so 100 per cent today. Eager to get my working day out of the way so we can have my celebration, I get up. The sun seems to linger. It goes by so slowly for the first time ever. Finally, we sit down for dinner and then I see it. Kate brings in a cake for me. It's a big 'R' made out of powdered milk, water and sugar, with one of our safety candles sticking out of it. I look at my brothers and sisters – their faces are glowing, everyone has a massive smile as they sing in unison.

As we cut up the 'cake', Kris leans over and says to me, 'Nine years old! You're getting so grown-up, BexyBoots.'

I know it. I feel different – I feel like an adult today.

*   *   *

It's a few months since my birthday.

My face is pressed into the carpet, its rough texture stinking of sour milk. It digs into my forehead. My breath is getting quicker, it shoots back into my nose, hot and full of this smell. Their hands are all over my body. Everyone in the house has been gathered here for this ritual. The Birmingham Home is now a fully working commune. All the rules are back in place, the schedules are being followed. It's full of new families and Leaders, including Uncle Jude. He is relentless, he is violent. He is a Watchout.

And he is our leader.

Jude is leading my exorcism. These aren't a usual part of our life. They happen very rarely when someone does something seriously wrong.

Like I have.

'Shadabadah, sheebadahbah, thank you, Lord.'

The mumbles of people talking in tongues fill my ears, which burn white-hot. I feel the red in my face, not that anyone can see, as I'm crouched over, partly in a position of prayer, partly because it feels safer if I can cover my head with my arms. I'm too ashamed to look at anyone.

The hands all over me feel like being enveloped in the sea, but the water is made of body parts. The soles of my feet are being touched. My shoulders. Every part of me. Their hands burn through the clothes I am wearing, skin on skin. The hands of people who are disgusted by me, disappointed with me, ashamed of me.

Uncle Jude's voice cuts through the swirling circle of people.

'Lord, we pray for this one who has been taken over by a demon, a demon with a deceitful tongue. This girl who has accepted this demon in and allowed it to speak through her, invading our home with her lies.'

'Shadabadah, sheebadahbah, thank you, Lord.'

The mutterings get louder. Some of the hands on me start to shake. I get hotter and hotter.

Is that my demon leaving?

The lie I told Uncle Jude was so stupid. I had written a note to my brother Joel to try and protect him. In a commune, there are informants everywhere. Sometimes people will trick you, trip you up and tell on you. And Jude's son Asaiah, who was 14, was actually one of *them*. They call them 'BellWethers' – a sheep that helps lead the other sheep. We call them 'Spies'. I could see him for what he was and I wanted Joel to be careful around him so I wrote to Joel, warning him. Joel had read my note and then shoved it down the side of the couch. Days later, it had been found by the clean-up crew.

Stupid. I should have double-checked. Always double-check.

After the note was discovered, the inquisition started. They interrogated us, one by one. I lied. Maybe we could all get away with this if no one said anything. Then they said no child would eat until the guilty one confessed and I knew it wasn't an empty threat because Jude never did that. I came forward straight away. As part of my punishment, or road to becoming 'better', I was to be exorcised.

'We cast this evilness out of her! We ask you to forgive her for her hateful unrighteousness.'

People shout in tongues. My face is still in the floor, it feels like I'm in a tunnel made of noise, hands and heat. Everything is shaking.

'Shadabadah, sheebadahbah, thank you, Lord.'

Uncle Jude screams, 'We will cast this evil out! We will call her Rebekah the Deceiver as a warning!'

I try to breathe. My eyes are swelling shut. I can't see, I can't catch my breath. The noise is too much. My hands are tingling. My arms are tingling. My chest squeezes, shutting the air out. I'm suffocating. Everything is closing in. I can't breathe.

I can't breathe.

CHAPTER 4

Mother Truckers and Mamacita: 15 Years After

'And so our adventure begins,' Sofi says with a laugh, lighting a cigarette as she grips the wheel of our truck.

I met Sofi in Berlin, she was in film school at the time. She's a writer, photographer and filmmaker. Raised by academics with an open, spiritual nature, she has the ability to crack open the universe in seconds. We bonded quickly over our love of dogs, dark humour and underground raves. I watch her while she drives our massive truck down the highway. Her wide blue eyes take in the road, white-blonde choppy bob bouncing as she smokes (and dances) at the wheel.

Three months ago, looking through my laptop into her high-ceilinged apartment in Berlin, an apartment that I had once lived in, I asked Sofi if she would come on an adventure with me – 'Let's go join cults,' I said. 'We'll make a document-ary, it will help us understand people. We'll meet kids who grew up like *me*.' Even with a plan that loose, she didn't hesitate. She'd recently graduated, she'd just split up with her long-term boyfriend and her wonderful father had died suddenly.

Perhaps she needed a way out as much as I needed someone bonkers enough to come with me.

We are headed through California towards our first group, the Ananda. We've spent a few days in San Francisco, getting the truck that we're going to be living in for the next few months into shape. Like a new couple moving in together, we headed to IKEA to fill her up with crap and make her into a home. She's a 1989 Ford beauty that looks a cross between *Breaking Bad* and Blanche from *The Golden Girls*' living room – comfortable, beige. Dated but still, somehow, badass. I'd fallen in love with her the minute I saw her. We christened her Mamacita – our caring mama of a truck that would house us and look after us on our journey.

I take Sofi through the history of the Ananda as we drive through the stunning mountains, red stone, green fields and open expanses. Views that are framed by my oversized truck window – a framing that becomes the one constant in an ever-changing American world.

The ideology and inspiration for the Ananda community came from a man who was born in 1893, in India. A man who was bafflingly ahead of the spiritual wave of the hippie revolution and whose ideology feels right at home even today, in the 'woke' minds of our generation: Paramahansa Yogananda.

'You don't pronounce it *Parmesan*,' Sofi laughs kindly. 'He was an Indian monk, yogi and guru, who introduced millions of Westerners to the teachings of meditation and Kriya Yoga.'

She takes over the history lesson – as a full-blown, level *bajillion* yogi, she knows more about this guru than I have written in my research.

In fact, Paramahansa Yogananda became so popular in the West that he ended up on the cover of a Beatles' album (*Sgt. Pepper's Lonely Hearts Club Band*) and was a major inspiration for Apple pioneer Steve Jobs, who read his book, *Autobiography of a Yogi*, every year until he died.

Yogananda created the Self-Realization Fellowship a few years after he landed in California in 1920. His ideals were to encourage 'plain living and high thinking' and to spread a spirit of brotherhood through kinship with God. He encouraged cultural and spiritual understanding between East and West and taught that we should serve mankind as a larger Self.

'It all sounds reasonable and progressive to me,' I say.

'He wrote this book in the forties, the *forties*! It was published just one year after World War Two ended,' Sofi says.

Yogananda was so ahead of a world that was so *behind*; this was the same year that women in the US were allowed to buy land and have separate bank accounts. And while he was busy setting up shop in the US, James Donald Walters was born in 1926, in Romania, to American parents. James went to school in four countries, spoke five languages and attended an Ivy League university. But he never finished his studies, because in September 1948, he read Yogananda's *Autobiography of a Yogi* and it completely transformed his life. He was so inspired, he bussed cross-country to Southern California to become a disciple of Yogananda – James Donald Walters was no more, he became Swami Kriyananda.

Yogananda spoke of creating communities to help the youth find happiness, freedom and jobs. Self-sufficient colonies that would live off the land, never judge or even *ask* if someone was Jewish, Gentile, Muslim or Catholic – instead, the membership criteria was willingness and good character. He wanted a place where people could learn that the first principle of life is happiness. And he believed that America was ready for this.

And in 1968, Kriyananda brought Yogananda's ideas to life: he created the Ananda community: a huge 840 acres with at least 300 residents. But Yogananda never got to see any of it – by the time that the Ananda village was built, he had already passed away. He died while speaking at a dinner in Los Angeles, Swami Kriyananda by his side. It happened as he recited his poem 'My India', managing the last line of it:

> *Where Ganges, woods, Himalayan caves, and men*
> *dream God—I am hallowed; my body touched that sod.*

'And then, he fell dead to the floor,' I finish dramatically.

I reach for my phone to make sure we haven't missed a turning but when I flip to the map, it's just grey pixels – the top right-hand corner of my screen tells me I have zero signal. Night fell without warning, the only thing visible in our headlights is cat's eyes and white dashes. The stars are bright. There are no streetlights and no GPS.

'We OK?' Sofi asks.

'It's cool,' I say. But I have no idea where we are. 'We need to stop at the next sign of life – a gas station or whatever, doesn't matter. Get some directions . . .'

'So, we're lost?' she asks.

'I *think* we're on the right track, I just want to make sure.'

'We OK for gas?' she asks.

Our gas meter is broken so I have to calculate this by mileage from the last fill-up. I thumb open the page on my notepad.

'I *think* so . . . Don't panic.'

Don't panic – two words that seem to inspire the opposite effect.

We drive silently through the darkness for the next half-hour.

'Look . . . Up ahead, a tiny glow. We're fine.'

As we get closer, the glow turns into the neon lights of a bar. We slow down, our tyres crunch on the stones outside and we pull to a halt.

The engine ticks.

'Go in together?' I say, my nerves betraying me.

We step into the smell of sticky beer and cigarette breath. The light inside is warm and red, the floors are made of wood and the walls are covered in the same, maybe walnut, panelling. Perhaps it's a classic American set-up, but to my alien eyes, it's thrilling and cinematic. I walk up to the bar as my focus moves to the crowd and my heart jumps in my throat. A man in the corner with a half-drunk beer in hand, the woman behind the bar pouring a pint, staring into the distance, the guy sat alone, an empty shot glass collection in front of him; their skin hangs like they've been drained of their blood, their features creep down their faces from the disintegration of flesh and muscle. It's eerie and unnerving. These aren't vampires; it's less dramatic and more sombre than that.

These kids have been devoured by meth.

*   *   *

A man with one leg propped up at the bar looks over at me as if I am the creature in their midst.

'Hi, we're looking for the Ananda?' I say.

'Welcome! You are here,' he says, his eyes smiling.

'You're kidding?' I say.

How could we have got it so wrong?

'Well, in a way, you are in the right place . . . The gurus are just up the hill,' he laughs.

I pull the passenger door open, grateful for the warmth and safety of the truck.

'I feel like we're starring in *Dawn of the Dead*,' Sofi says as we rumble up the hill.

I squint into the darkness. 'This is the turning, just pull in here to the left, see . . .'

We roll into the Ananda. There are no gates to keep anyone, fictitious or otherwise, out of their hallowed grounds. As my eyes start to adjust, I see the outlines of trees, bushes and a blanket of mist on the ground.

'What the hell is *that*?' Sofi yelps.

'Jesus Christ!' I jump in my seat as glowing eyes split through the mist. Bright yellow, some almost green, they seem to be circling all sides of the truck. 'I think it's just coyotes,' I say.

'You *think*? These could be werewolves for all we know . . . considering what the townspeople look like!' she laughs.

Nervous energy has filled the cabin, our breathing shallow and in tandem as we drive through the pitch-black, glowing eyes and low mist.

My thin voice breaks the silence: 'We don't have to stay here tonight if it's too much.'

Sofi stares hard into the dark, maybe considering it.

'I mean, it would be pretty lame if we were bitten to death by guru monk vampires in the *first* group we stayed in,' I say, adding a laugh that sounds fake at best.

'We'll never finish the film then,' Sofi says, matter-of-factly.

'These guys are harmless,' I say, convincing and reminding myself that the reason we chose this particular group as our first is because they are mild, safe yogis – 'A dry run,' I'd told her. 'Everything will look entirely different in the morning when the mist has gone and the coyotes have scarpered.'

'Yep,' she says. 'It will all look different.'

We park up near a set of buildings, deciding the safest thing we can do is just get straight to bed. I clamber into the bed next to Sofi, pulling the blankets up around my neck, fully clothed. Not sure if it's for warmth, or because something inside is warning me to be prepared to run. The sounds of the engine start to fade, the ticks of the truck become quieter, the metal cooling down.

'You OK, Angel?' I say.

'Yeah, 'course,' she says (also fully clothed).

There is a pause in the sounds of the truck, our breath slows down, its rhythm in tandem.

'I need to wee,' I say.

'You want to go out there?' she says, smiling.

'No fucking way!' I laugh.

'Just pee the bed,' she laughs. 'I won't tell anyone.'

Sofi pulls out her phone and hits 'Record'.

'What you doing?' I say.

'Don't you want to say goodbye to your loved ones?' she says with a smile.

We film ourselves sarcastically saying goodbye to our families, *just in case*. And then actually send the footage.

Just. In. Case.

*　　*　　*

The morning sun wakes me as it fills our makeshift bedroom with a golden light. I poke Sofi under the covers and whisper, 'We made it through the night, babe.'

'Really?' she says, rubbing her eyes, her blonde hair catching the light like a halo.

'Yeah. *And* I didn't wet myself,' I say proudly.

I pull the beige curtain back fully to see that everything *does* look different. A harmless set of buildings sits in front of us, trees of all colours, shapes and sizes surround us – orange, brown, green, bursting with life and colour. The aroma of coffee floats through the truck from the group's kitchens. People float around serenely in colourful robes of green, blue and orange.

And not a single creature of the night in sight.

We step out, stretching our limbs out and taking big gulps of the beautiful fresh air. Hands on hips, I spin slowly to take it all in.

'We're standing in the manifestation of Yogananda's dream ... this is bonkers.' It's pretty remarkable this is a dream that started all the way back in the 1920s. 'Sofi, did I tell you who Kriyanda bought this land with? Richard Baker, Gary Snyder and Allen Ginsberg ... *Allen-bloody-Ginsberg!*' I say this rather grandly, hoping the fact that I only very recently found out who these guys are isn't obvious. 'So, a monk, a Zen master, a Pulitzer Prize winner and the father of the Beat movement bought some land in Nevada.'

'Sounds like the beginning of a bad joke, doesn't it?' Sofi says.

But this is no joke: it's a living, working commune and it's huge. We walk around freely, get coffee, snoop about in their thrift shop. Smiles, hellos and howdys are handed out by everyone we pass by.

'Hey, girls, can I help you?' a man in overalls says.

'Thanks, we're good.'

We've been found out.

'Would you like a golf cart? You'll be able to get around easier,' he says.

'WOOOHOOOO!' screams Sofi as we speed up the hill in our new set of wheels.

'I mean, where even are we?' I say.

We head towards the home of Swami Kriyananda. Although he died some time ago, it has been left exactly as it was: calm, serene, simple. We wander around his garden, which explodes with statues. Buddha, angels, and even some of Jesus, dappled sunlight gives a sense of aliveness to a collection of stones that perhaps proclaim '*all are welcome here*'. A feeling of calm envelops me, as does a sense of strangeness – it's just odd this oasis exists in the middle of a town in Nevada.

As we putt around on our golf car, breathing in clean, crisp air, the smell of ferns around us, I can imagine this as a scene from a utopian sci-fi film. The swamis floating by in colourful robes, the *perfectly* manicured grounds. The weather is mild, blue and bright without being too hot. Everything is *just so*. It's harmonious and otherworldly. *Spooky.* The inspiration behind it is 'plain living for higher thinking' and I can see how a world that's this balanced could leave you with enough room to think better and clearly.

We head to meet up with a kid we met in the community thrift shop this morning. He'd asked if we wanted to come for a walk with him and his dog in the woods, and offered to show us around the Ananda.

Jared is a 12-year-old boy with dirty blonde hair that goes just below his ears. He has pale, clear skin and sharp blue eyes. It's clear he is fiercely intelligent – his eyes dart back and forth, computing everything at high speed. We follow him and his black dog through the forest, through beautiful winding tracks with skinny, but giant ferns towering over us. This new world is enveloping me so quickly. Just a week ago, I was in San Francisco in a completely different state of mind – it feels so much longer.

Another world, where I sat alone in my friend's beautiful home. Writing in my journal, wondering how this, being here in the Ananda, would be today. I wince as the feelings of that night come back.

It's 9pm, Friday night. I am alone.

I am in a busy city where I know people, and yet I feel starved for human contact. I sit in this empty house and I know that I should be working. This film is well above my pay grade and my skill set. I need to concentrate and get myself into the right mindset – healthy, calm and ready.

But all I can think about is getting wasted.

Anything to distract me from the fear that I feel about what I am about to do. Not just fear of the groups that I am going to join, but fear of failure – in fact, all the things that everyone else seems to be worrying about, that I'll end up in a cult, lose my mind, or get kidnapped – that all seems far-fetched. Failure, on the other hand, is very realistic. Fear that I have no right to be doing what I am doing. And that I am in over my head.

While I was on the flight to San Francisco, I wrote a list of all the things that I thought could go wrong:

We don't film anything and come back empty-handed.

I run out of money.

Me and Sofi fall out and never speak again.

One of us has a total meltdown.

Sofi wants to stay in one of the cults or abandons me somewhere.

The trip is pointless and a waste of time.

Everyone thinks I am mad/an idiot for doing it.

Kidnapping doesn't make the list.

I know I am in a state of 'need', and that is never the right time for me to go out. The want for escape rather than to experience joy. The intention is not healthy – this is when I can be at my most destructive. I feel needy. And it feels nauseating. Nauseating because I recognise it, I hate the sight of it, it's ugly, pathetic appearance is staring right at me. I check my phone; check my mail, hoping that someone in SF has contacted me. I simultaneously want to retreat from the world and go out into it, feverishly consuming and self-medicating until the fear fades. I know the drill – drown the feelings tonight, drown in them tomorrow morning.

Should I just take a sleeping pill and sedate myself to keep out of trouble? Hold on, there's my phone.

Gagging on the memory, I physically shake off the feelings of that night, jam my boots into the earth to bring myself back.

I look up at the trees, the sky and listen to the crunch of the woods under my feet. Bring myself back to where I am standing now, in this moment. And it starts to make sense, what being somewhere like this can do for you and your mental state. Even just the physical make-up of a community like this, where everything is taken care of and runs on its own rhythm, can shrink the anxiety, make you feel like that other life of fear, failure and terrifying realness is irrelevant, or of no consequence. The distance soothes. This place is a refreshing, calm tonic – who wouldn't want to take a sip?

We come out of the woods and Jared starts his tour of the community.

'This is one of the temples you can meditate in. People spend hours in here,' he explains, taking us into a wooden structure that's empty except for a few framed photos of Yogananda on the walls and some rugs on the floor. The temple has large windows with views of a calm, beautiful lake that sits in the middle of the commune. I touch the glass, my breath mists the view – I could spend hours in here, looking at that peaceful water.

He walks us through the grounds, explaining how the colours of the robes work.

'There are the swamis that wear the orange robes, this is pretty ubiquitous amongst yogic monks. However, Swami Kriyananda felt inspired to establish a new swami order, called the Nayaswami (or new swami) order, who wear blue. You can wear this if you are married or unmarried. The blue is about calmness and inner state.'

'So, those who wear orange robes, does that mean they're celibate?' I ask.

I regret my question as soon it escapes, realising that I've just asked a 12-year-old boy about the sex life of the monks. He nods, completely unfazed.

Good, glad we got that out the way.

He doesn't seem embarrassed by the question.

'Do you wanna come for dinner at my parents' house?' he asks.

Jutting out between the trees is a breathtaking property that's built into the forest. It's incredible, the kind of place that you put on your Pinterest page and imagine you'll live in one day when you have your shit together. Double-height ceilings, giant windows that make the structure seem to blend with the trees, beautiful wooden beams and state-of-the-art technology that we haven't seen anywhere else in the community. They also have an outdoor pizza oven.

Jared's mom greets us: 'We're having a build-your-own-pizza night and we are *so* excited to have you here to share it with us!'

We are thrown into a welcoming, pesto-infused family night in. It feels so normal and natural. Within minutes of being here, Sofi and I are wearing aprons and assemble peppers, onions and other bits and bobs on floury bases.

'We have gluten-free and vegan, if you need it, girls.'

I look over at Sofi, baffled.

'What the fuck?' she mouths.

I giggle.

'Dreamland, thank you!' I say.

Their big, beautiful, high-tech house is like stepping into another world within a world. It *is* a dreamland. The Narnia door that leads into a palace within a commune. The other houses here tend to be small, simple wooden bungalows with two or three rooms.

Nice, but basic.

The family has been here for three years: after Jared's dad made enough money from selling voice recognition technology he created to retire with his family into yogic life. We don't pry, but are told by someone the next day that he invented 'Siri'. I wonder if he found out about this place because Steve Jobs was such an avid follower of Yogananda's book. Someone else tells us he supports the entire community financially, so his house is extra special and, of course, he built it himself.

We spend the evening having an enjoyable and 'normal' family night. Occasionally, something happens that reminds us that we are actually in a commune. Someone will say, 'One vision that I had' or 'Remember Jared's premonition?' or even a spiritual joke, 'That third pizza's not going to bring you enlightenment, honey. Maybe you've had enough.' Normalising self-realisation for us outsiders. Whether they are doing it for our benefit, or just because it's a part of how they exist here, spiritual, sarcastic, enlightened and down to earth, whatever it is, it's charming as hell. As I laugh at their jokes through mouthfuls of homemade pizza, I wonder if this is how communal living and spirituality can be. Where you can have a kind of balance. Where you can have nice things like a big TV, take the piss out of your faith, but still be deeply connected to it. It's not something that I had experienced before – my group was the all-or-nothing approach.

* * *

After dinner, Sofi and I offer to wash the dishes. We soak our hands in sulphate-free, vegan soap bubbles, eyeing each other up, sharing the private joke of the world we have stumbled into.

'Girls, do you want to see what the school is like here?' Jared's mom's voice interrupts us. 'I'm sure you can tell that Jared has an extremely high IQ – we were looking for some- where to put him where he could explore that intelligence but where it wouldn't become the only focus for him,' she explains.

'We would *love* to see the school,' we almost chime in unison.

The next day, we pull up in our golf cart at the 'Living Wisdom School'. It's surrounded, of course, by nature. It's first period and we walk into the big wooden schoolhouse over- flowing with the sounds of children running and laughing. The whole place has huge windows and is bathed in natural light.

While I'm still figuring this trip out, one thing that I am sure of, and have been sure of since Walter's house, is I want to understand the perspective of children. I feel that adults have the right to follow whatever religion they want. It's the conflict between what an adult wants to do and how it affects their kids that interests me. Like me, the kids have no choice but to follow their parents' religion and the lifestyle that comes with it, so I can't wait to meet them en masse.

We follow Jared into a room where there are children of all different ages. He says that they are going to explain the 'Education for Life' to us and the curriculum they're study- ing. I wonder if I should tell them I haven't been to school. It's something that I share with care. Never attending school had a massive impact on me. Not just from an educational per- spective. Like many people who don't have something, you can become obsessed with the idea of it. What you missed out on, what you 'could' have been. It's easy to blame your failures on it. Many a kid I grew up with proclaimed they could have been a neurosurgeon if they'd attended school. Perhaps. But probably not. As an adult, never attending school did make me completely unsure about what I was thinking, saying and the validity of what I had learned. Most of my life is spent on the edge of conversations at parties, work or wherever, smiling and nodding and HOPING that I don't say something completely stupid.

Stay around the periphery where it's safe.

What did I learn in 'school'? That Heaven was a giant pyramid in the moon – literally *inside* the moon. On a clear night, squint and you can see it. That world was only 6,000 years old. Even my biblical knowledge came with a twist. That Jesus was sleeping with Mary Magdalene (she washed his feet that one time – and she was a reformed prostitute – so it's not *too* far a stretch). That Noah cursed Ham 'black' because he was gay and that's how we have black people and why they have such a struggle in Africa.

Yeah, best keep that education under wraps.

In contrast to my lack of education and the obsession I have had with getting one, I've also read the theories about the Western world's schooling system and its fallibilities; where the subjects that mattered most during the Industrial Revolution still have the highest precedence now. Maths, English, Science. And in the style of an industrial factory, kids are put into classes by their 'date of manufacture' rather than their skills, aptitude or desire to learn.

I wonder how I would have done in 'real' school?

The kids gather round, eager to talk to the girls with strange accents. I ask a little girl who must be about eight what her favourite subject is and she says, 'Earth and the Universe.'

'It's all about understanding the wholeness of the universe and how everything works together to make it, so it's a little bit of physics, astronomy, chemistry, biology, general science, botany, geology and anatomy,' she explains.

I can't think of an eight-year-old I have met who talks like this.

So, here, it's not just about subjects in isolation, it's about big, meaningful topics, helping kids understand their context. Another subject they study is 'Personal Development'. Kids as young as six years old are taught about physical, mental and spiritual development. This class includes lessons on how to expand your memory, how to remain centred, joyful and self-disciplined and teaches them the secrets to happiness.

'Do you have any spaces left on this course?' I ask the teacher.

I am only 50 per cent kidding – and 100 per cent jealous.

I want to know how, or if, they discipline the kids here, assuming they use 'time outs' or 'detention' – the New Age-style curriculum makes me feel it would be inventive. The teacher says, 'Have you heard the phrase "spare the rod and spoil the child?"'

'I know that saying *very* well,' I say, my body becoming rigid, alert.

'Well, we believe that it *is* possible to spoil a child – to raise him in the belief that he can always get his own way, perhaps by temper tantrums, perhaps by playing one adult against another.'

'Uh, huh.' I nod, still coiled, waiting for something fucked-up to come out of this sun-soaked classroom.

'However, we also believe that the use of the "rod" can spoil the most beautiful aspect of a child's nature, the quality of trust,' she says.

A wave of relief runs through me. What an important way to describe the deep consequences of physical punishment: ruining a child's belief in trust. I think about my trust issues and the depths that they run to. The teacher has hit an old nerve with a sledgehammer. I exhale, my breath pulls me back into the room. And perhaps the teacher notices my shift as she says, 'Do you guys want to come play music with us?'

* * *

As we float away from the school on our golf cart an hour later, I ask Sofi, 'Is it all just a bit *too* nice? Does it feel a bit, I don't know, Stepford wife?'

She looks at me, an eyebrow raised.

'I mean, they seem really nice and balanced, that school is so nice I want to enrol in it, they GAVE us this golf buggy and . . .'

'They must be hiding something,' she says.

I can't tell if she's sarcastic or serious.

She laughs.

'Truth Joke,' I say.

As we bob over the hills, the woods fly by in out-of-focus greens and I think about the Ananda's ethos and how it connects to so much of the *need* of our generation. I am thousands of miles away from my home, but even the time I spent in San

Francisco and New York on this trip showed me that young people (and probably *all* people) are clearly looking for purpose, connection and community. Cities hosting cocaine-fuelled nights, people arguing about gentrification, how we should live off the land, how yoga changes lives, 'This-one-time-in-an-ashram'. We sit in warehouses, drinking boutique beers, talking about global warming, while chopping out lines of expensive chemicals. We're becoming flexitarians, farm-to-fork, we are a generation full of contradictions looking for a purpose.

We drive by the small wooden bungalows the Anandans live in and I wonder how many people would look at this way of life and be *into it*. In fact, if you attached a £3,000 price tag on spending a week here learning how to be a Guru or Guvri, the Ananda could have a pretty profitable business from the hipsters in London alone. The quests we've been on, from white linen beds in Ibiza drinking ayahuasca with 'genuine' shamans to puffing on DMT (a hallucinogenic drug) in council estates, experiencing life after death, or even ingesting the poison of frogs as a boost for our immune system and a spiritual cleanse show that we're searching and expanding – or vulnerably swaying from spiritual charlatan to shaman – in the quest for self-realisation and authenticity.

We are so much closer to being ripe for this way of life than we think.

'Shall we go back to the thrift shop in town and buy some shit?' Sofi breaks my internal monologue.

'Sure, let's check out town too . . . be nice to see in the light of day,' I say.

* * *

The Ridge is a unique town where micro-communities, lifestyles and cultures converge. It's home to not only the Ananda, but to 'regular' townsfolk, the bohemians (in the 1970s they 'brought their drugs and their dogs,' said the grocer) to meth cooks, weed growers and two naked (and 'incestuous', according to the gas attendant) Germans, who reside on the beach. Comparisons to the Wild Wild West have been made, people call it a haven for outlaws and dope-growers ('which is offensive,' say the regular townspeople), while the town dentist told us it's a 'complicated, but beautiful mosaic'.

There's a shop called 'Mother Truckers', a thrift store and a vegetarian café. Opposite these is a car park currently *teeming* with half-naked hippies, white kids with dreadlocks and unwashed Europeans, looking to make a buck on their road trips – all of whom have stormed the town for weed-trimming season.

Californians have got to get their medicinals from somewhere.

And there's another commune in The Ridge, one that resides deep in the woods past the edge of town. It's 30 people-strong, with a handful of kids too. What the commune ('freaks in the woods') believe is a mystery. But what we do know is that they 'wear clothes made of animal skins and eat roadkill' and are led by a woman called Star Compost. Desperate to meet them, we head up with bags of almond milk and cereal (the guy at Mother Truckers told us it's their favourite). We stand looking through the wire gate at children's toys strewn ominously across the land and thousands of crushed cans, perhaps to sell, that fill up the grounds. But no one comes to the gates. We wait long enough in the woods to spook ourselves out, leave our gifts and head back to town.

There is a specific smell to thrift stores: it's musty, dusty, foisty. Like the back of Nana's knicker cupboard, and this thrift store is no different. It's a hoarder's paradise, full of stuff – old cameras, fur coats, clocks, used batteries. Bits that could have been sifted out of the trash sit next to objects that *could* be priceless – everything fused together by a carpet of dust.

'My name is Tiger.' A sing-song voice floats from the front of the shop. Nosily, I peek over the rack of coats at a girl draping herself on the counter, talking to the guy who runs the place. Her woollen bikini top reveals tattoos all over her back and shoulders and she fiddles with the hoop through her septum as she speaks.

'That's an unusual name,' he tells her.

I sift through a box of battered cameras close by, listening in on Tiger's chat. She's sleeping in a van across the road in the car park, she tells him. She's from Ohio originally but doesn't consider herself 'from there' anymore as she's travelled *so* much and is hunting around for some trimming work. I catch myself eye-rolling each new bit of intel.

'If you hear of anything, you'll let me know, won't you?' As she hands her number to him, she strokes his wrist heavily on the way out.

'Nicely played, Tiger – grrrrrrr!' Sofi says under her breath.

'Ha!' I say, pleased that perhaps I am not the only one being super judgemental.

I walk over to the softly spoken man behind the counter: 'Wow, you get all sorts in this neck of the woods, don't you?'

'Yeah . . . You guys here for trimming season too?' he asks.

'God, no – not green-thumbed in any way! We're doing a project on new religious movements, we're staying up at the Ananda community,' I say, waving my hand towards the hill.

'Woah!' He cocks an eyebrow and leans in towards me. 'Well, I know a few things about *that* place.'

Sofi and I close in on him, slowly and calmly, so as not to scare the man in our midst.

'Really? That's interesting.' Almost deadpan, I dare not show how excited I am. But I don't want to start this conversation here, disturbed by a trim-hungry hippie every two minutes.

'Maybe we can take you for a drink later on and you can fill us in?' I say.

He looks the two of us up and down.

'Well, when was the last time you gals had a homecooked meal? You could come over tonight and I'll make my specialty pasta.'

I shoot Sofi a look that goes something like, *What do you think? Is this safe? Is this guy a creep? Also, we JUST had pizza night!*

She responds with one that feels like, *Seriously? This guy? AND you can never get TOO much free/homecooked food.*

And we agree to go for dinner.

*   *   *

Later that night, I snoop around Josh's house. It's like creaking round the bowels of a boat. Knots peer out from the wooden panels with wild Picasso-style faces. The scent of garlic, onions and tomato floats through the air, giving the whole home a steamy essence of creature comfort. Josh brings his work home with him – there is bric-a-brac on all the shelves. My thumb strokes an old wooden figurine, wondering what life it may have had before coming to sit on here, with front-row seats into Josh's life.

'You looking for the restroom?' Josh shouts from the kitchen.

'Nah, just being nosey,' I say.

'Well, food's up,' he says.

Like hungry children, Sofi and I sit salivating as Josh piles our plates with spaghetti and pasta sauce.

'Is that enough for you?' Josh asks through a handsome set of teeth.

'Mmmmm!' we say at the same time. The two of us have started to meld into one – worn-out flannel shirts, old T-shirts underneath, threadbare jeans ... We've both removed our trucker caps – to be polite. I don't know where the rule comes from, but I know it exists.

I am halfway through my plate of food when he lays some photos of a beautiful, mixed-race woman on the dinner table.

'This was the love of my life ... my ex-wife,' he says.

I drop my fork and lean in. The air in the room changes as a window to the past is opened.

'We moved here ten years ago to live in the Ananda together.' As he tells us this story, and perhaps has told it a hundred times, his voice drops a semitone, perhaps with loss. 'Everything was OK for a while – actually, we loved it – but we'd been in there for a few months and there was a distance that was growing between us and it felt like it was getting bigger every day. And then ... You know when you feel that your partner is drifting and you become more desperate to hang on to them? And they feel it straight away and it's kind of gross to them? Yeah, that.'

We're both nodding. I know 'that' so well – the desperation that somehow stinks so bad, it repulses the very person that you are trying to hold on to.

'And I was beginning to blame the group, which may have been wrong to do . . . but I was angry . . . and she was getting more and more into it, I guess, and that became a wedge. I ended up giving her an ultimatum: "them or me".'

'Ouch! Ultimatums can be risky,' I say.

'Yeah, I didn't know how risky. Obviously, she chose them. I left and found out that not only had she started sleeping with the guy who was the "leader" of our course, but that she was pregnant.'

'Oh, God!' Sofi says.

Josh didn't know if the baby was his or not as there was crossover and he says he still doesn't know. He's decided to live in town and stay in contact with his son just in case. He couldn't go back to the group and couldn't leave. I wondered if he could ever move on emotionally, mentally or even physically.

Limbo in The Ridge.

The swirls of spaghetti and tomato sauce on my plate have gone cold – I can just taste heartbreak. I can't look directly at Sofi, we both know love-loss so well. She takes my hand under the table.

'I am so, so sorry, Josh . . . That is deeply . . .'

'Well, it's old news now in a way. Would you like some wine?'

'Sure,' Sofi says.

I feel he needs to move away from this moment, this vulnerability – the news might be old, but the hurt feels fresh.

There is something about how he told his story to us with such brave vulnerability that makes me feel like I should give him something back.

As he pops the wine, I say, 'I haven't experienced what you experienced, but I do understand first-hand how living in a community can break your heart, and while I haven't ever had a partner taken from me, a religious group did split up my family . . .'

I tell him about my upbringing and that I understand how belief systems and communities can break down a family – because the group *is* the family. There is no space for 'blood' over the group and what it needs. And when people become *fully* in, the collective identity and their beliefs can become more important than anything else – their lovers, even their children. He looks at me nodding, agreeing.

Is what I'm saying making him feel better? *I want to make him feel better.* That he is not alone in his experience. Because he isn't. I'm not telling him his wife isn't culpable, it's not that simple, but it's more complicated than that.

He interrupts me: 'Yeah, there is that. I know it's about identity and human needs, but there's also the sexual corruption that can come with power,' he says.

I nod energetically, knowing more than I want to about this topic.

'Did you hear about the court cases involving Swami Kriyananda and sexual misconduct?' he says.

I think back to being in Kriyananda's courtyard, the peacefulness, looking through the window into his serene home at the top of the hill. What terrible things could have happened in that serene space?

Shouldn't I have known it? Felt it?

'Eight women from the Ananda took him to court, accusing him of trying to have sex with them when they would come in to check on him while he was meditating.'

'Filthy bastard!' Sofi says. 'I knew they were hiding something.'

* * *

The next day, among the smells of chai lattes and roasting aubergines, Sofi and I sit in the vegan café, searching online for proof of the court case. Lo and behold, there it is. Pretty much exactly as Josh had told it the night before. There are times, dates and transcripts. Kriyananda's defence had been that the women had tried to sleep with *him* when he was trying to meditate. Same story, just flipped. The women had strength in numbers on their side when it comes to 'he said, she said'. However, as in so many cases, whether in Hollywood or the Senate, when the voices of many women are pitted against one powerful man, strength in numbers can be meaningless.

Our food arrives as we pull the transcripts up.

'So, this is an expert witness they called to the stand, a Reverend Pamela,' Sofi says.

'S'pose they got someone who is a woman and religious so they can kind of tick the non-bias side of things,' I say.

The café starts to get busy. I look around, worried someone might be waiting for our table. *Why do I care about stuff like this so much? We have something so important to do.* I take a bite out of my sandwich – 'Pretty delicious, actually,' I say, handing it to Sofi to try. She ignores me, mumbling to herself, then says, 'Ooh, Reverend Pamela sounds like a *badass*! Listen to this . . .'

It is my opinion this constitutes a clear-cut case of a religion's minister's [J. Donald Walters/Swami Kriyananda's] conscious and deliberate sexual abuse and exploitation of a person clearly under his spiritual care and jurisdiction.

The abuse by Kriyananda was all the more damaging because this minister misrepresented himself as celibate, holy and having only her best interests at heart, and thus betrayed her trust as an initiate in his religious organization.

'Well then, he definitely shouldn't have been in orange robes. Demote him to blue or whatever, the dirty old bugger!' I say.

As with rape, any minister's sexual or romantic involvement with a parishioner or member of his/her religious community is not primarily a matter of sex or sexuality but of power and control. Probably the most important factor in this case is that there can be no authentic consent in any relationship between a minister and his parishioners/followers because the relationship has by definition such unequal power.

'Yes, Pamela! That means that even if *they* initiated it, it's still not really consent. Also, it's huge when it comes to understanding consent overall when it comes to power dynamics and sex,' I say.

Pamela really is a badass. When there is unequal power, consent becomes more complicated, or perhaps impossible.

'She goes on to describe the pattern here,' Sofi reads.

He singled out women to perform sexual services for them, in a pattern of sexually predatory behaviour. When confronted, threatened the victim with exposure and shaming in the community. He would then turn the responsibility for the sexual behaviour back on her and confusing her, that she was at least consenting, was seductive, or even initiating the sexual activity herself.

'I mean, I feel you could apply this to a lot of sexual misconduct. This could be describing corporate sexual harassment just as easily,' I say. 'And even darker than that, it's not too dissimilar to grooming and abusing a child. How old was she when this happened?'

'Twenty-eight.'

'And Kriyananda?'

'Sixty-eight.'

'Gross!'

'This pattern of blaming the victim is similar to the dynamic with rape survivors who usually feel that they are the ones who are on trial,' Sofi says.

'It makes me so fucking angry,' I say.

'So,' Sofi continues, 'they find him guilty and he is ordered to pay damages.'

'How much?'

'A million dollars.'

'Not enough.'

* * *

I am disappointed by the news, validated by it, saddened by it and relieved in some ways. Like an invisible tension around this place shattered. Now, Swami Kriyananda is dead, this commune is to be run more like a happy mindfulness corporation with nice middle management and an alternative private school for kids.

And during our café research we find out that Kriyananda was chucked out of the Self-Realization Fellowship (the group that Paramahansa Yogananda created) – just *before* he founded this community. The SRF said that his behaviour had become 'self-serving'.

I start to tug at the simplicity of the phrase 'his behaviour being self-serving'. So simple, yet these basic words can be the beginnings of a rot when it comes to a person who is preaching enlightenment, claiming to be a channel to a higher place, or a guide to the divine. Whether the leader of a commune, a cult, or even a shamanic ritual, to be in the world of spirituality is to be 'in service', not to self-serve. I think of other groups, including my own, where the rot of 'self-serving' can turn to corruption and abuses of power. This happened with David Berg and it happened a lot faster than most people want to admit.

Over the next few days, I become interested – perhaps distracted – by The Ridge itself. What is this weird hotbed of spirituality, drugs and folklore? What makes this tiny town a magnet for all sorts of misfits, swamis, communes and tech entrepreneurs? Why has it attracted beatniks, poets, monks and now two girls in a truck? We lose a few days to stories, people and new friends. Someone offers us a yurt to live in and Sofi and I seriously consider it – 'Remember when we lived in a yurt in Nevada?' we say to each other at least five times a day. But I realise that while we could easily do an entire film about The Ridge itself, what we are seeking lies beyond the boundaries of this town.

We make our plans to leave.

* * *

On our last night, we head into town to toast the Ananda and say farewell to the town. We order pints in the bar we went into for directions on that very first night. The sight of the people whose youth has been eaten away by meth is as shocking as the first time, maybe more so now that we've been living with the blissful and pure Ananda group. We grab a couple of pints and prime seats to people-watch. Karaoke is on tonight and the weed-trimming hippies, meth heads and townspeople have all come together over their love of singing eighties ballads, loudly and off-key.

A guy in baggy jeans and top sways towards us. As he gets closer, a heavy chemical stench bites the back of my throat. I hold my breath as he sidles up to me.

'This song means so much to me,' he says.

'Really?' I take a sip of air in from behind my shoulder.

'Yeah. It's the song that was playing when they arrested me and my mom for cooking meth.' He smiles, revealing broken and missing teeth.

'You're joking?' My voice nasal and full of badly disguised shock.

'She took the rap for that, God bless her,' he says.

'How old were you when that happened?' I ask.

'Sixteen. Isn't she amazing for doing the time for me? I could have lost all of this . . .' He motions his clammy hands around the bar, jammed full of misfits singing (shouting) the chorus to 'Livin' On A Prayer' by Bon Jovi.

'That's motherly love for you,' he hollers.

'That's one way to put it,' I shout back.

CHAPTER 5

Silent Lambs: 5 Years Before

It's still dark outside. I am wide awake, waiting for the song that rings in the beginning of each new day at the Birmingham Home. The room is full of the sounds of sleep – shuffling, breathing, the crumple of kids turning over in old sheets.

'Revalieeeee, revalieeee!'

There it is, the first part of a sequence of the day that never changes:

Wake up to this song.
Breakfast in half an hour.
'Jesus Job Time' for an hour and a half.
Devotions.
Scheduled Work.
Lunch.
Quiet Time.
Get Out Time.
Work.
Dinner Time.
Prayer Time.
Lights Out.

Uncle Job sings to us from the landing outside our bedroom, clumsily strumming on his guitar. The number of amateur, yet madly enthusiastic musicians this place turns out is breathtaking. I suppose with only one or two 'hobbies' allowed here, it's no wonder music is taken up by everyone, even by the stone-cold tone-deaf. It's not always the same person who is assigned this early morning job, but it's pretty much always this same song that we wake up to.

The door swings open, the tip of his acoustic guitar pops into the room as he breaks his off-key strum for a second to flick the lights on. Yellow light fills the crowded dorm as girls' faces poke out of blankets and duvets. The bunk beds and trundle beds are like a stacking system – up to five girls can sleep on the footprint of one single bed, like putting cans of beans in a cupboard. It's a good way to get 17 of us in a room that's about 15 × 15ft square.

Heavily lidded with sleep, my roommates shuffle robotically out of bed. There's Naomi, who has such bad asthma that she hallucinates in the night; Eden, who's got a skin condition that she scratches so loudly, it sounds like someone is grating a fresh carrot; then Saphira, who mumbles conversations, sometimes arguments, with herself in her sleep.

I know everyone's night-noises here.

Kate, who sleeps as lightly as I do, grumpily makes her bed, her brown curly hair tied back in a low ponytail, her green eyes somewhere between the Land of Nod and morning moodiness. I catch her eye and stick my tongue out. Her lips fold in on themselves in response, resigned. I think back to when we lived in Africa and how different our bedroom scenes were. Every night, I would climb into bed with her and wrap my skinny arms and legs around her as she slept, even though this pincer move would make her so hot, I would end up being kicked out on the floor. I'd wake up there, unsurprised and determined to try again the next night.

Things are different now at the Birmingham Home. We fill the dining room for breakfast, do our first round of jobs and have our work inspected, just as we do every morning. I can sail through the first few parts of the day without being noticed. Until JJT (Jesus Job Time), we have a schedule that lays out what everyone's jobs are for the three *main* sections of work in a day. This can change, or you might be given something chunky to work on, like when Kate and I ran the commune nursery. JJT consists of smaller cleaning tasks, like all the bathrooms in the house, that morning's dishes, the nursery's terry towelling nappy laundry, followed by an inspection.

Inspections can be more about humiliation than cleanliness. I realised this pretty early on, so depending on who was in charge, I knew what kind of job to do. Some people needed one clear thing they could tell you off about, others needed things absolutely spotless. But whatever happens, don't talk back, get through the inspection quickly.

The sound of the guitar plays again, this time signifying that we are expected in the living room for devotions.

My hands smell of bleach. I press them up to my nose for a good sniff as I walk through the hall and see Joel wildly stuffing towels into a laundry bag. He's running late, again. I raise an eyebrow – '*Hurry Up,*' it says. His eyes cross as he pushes his tongue into his bottom lip. A classic Joel face – mocking me. I roll my eyes. Joel, 'the brave one', or 'the stupid one', depending on your point of view. He's always doing things that make him stand out and get him into trouble. During devotions, he says things that he hopes the kids will laugh at, is always behind on his work and even got caught with chewing gum. I once heard Kris say, 'Joel doesn't give a rat's ass.'

I quicken my pace to the living room and sit on the floor. This living room that only a few months ago looked like an alien landing had ripped through it. Now it's filled with old couches, carpet and more yellowy lights. The same carpet I had my face pressed into for my exorcism. The smartest thing to do is to be a little out of the eyeline of the people 'giving' devotions. I tuck myself away, but not *too* far away, not so much that I look like I'm *avoiding* devotions. There are certain things that I can do to seem like a willing participant: join in on all the singing, clap my hands to the rhythm, talk in tongues and maybe ask one question. But it's important to be careful how I word the question. They can spot it immediately if you are trying to 'be clever' or use the time as your own platform to speak. It's a delicate dance that we figure out the new moves and rules to every day.

'*There's a cry of revolution in my country . . .*' we sing, as more and more kids and Teens take their places.

We stand for this part, until we have done our first prayer.

'*There's a cry of hatred and idolatry,*' the song continues.

The room is almost full. I see Joel come in. He's not the last one.

Thank God.

Kris plays one of the guitars leading the music. He is actually quite good, but he is quite good at everything. I wait for him to notice me, patiently clapping and singing. He spots me and gives me the *tiniest* wink that no one else will have seen. It would have looked like the smallest blink ever, but I know it's for me. As I flicker a tiny-corner-of-the-mouth smile back, a warmth spreads through me. I look around the room for Kate – I know she'll be somewhere at the back, blending into the walls.

Uncle Jude sits at the front, leading today's devotions. I tuck my legs under and sink into the floor, hoping to become as small as possible.

'Today, we have something really special from the Lord,' he begins. His eyes slowly move across the motionless kids, all praying his gaze doesn't linger on them. 'But before we start, something has been brought to my attention.'

Jude gets out of his chair, slowly and deliberately. As he walks into the middle of the room, it's like he grows in front of us, puffing up, becoming taller and broader with every step until he towers over us.

'This was found in the cutlery drawer,' he growls. He holds a fork. It looks ordinary enough, but on closer inspection, we can see a piece of food, the size of the end of a knitting needle, on it.

'Everyone who was on breakfast clean-up, stand up.'

Four teenagers automatically stand in a line in front of him, Kate is one of them. I bite my lips to stop them trembling.

'So, this fork would have got through Naomi the slop washer, Kate the washer, Caleb the rinser and Noah the dryer?

'If four people can't be "of the Lord" enough to wash a fork, then how are they going to survive the End Time? If the four of you are *that* distracted by your own carnal thoughts or numbed to the world around you, what will we do in the End of Days?'

The fork is passed around the room, so that everyone can look at the offensive muck on it. My eyes are on Kate. I feel the pain of her standing in the middle of the room being ridiculed. She is stony-eyed, appearing unafraid, but perhaps using up all of her anger and willpower to just not look weak or upset by this. I look to Kris for comfort. These looks are tiny, invisible. We cannot get caught communicating with each other, especially while Jude is in a state of outrage.

'Double demerits for all of you,' he says. He walks along the line of Teens with his finger millimetres from their faces. 'Actually, "chalk up" a triple.' Three of his fingers swoosh through the air as he makes a giant and damning *tick*. I heard him once say it is his 'trademark' – he seems proud of it.

'Let's move on,' Jude says. 'Today is the start of our new series called "Teen Specials". These have been written specifically with you in mind. Isn't that beautiful? That you are being spoon-fed this *beautiful* word from Dad? I just hope that some of you will grow into the kind of Teens who actually *deserve* these words. I hope that Dad is not casting his pearls before swine.'

The Teen Specials are stories from some of our Leaders, stories from the 'outside' when they were still in the 'system'.

'You are so incredibly privileged to have been born here and to never have experienced the woe, sadness and evil that is *out there*.' He stabs his finger towards the window and perhaps up towards the road beyond it, which leads to a city that we will probably never see.

Jude develops a glob of creamy spit between his lips when he speaks, thick spit that pools on his top and bottom lip and makes a string between the two; it gets thicker the more excited he is. That's his *real* trademark. When he shouts, it breaks – and it looks on breaking point already.

We're only five minutes in.

He's fired up. I fade out. Even though he is fully engaged, fully inspired and this is supposed to be fresh words straight from the mouth of 'Dad', I have heard it all before: We are the chosen ones, our lives are an honour, etc., etc., etc. I sit stinging from my sister's humiliation. As he talks, my finger traces out silent letters in the carpet next to me:

I

My nail digs into the stinky threads, I carve out a message:

H
A
T
E

'Do you have any idea how unbelievable it is that you were born here? What a miracle that took?' he says.

Y
O
U

Each letter is stacked on top of the other and only takes up about an inch and a half square. No one would ever know what I'm writing, but my finger talks to the floor in a way that I can't talk to anyone else. I don't know when I started to do this, but carving my anger into the carpet is my way through devotions. I look at him, pretending to care, but my finger writes what I *really t*hink. Maybe there is someone in the floorboards, a ghost who might get it, or an understanding angel collecting these silent messages for safekeeping.

I stop just before I finish my message. Even though I am sure that my letters in the floor are untraceable, I hesitate before I write the word 'Jude', just in case.

He goes on, 'Do you have any, *any* idea of the sacrifices we have made to ensure that you have this privilege?'

I think back to being face down on his musty bed sheets just yesterday, the feel of his leather belt across my back, and write out the letter '*J*'.

Now it's time to read a 'Mo Letter'. We get these from Moses David every week. He has written thousands of them, and they started years and years before I was born. They come as a few pages stapled together, sometimes with pictures, sometimes not. When they add up to a few hundred they turn them into leather-bound books, creating a library of his words, dreams, and even sometimes just conversations with Mama-Maria. The adults seem to live in excited anticipation of them; What prophecies has he had? What changes will happen? What messages from God will be typed out on these printed pages?

Jude begins this week's; a story about Auntie Crystal's life before she was 'saved', it's called 'Tried Everything and It Was Husks, Husks, Husks'. Crystal grew up in a house where she was beaten by her father daily, controlled by him and gang raped at school. It's one of the first stories where I don't pretend to be listening. This story is dark and horrible and it features a girl.

Jude has my full attention.

He goes on . . . Crystal had sex with a man when she was 15 and refused to tell the authorities his name. Jude reads, 'In the system, if an adult man has sex with an underage girl, even if she asks for it, the *man* can be charged with a serious "crime" called "Statutory Rape".' He pauses over both words and puts air finger quotes, almost comically, around them.

Then Crystal ends up in a paddy wagon (police van) with 12 men. One by one, she is raped by both them and the policemen – 'Going to the paddy wagon was awful,' she finishes. Seems like a bit of an understatement to me. Jude looks around the room, a signal that it's time for the discussion points – we have them every 15 minutes or so to ensure that we're listening and really get the message.

He reads: 'Point 16: If you as a teen girl were in a situation like this in a paddy wagon, with 12 men wanting to have sex with you, what would you do? How would you handle it? Being a Christian, what would you do to show the Lord's love? The first impression that some of you teenage girls might have is "oh gross" or "how terrible". But if you think about it, Auntie Crystal wasn't being harmed, was she? She wasn't *really* hurt. And please bear in mind that this might be the last chance for these men to hear about the Lord. So, what would you do to win these men over to the Lord?'

I look around the room – which one of us girls is going to give him an answer, what we would do in that paddy wagon? It's clear what we *should* say. My vertebrae shrink into each other, my bones desperate to assist my disappearance. Jude doesn't hide his irritation with the *pathetic*, mute girls in his midst. He inhales loudly, his nostrils flare:

'Women in the system make *such* a big deal about sex. It's ridiculous, so many of them calling it rape. It's *just* sex. GET. OVER. IT!'

Uh, oh.

His spit string just broke.

He's found his flow as he paces and rages.

He's getting more and more excited, his voice is getting louder, his eyes widening.

This is the moment to hone my skills. Now is the time to try and rouse the dormant powers that I know are waiting to explode out of me.

I concentrate on his hand that's holding the Mo Letter.

Don't blink.

I slow my breathing down. Long and deep, in and out. I don't move my eyes away from *that* hand. I narrow my eyes so that everything around the hand becomes a blur.

The Mo Letter starts to darken in one corner, then a small flame flickers and it catches fire. Jude throws it on the floor and wildly stamps on it to try and put it out. *Nobody* helps him. As he leaps around like a bouncing sucker, the hand that held the letter bursts into flames too. Still, no one moves. He runs around the room fully ablaze, burning, melting, whimpering and then screaming for help. *We all just watch.* He drops to the floor, kneeling before us pathetically, face melting, before crumbling into a pile of ashes.

'Which brings me to my next point . . .' His voice snaps me back into the room.

My powers will come one day.

'The reason that Dad is bringing out these Teen Specials, is because there have been some instances recently of teens, your age, rebelling,' he spits the words out. He holds the room's attention now.

How far did they go? Were they just having doubts? Did they leave for real? Did they run away? You can almost hear the racket of thoughts ricocheting around us.

'Some Teens have actually wanted to GO OUT INTO THE SYSTEM, the one that *we* saved you from. These rotten apples want to turn their backs on the Lord, for the sake of the Whore of Babylon.'

Ah, so maybe they didn't make it that far. Not even as far as Solomon did when he made it to the border with his photocopied passport.

'And because of this, we have started something called the Victor programme. Which many of you here – in fact, most of you – will be joining.'

Coldness fills the room. There is no whining, no one protests, no questions, not even from Joel. We are all, as my dad loves to quote, 'Silent, like lambs to the slaughter.' Because we can feel that that's what's coming.

'There are varying degrees in the Victor programme,' Jude continues, 'but I am excited about it. Over the next few weeks, things are going to change. More Teens are going to be brought in from other homes. A few of the families here will be moving out and this home will become a Teen Camp for Rotten Apples.'

We're moving out.

We *must* be one of the families that are moving out. There are only four families here. And I'm not a teen, I'm only ten, so there is no way that they can keep us here for this. I shouldn't even really know about this plan because this is for JETTS

(Junior End Time Teens) and Teens. I am an OC (Older Child). And surely, if they are bringing in more Teens, our family will *have* to go. There are nine of us now, 11 if you include Mom and Dad. We take up so much space as a family, there is no way there is room for all of us.

Kris will know, I'll ask him later. He always seems to know.

I sit up straight, filled with excitement at the thought of getting away from Jude. Those triple teeth, sunken-in eyes, that glob of spit . . . I might never have to see him again.

'You'll all be told individually what your status is, but the programme, while it's for Rotten Apples, will turn you into VICTORS, to be victorious for Jesus.'

Later, when the bell rings for lunch and I have about five minutes when I won't be accounted for, I take my chance to find Kris. I scan the downstairs landing. Everyone makes their way towards the food and I run against the flow of people into the 'boys' room'. I find Kris sitting on his bed. His face is crumpled, gaze in his lap, arms limp by his side. My brother, who is like an electric current of energy, is extinguished. I am almost too scared to ask him what's wrong – and I don't have to.

'Bex, I have to go. I'm being moved to another Victor Camp.' His voice breaks as he speaks.

This can't be right.

'But *this* is the Victor Camp, Jude just said it,' I say as I slip my small hand into his bigger one.

'I'm being moved to a different home, I don't know how long for.' His voice lowers to a whisper. 'So we shouldn't even be talking right now.'

'What are you going to do?' I ask. I can feel my chin starting to wobble. I have so many questions and this seems like a stupid one to ask in our limited time together.

'I'm going to speak to Mom and Dad,' he says. He sits up straight, inhales and says in a steadier voice, 'You should get downstairs to lunch.' He rubs my frizzy head, smiles and winks as he adds, 'Being around me is going to get you in trouble, OK?'

I run down to the busy dining room while I fight back the tears that I don't have time for.

Today feels like being trapped in a maze, running around desperate for a way out, frantically looking for answers in the slivers of time I have between my skintight schedule. I want to speak to Kate, to see if she knows what's going on, but she is working in the nursery so there is no time for me and my questions. Joel never knows anything – I am the one that tells *him* stuff. I see Mom and Dad packing up their room, but the looks on their faces clearly say 'Do Not Disturb'.

But, they are packing and this confirms we are leaving.

* * *

Night has been and gone, dawn cracks through the curtains, it's hours before the sound of 'Reveille' will snake through the darkness. I am wide awake, thinking about Kris. He was gone by dinnertime yesterday. I wonder where he is now, what home he ended up in.

I hope he is OK.

I already miss him; my protector, the one I have relied on. Kris always had my back, he always explained things to me, and he always had a joke or a cuddle when things got hard with Dad or Jude. He taught me swear words that I could use in private like 'dickhead' or 'sonofabitch' and the most blasphemous one of all, 'Jesus-shitting-Christ' although I never use that one, just in case.

Kris is strong, he can handle anything.

I lie listening to the night chorus of the girls, the carrot-grating itches, the asthma delirium, and I can just about make out the marks on the ceiling above me, maybe water marks popping through where we have painted. I wonder who else has looked up at this ceiling before in this very old house. Before *we* came here. A Victorian child trapped in this room in quarantine? A mother held against her will? Maybe someone else who was split from their brother, who had felt the same way I do now? I crack open a hatch through the ceiling into my daydreams, escaping in this splinter of time before the next day begins.

But today, there is hope perhaps. Because today, we are on the move.

'Uncle Jude wants you.'

I look up from the giant vat of wheat flakes that I stir for lunch. My hope has only lasted halfway through the morning and collapses as I hear these words. I glance around at the other girls in the kitchen.

This cannot be good.

A soundless sympathy emanates from my fellow kitchen workers.

My feet weigh a thousand kilos as I climb the stairs. Small, black plimsolls, unmatched socks dragging up to Jude's room. The carpet's pattern of roses hides the tread of 40 kids going up and down these stairs every day. But right now, it's just my shoes on these stairs. I'm alone, the house feels silent and still.

Knock, knock! My fist bangs on the cream gloss on Jude's door that I am so familiar with, my small hand outlined by the streaks and drips of an amateur brush.

'Come in.'

Jude sits at his desk and motions for me to sit on the bed. It's made with the floral bed sheets that I know and hate so well. Light comes through his window, grey clouds unable to hold back streaks of sun that fight their way into this hole of a room.

I'll concentrate on that.

'I have news for you.' He is smiling as he says this.

A smile with nasty secrets.

I adjust myself on his bed. Steady. Calm.

'I know you're an OC and therefore too young in many people's eyes to be on the Victor programme. But we have prayed about it and your parents have prayed about it too. And we have decided that you will be joining the Teens on the programme.'

I stay silent, but my mind is ablaze: *How can I be on the teen programme? I am ten years old. And wait, weren't Mom and Dad packing?*

'Rebekah, your lying, your unyieldingness, your fascination with evil, your resentfulness and constant daydreaming are why you are on this programme.'

My eyes start to burn and I wonder whether, if I stare at him long enough, now is the time I can get my powers to work. My finger starts to write in his bed sheets, jammed between my leg and his bed so he can't see.

'You should be glad that we still feel that there is some hope for you.' He smiles again, as if this is good news. 'Your parents have moved out into a caravan at the back of the house to make room for the Teens that will be joining us and for the new Leaders who are coming to work on the camp.'

Now it makes sense. I feel the burn of my tears on my cheeks. I wish I could stop them. I don't want *him* of all people to see this. As they flow, I feel a flash of joy in his eyes. His face then crinkles with disgust, like he smelt something rotten.

'The biggest change for you will be that you are now on Silence Restriction.'

I look at him, confused.

'On Silence, you cannot communicate with anyone other than me and your assigned Leaders. When I say communicate, I mean no talking, no hand signals, no eye contact. This will give you more time to commune with the Lord.'

My brain starts to churn up an internal defence while my lips say nothing. *Did I do all those things? Could I influence people?* I knew I made fun of certain adults and I *did* have questions about some of the stuff that was read out to us. And I knew I had lied before.

'For how long?' These words come out without realising.

'Rebekah!' A flash of white-hot anger shoots out of him. 'It's not about the length of time. THAT'S NOT THE POINT, IS IT? You can go.'

I leave his room as he shouts behind me, 'Effective immediately!'

* * *

The walk down the stairs is a daze. There must be noise in this house full of people but all I can hear is the sound of heavy marching in my head. *Thud, thud, thud.* An army of blood pulsing through my ears and it's deafening. I walk into the kitchen where the girls are still making lunch. They haven't moved. How can they be in the exact same positions but *everything* is different? Flipped on its axis.

I keep my head down as I walk by. My feet get quicker. I fling the back door of the house open and fill my lungs with a gallon of cold air as I break into a run towards the caravan that my parents now live in. My fists punch the plastic caravan door.

By some miracle, they're in.

'Mom,' I whisper, desperation binding my throat. 'Mom, they put me on Silence Restriction. How can they do this? I am not even a teen.'

I look up at her, hugging her waist, clinging to her. She gently pushes me off and says 'Shuuuushhhhh!', her finger going up to her lips.

I can't tell what she's thinking. *Is she sad? Is she scared? Is she maybe just as scared as I am?*

My dad sits at the other end of the caravan, he looks detached. 'You can't come in here, Bex,' he says.

*   *   *

Things at the Teen Camp change rapidly. Families leave and within a week, 21 teenagers ranging in age from 10 to 18 take their place on the Victor programme. It's not that many – some of the teen camps that we've heard about house hundreds.

Our routines become a severe combination of army training and a spiritual camp. Everything is amplified. There is a cruelty with this new regime and it is strong and encouraged. We used to be told the words 'this hurts me more than it hurts you' when we were being disciplined, but now, it feels like it's open season for the adults to come up with tools that are not just physically violent like the public beatings, but feel like psychological torture – silence restriction, isolation. The Philippines is considered to be making the best strides with their methods, methods that came with the following instruction: 'When a child is having serious problems and is fighting heavy spiritual battles, the key question is not so much *which* method to use but *when* to use which method'. They want to beat the devil out of us. Isolate us. But for me, well, I'd rather take a beating a day than be on Silence Restriction. It takes everything away – humour, cheekiness, needs, being 'seen'.

Silence makes you invisible, disconnected, to walk into a room and for everyone to look away creates a level of daily, underhanded abandonment. To never share a joke, or a story, or even a look with other people. It confirms every day that you are perhaps worthless and meaningless. It creates walls around you that are transparent, but feel real and are heavy with heartache. The only thing that all of us can hope for is that this is just another one of Moses David's phases: that it will all be over soon.

*   *   *

I sit in the dining room with an A3 piece of card and a red permanent marker in front of me. It's four months since I have been put on Silence Restriction. Nineteen of us were put on it in total – at least I'm not alone. The smell of the marker makes me dizzy, but in a nice way. I once took a big sniff of this pen and it gave me a headache for the rest of the afternoon.

Got to be careful with this stuff.

I am writing out my fourth, maybe fifth sandwich board since I started the Programme. I draw big thick red letters that read: 'I AM ON SILENCE RESTRICTION'. On the other side, it says, 'PLEASE DO NOT TALK TO ME'.

Four months seems far too short. I can't quantify it. So much and yet so little has happened. The days have all felt the same because they are, exactly, the same. I make holes in both pieces of card, tie them together with string – two double knots to keep it secure. I don't know why I have to make and wear this sign; *everyone* knows I am on 'Silence'. Pretty much all the Teens are on 'Silence'. Kate isn't, but that's because she is silent and invisible anyway – she made herself that way for protection.

Smart.

The only difference in the days that go by, in the weeks and months, is *who* is in trouble for what and what new way they have chosen to punish us. Saphira is in a caravan, way out in one of the fields. For almost two months, she's been in isolation. Particularly rebellious, she is maybe one of the worst – she did things that were deliberately disobedient, pretending to be the Aunties, sexy dance, she flipped someone a middle finger. Once she was told off and made to stand in another room but we could see her shadow dancing around madly to make us laugh.

The Lord tried to break her one night when she was making dinner and a 10-litre pot of boiling water fell on her and poached her arm. That was the first sign of her 'going wrong' and His judgement of her.

Shiloh was put out in another caravan for a month. She learned her lesson very quickly.

I know that it's the *worst* to be in isolation, but at least they don't have to do the 'End Time Army Training' that the rest of us have to do. We run around fields endlessly, digging holes and filling them back up. We lift concrete stones or bricks while being screamed at, all in an effort to get us into shape for Armageddon. But, I suppose, the army training makes sense. If we are to spend the next seven years fighting Antichrist soldiers, we should be strong and able to run. Preparing for the end days, the days that the lasers will come out of our eyes and fire from our mouths to burn Satan's men.

I can't wait for that.

I look at my sandwich board: this is pretty much ready. I pick it up by the strings, slip it over my head and straighten it up so the message is loud and clear.

Better get back out there.

I walk into the kitchen to start on the dinner prep. I pull out the big white vats where we keep the wheat flakes. I've tried *everything* I can with this rough ingredient to make it edible. I've made it into granola by laying it out on trays and putting it in the oven to crisp. I've turned it into porridge. I've even tried to grind the flakes up to make them into bread – it just turns into bricks. But the white vats are all empty.

We can't have run out.

I know the wheat flakes are kept outside in the barn, but I've never been out to fill the vats up from the source. Usually an adult does that. The concrete outside crunches under my shoes; I've wearing super old black plimsolls that smell of rubber and I can feel the cold of the ground underneath them as if I'm barefoot. Before I was in the Victor Camp, I used to stand on tiptoes in these and pretend that I was wearing ballet shoes.

Can't get away with that now.

I push the big wooden door of the barn; it swings open with ease and I slip inside, dragging my vats. The smell of must and mould hits me. It's not gross though, just different, with a kind of woodiness to it. There is only one window in here and it's boarded up. I walk slowly in the darkness towards the shapes of the sacks.

As I pull the wheat flakes into the vats, my eyes adjust to the darkness and I start to see clearly. My hands go in and out of the big sack. Then I start to make out shapes on the sack itself. There's a large, almost life-size head of a horse. Underneath in capital letters it says 'BRANFLAKES' and then 'HIGH-QUALITY HORSE FOOD. 50 KG'.

No wonder!

Of course it won't make good granola, it's for horses. And it's stale, expired for over a year. I feel vindicated that we couldn't do anything good with these stupid brown pieces of wheat. And it's not even WHEAT! I think about all the kids trying to chew these for hours, getting unbearable jaw-ache and it all makes sense.

HA! Kate is going to love this.

I wonder when I'll be allowed to tell her. She sleeps just feet away from me, but of course, we haven't spoken in months.

I drag the vats of horse food into the kitchen. The other girls are assembled at their stations, everyone looks down as I walk in. Out of habit I look down too – it's the easiest way to avoid trouble, just look down at the red stone floor.

Keep looking down.

I sit at my spot in the kitchen and start to prep, noticing I've already got a splash of water on my 'Silence Restriction' sign. Anxiety flutters through me.

That isn't going to go down well.

*　　*　　*

She sits on the end of my bed. It's dark, but I can see her clearly. Her brown hair is so neat, it's as if she has just brushed it. Side parting.

I could never get my hair that tidy.

She wears a polka-dot dress with a white bib with ribbons on it. Her hands are folded in her lap.

'You'll be OK,' she whispers into the dark.

I want to believe her.

'This kind of thing happens all the time. I've been sick and I haven't seen my brother in six months too. But he is OK and I am OK, it just feels bad right now.' Her eyes are big and she looks straight at me. She smiles and looks around our dorm. 'I have always lived here, this is my room,' she says.

A chill runs through me; I want to tell her it's not safe to talk to me.

'You can always talk to me,' she says, her hand reaching out to mine.

I open my eyes and she's gone.

*　　*　　*

I am six months into the Victor programme.

I gently touch my thigh, feeling the welt and bruise through my bobbly trousers. My finger traces the bumps like braille across my skin from the paddling that I had earlier today. It's not unusual for these to happen and it's easy to get one: you only need 12 demerits in a week to warrant one, or four in one day, and you can get a 'double d' for dropping a plate. And like braille, paddlings are used so we receive a message:

'Were you daydreaming?'

'You clearly aren't HERE!'

'Your mind is not on your work.'

'You are not being *of* the Lord.'

The public beatings started as soon as the Victor programme did. And they became more inventive with each new leader that came to the camp. One afternoon, about 20 of us had to sit and watch my brother Joel get beaten with an oversize chopping board with a dozen holes drilled into it so that it could 'break the air' easier.

This one was particularly brutal. Joel had been particularly rebellious. Even though these paddlings happened almost daily, this was one I will never forget.

Mary Malaysia was reading Grandpa's new letter, 'Make Love to Jesus'. She was explaining that we can start to commune with Jesus in a new way. The adults in the group could 'trip out' while making love and actually have sex with Jesus. The comic-style drawings showed people in all kinds of sexual positions with Jesus. Conjure up His spirit and show how much you really love Him and are dedicated to Him. This is supposed to be done in private, unless you are an adult.

But here, there really is no privacy.

At the end of devotions, the speaking in tongues starts:

Shadabadah
Sheeebahdaabah
Shaaabahdaahbah
Thank you, Jesus. Praise you, Jesus. Thank you, Jesus.

The overlapping rumble of voices gains momentum:

Yaaabaaashaaabahh
Sheeebahdaabah
Shaaabahdaahbah
Hallelujah. Praise you, Jesus. Thank you, Jesus.

It gets louder and picks up speed:

Shadabadah, deeebaaadaaaabahhh

Then, cutting through the tongues is Joel's voice:
  'Yes, Jesus. That's it, Jesus.'
  His sarcastic tone that I know so well.

Sheeebahdaabah

'COME ON, JESUS!' he says, louder.

Shaaabahdaahbah

'Fill me with your SEED, JESUS,' he mocks.

Thank you, Jesus. Praise you, Jesus. Thank you, Jesus.

'FUCK ME FROM BEHIND, LORD, AND FILL ME WITH YOUR SEEEDS!' he shouts.

The speaking in tongues stops dead. All eyes are open. I want to laugh but the whole room is as paralysed at his outburst as I am.

* * *

A few hours later, and it's time for the punishment.

Joel walks in, head down. Titus, the leader who is going to paddle him, takes his position. Joel not only mocked a Mo Letter, but he brought in homosexuality, which is a sin.

This is going to be bad and there's nothing any of us can do to save him.

A blaze of fire rushes out of my mouth, quick as lasers and hotter than brimstone. It burns a giant hole through the wall, revealing a golden path on the other side. I climb through it.

'Joel, quick! COME!' I hold my hand out to him through the burning wall. 'LET'S GO!'

SLAM!

The first blow brings me back into the room.

Joel yelps like a puppy that's been kicked.

A sharp intake of breath follows. He normally doesn't make any sound at all. The holes in the chopping board are doing their job, what Titus wanted.

Public beatings are cunning and effective. For most kids, like me, it's harder to watch a beating than take one. I sit next to Saphira, who was allowed out of her isolation to watch this. The bandages from her boiled arm are a rank orange colour and stink of old meat. Or maybe the smell is because she has to go to the toilet in a bucket – I would puke if I wasn't so scared.

SLAM!

'No, No, *No! Please! NO!*' Joel cries.

Two adults hold him in place because he keeps trying to wriggle away from the paddle's path.

I can't bear to watch; I wish I could close my eyes. We're not allowed to look away, we have to bear witness to it – it has to be remembered.

It *will* be remembered.

I will *never* forget this.

* * *

Later that day, I walk in on Joel with his trousers down in one of the bathrooms, trying to patch himself up. None of the toilets have locks on the doors, these are not allowed. I catch sight of the skin on his bottom so badly bruised that it's broken. It looks like marble, but all the streaks in stone are the cracks in his skin and they are bleeding. I close the door before we get caught.

The next day, we have a new tactic sprung on us.

'We are changing how we discipline you. We have noticed that some of you are holding on to resentment against the Leaders who are administering the paddlings. This is not right, as the paddlings are done out of love and are from the Lord. But to make this situation easier for the Leaders, we will be doing the paddlings individually and blindfolded.'

I welcome the news – I never want to see my brother in that state again.

It's foolish for them to think that we won't know who has done it just because we're blindfolded. Every leader here has their signature bruise. The square buckle of the belt is Jude. Mary Malaysia likes to use a switch, which gives you tiger stripes. Titus goes for a big paddle, which results in a larger spread of bruises and cracked skin.

The purple and red shapes tell-on them.

So, today, when I went in for my paddling, there was no group of kids to watch, no Saphira with her stinking arm, no brothers and sisters to get hurt by my lashings. Just three of the Leaders, a switch rod and a blindfold.

For the first time in a long while, someone looks me in the eye to speak. Which is almost more startling than the sight of the blindfold.

'Rebekah, you know why you are here?'

I nod.

'You know that this hurts us more than it hurts you?'

I nod again.

'Look in my eyes. Let me see you smile. Do you still love me?'

I smile, I nod.

And the room goes dark.

* * *

It's nine months since I have been on the Victor programme. Nine months since I have had a conversation, since I stuck my tongue out, nine months since I heard the sound of my own laugh.

Nine months since I became invisible.

I crouch on a flight of stairs, gripping on to a dustpan and brush. Dust gets in my eyes and fluff collects in little balls of grey as I brush all the corners. The smell of these stairs is almost comforting. Out of all the jobs, it's not a bad one – it's better than cleaning the bathrooms. *Gross.* It's also fast and loud. Sometimes it's nice to make noise, even if it's just with a brush, or a mop, or a vacuum cleaner.

On the landing above me some of the kids talk in hushed voices. Sure, I shouldn't be 'listening in' as this is still communicating. But I listen in, carefully choosing when I bash my brush, so that it looks like I am very, *very* busy.

BASH, BASH, BASH.

'New Leaders', 'Some new Teens', 'Kris Scott coming back.' The brush drops. My heart punches through my chest. *Kris? Coming back?* He's been gone since the day they announced that this was going to be a Teen Home. My eyes go dry with excitement.

Kris is coming back. My protector. My brother. Kris is COMING BACK!

I pick the brush back up and start pounding the stairs.

I wonder what he's been through, how many paddlings, how much trouble he has gotten into. I can imagine him standing up to the Leaders and calling them 'sonsofbitches'.

By the time I get to the bottom of the stairs, I am sure he is coming back to rescue me. I ignore logic; that people, especially these kids on the stairs wouldn't know about it if that was the case. My heart is set on it. I imagine us running away, up that driveway, on that road that leads to that city. I see Kris getting really, really angry when I tell him how I've been treated. I'll tell him about Mom and Dad and how they haven't spoken to me

since the day after he left. About how much I hate the Leaders
and the *horse food* and everything.

Who knows what he will do?

I start to plan how I will do it; I need to be clever, I can't
just run up to him. He's been on the Victor programme too. I'll
have to wait for the right moment; be sneaky.

I can't believe that he is actually coming back.

* * *

The half-seconds, seconds, minutes and hours of the day
go by in slow motion; people move in and out of focus in a
sticky, sludgy forever-of-a-day. It gets dark and *still* no Kris.
It hits me, it's not true. I feel the bile of anger rising, angry
at the stupid kids on the stairs, angry at this stupid, slow day
and really angry with my stupid self. Why did I let myself
believe that he was coming? So stupid. This is exactly why you
shouldn't 'listen in'.

It's dinnertime. We file in line and slop liver and potatoes
onto our plates. I can't tell if it's rust from the pans or the meat
that smells metallic. I take a seat at the end of the table and concentrate on looking down at my food.

'Can I have your attention, please?' Mary Malaysia stands
on the stairs that lead to the dining room, giving her a little
height that she so desperately needs. She is as small as me but
that doesn't stop her from being one of the cruellest Leaders in
the country, renowned for her brutality.

'We have two new Shepherds we want to introduce you to.
They will be your Leaders and keep this Victor programme in
shape, keep you Teens on fire and make sure that we don't have

any slackers,' she says through moustachioed lips. She tosses her thick black hair over her shoulder as she moves to the side of the stairs to make space for the new Leaders.

'Some of you already know them, Ezra and Kris Scott!'

My fork slips. My hand shakes. My ears generate a high ringing sound inside them.

Have they turned him?

Kris walks in. He looks taller, he looks different; he looks more like a man, more angles in his face, his freckles seem to have faded. He stands straight with an expressionless face. If he does see me, he stares right through me.

A piece of liver cements to my throat. Stuck. Dry. Trapped. The rest of my food fights to come up. Every hair on my body prickles as a rush of nausea runs through me.

This must be a trick. This must be his plan. This can't be real.
Or maybe he really is one of them.

* * *

The next month with Kris is like someone else has taken over his body. He looks and sounds like Kris, but all the things he does are not him. Whatever it is, to have *him* here but have my *brother* is like living with a ghost.

Every day, I spin dizzily back and forth as to whether it's an act or whether he has been turned, never truly knowing. He tells me off. He gives me demerits. He leads devotions. But, he never beats me, he never lays a hand on anyone and I never see him be cruel.

Some days, I am sure he is one of *them*.
But is he?

If he isn't, he never lets the act slip. Not even in private, not even for a second.

* * *

A shroud of sweat covers my face – hot, sticky, frantic sweat. I have been lying awake for hours. The sounds of the room are in full swing, the scratch of the eczema skin, the babbling sleep chatter, the rasping asthmatic breath. But the night symphony faded into nothingness when the voices started. First, they whispered, then they murmured, then they screamed.

My arms and legs fight against sheets that feel like restraints, my blanket a noose. The voices are trapped in this bunk bed with me. Close. And loud.

'There must be something wrong with you.'
'Not everyone in here can be WRONG, BUT YOU.'
'What makes you think that YOU know more than THEY DO?'
'There is something WRONG WITH YOU.'
'You need to be broken.'
'Let yourself be broken.'

I can't tell if the voices are God's, the devil's or my own.
Splinters of myself at war with one another.
I run my fingers across my forehead, slick with sweat, hoping to calm its manic fire. The insides of my head feel like a ball of yarn that's fallen into the grips of a cat, a cat that claws away at the threads of my sanity, snatching and pulling relentlessly.

I have been fighting this, *them*, my whole life. Battling, because this, this home, these rules and this life, has not felt *right*; to see this violence towards my siblings has not been *right*, to feel this trapped . . . surely, it's not *right*?

I raise my heavy head to look around the room of sleepers. Do their minds house the same voices as mine? Are they, too, in a constant state of unravelling? Or do they have peace because they have surrendered? Have they been given a cure? Is God the medicine that they tell us He is? Is *that* how they sleep?

I have to find a way out of this and if there is no physical door, perhaps surrender is the key. The Leaders, my parents, the kids around me, how can they all be wrong? How would I know what's right?

How dare I?

I want the yarn back, I want the scratching to stop, I want it safe. I want the vicious tugging of my mind to cease, I want some peace from the ruthless scratching.

I must surrender.

Silently, I mouth these words into the night: *Please, please God, show me the way. I know I am a bad girl and I have lied, and I deserve to be where I am.*

I turn over, face down in my pillows so no one can hear me.

Please break me and make me a good servant.

Rough cotton fills my nose and mouth. It is old, worn and suffocating.

I am a bad girl and I have lied, and I deserve to be where I am.

I bury my head in further.

Please break me and make me a good servant.

I repeat the words over and over and over until I lose count.

I hope that the more I say them, the more likely He is to hear me. If He hears me, if He believes that I mean it, if I can make myself worthy, He will release me from how I feel.

He will set me free from these invisible bars.

CHAPTER 6

The Twelve Tribes – Stolen Children: 15 Years After

'How are you feeling about the Twelve Tribes?' Sofi says.

We're driving down from Northern California to our next group in San Diego. Our big beige truck thunders beside cliffs, around creeks and over beautiful arched bridges. My face flops out the window like a goofy dog, tongue out, lapping up the tastes and smells of adventure. I want to feel *everything*. Metallica, German Techno, sometimes classical music pumps out of our ratty speakers, the soundtrack to long stretches of highway so straight, they start to mess around with my perception of time and space.

'Well?' she says.

I pull my head in, dry-mouthed. 'It kind of feels a bit abstract that we're going into something . . . a little more real.'

'I am a bit worried, I think,' she says.

'Oh yeah?' I reach for the volume on the music and turn to look at Sofi, hoping I can read how worried she really is.

'Well, I know you are a tough biscuit. But you are interested in this group because they remind you of how you grew up, yes? What if you regress in there? What if we see some really dark shit and it triggers you?'

'And I go back to being a scared kid?' I smile.

She nods, keeping her eyes on the road, but I can feel the concern radiating from her.

'I have thought about that, yes.'

I have, but maybe not taken it seriously enough.

'Well then, do we need a system?' she says.

We have been creating systems for everything – how to survive without hot water, how to keep 'vegan healthy' by eating things like 'magical yeast'. We're figuring out the intricacies and idiosyncrasies of our van: flipping between a pair of gas tanks because we never know which one is full. Figuring out that our shower is better used as storage. We have these systems so we don't break down on highways (and now so we don't break down in more ways). We sing stupid songs, crack inside jokes, create our own language, acronyms like WWFIO . . . Whenever we get stuck, we shout, 'WEEFEEEOH!', which means, 'We Will Figure It Out' – a declaration of our attitude to being in over our heads. WWFIO camera equipment, WWFIO film funding applications, WWFIO the gas tank, WWFIO dinner and WWFIO getting ourselves into the next commune.

We try, clumsily and unsuccessfully, to flirt our way out of speeding tickets. We sleep under the stars and wake up to sunrises in the hills, or sometimes in the car park of a Walmart. Occasionally, we treat ourselves to nights at what we call 'Murder Motels', the ones in movies like *True Romance* that are anything but romantic (where you definitely wouldn't want to flick on a black light). But still, they are a *treat*; we have hot showers, drink burnt coffee and eat rock-hard baked goods known as 'breakfast included'.

'Yeah, we probably do need a system – and to keep a lookout on each other.'

My reflection in the wing mirror challenges me: *Are you going to lose it in the Twelve Tribes?*

We can do it, we'll be fine. Twelve Tribes are small fry in comparison to where I am from.

* * *

The Twelve Tribes have been on my radar for a while. I had seen similarities to the Children of God – they are Armageddonists who believe in the second coming of Christ. Although the Twelve Tribes call him 'Yahshua' because Christ is apparently possessed by Satan – the devil moved in a while back, but most Christians *just don't know about it yet*. The Twelve Tribes believe that after the Rapture, believers reign for a thousand years with Yahshua before the Last Judgement. The Last Judgement is a pretty big deal for a lot of Christian faiths. It's kind of like their Oscars, a massive event where there are winners and losers: the *righteous* and the *filthy and unjust*. The filthy are sent to the Lake of Fire, while the righteous live for all eternity. I'm pretty sure which camp they would believe I belong in.

Filthy as.

Best get my swimsuit on for that lake.

Other similarities with the Children of God are their friction with the establishment and how they shunned the Churches. Another strange coincidence is the name of the café the group started in: The Lighthouse. The same name as one the Children of God started in. Gene Springs, their founder, created it as a ministry for teenagers in 1972. I had to double-check if it was the same one, but no, this one was in Tennessee. Maybe there's a book, *How to Start a Cult for Dummies*? Part One: 'Getting Café Branding JUST Right'.

The group is an attempt to recreate the first-century Church in the Book of Acts: 'All that believe were together and sold their possessions and goods' (Acts 2: 44, 45), a scripture I know off by heart. It's one of my parents' favourites to prove that communal living was conceptualised by Jesus himself. Not by wacky cultists trying to get their hands on your car, house and cash.

The Twelve Tribes give this explanation of why they live as a separate holy nation:

> As we studied the history and prophecies of the Old Testament, there had to be a holy nation that proved their love for Messiah before He could return to the earth. There would have to be a people separate from the nations of the world who would live their lives obeying His commands.

The only time they participate 'in the world' is when they preach and dance (Hebrew-style) and by running their Yellow Delis, which is a way for them to financially support their communities and recruit members. They are sometimes called 'The Yellow Deli People' because of their bustling restaurants serving organic (and delicious) food, matcha lattes, bean salads and homemade burgers.

There are some stand-out classic ingredients here. Heroes (them), villains (the system), the rebellious youth, a charismatic leader and then a structure and story that wraps around the whole thing to make 'sense' of it. Creating a world *outside* of society is so much easier if you are in glorious battle *with it*. But the Twelve Tribes take it a step further. The group believes that *all* other denominations are fallen, that the world is the filthy Whore of Babylon. The Twelve Tribes are the new Israel, creating a righteous generation to ensure that the rapture happens. Within all of these familiar beliefs, the one that really interests me is their aim of 'raising a generation that are pure'. How does this play out? How does this affect the children growing up in the TT communes? Are they allowed to play? Are they allowed to be kids? Do they have the freedom to speak?

'What is it with people trying to turn their kids into the "Bride of Christ" or soldiers?' Sofi asks.

'I think they thought if they raised us right, without outside influence and completely clean of the "system", it's like they are, I don't know, finding a *cure* for the world in a way.'

I realise I have slipped into talking about my childhood.

Is their world already mingling with mine?

The Twelve Tribes wear matching outfits – gold-rimmed glasses, maxi dresses or balloon pants, tabards and Birkenstock-style sandals. Besides the tabard accessory, I've seen this look in San Francisco, London and NYC on many an organic hipster. But these clothes are designed to create modesty and unity between the members rather than a sign of being 'woke'.

* * *

We pull into the small town outside of San Diego, where we are meeting our Twelve Tribes contact. The meet-spot glows green with the light from a gas station, it's dark and quiet, with only the occasional sound of a car passing. I flick on my phone, our faces instantly bathed in a blue glow that changes to red as I hit 'Record' on voice memo: 'So here we are. We move into the Twelve Tribes tonight.' I pull the glow closer to my mouth.

'We're tired,' Sofi cuts in over me.

'It's taken so much longer than we thought it would to get here,' I say.

'Mamacita has her own way of riding the roads, she will not be confined by ETAs,' says Sofi.

BANG-BANG-BANG!

The sharp rap of knuckles on the window pane makes me jump. A woman's face stares through the glass, an inch from mine. She wears no make-up, her grey hair parted down the middle.

'Jesus!' I say as my phone leaps out of my hand.

'Are you the British girls?' she says with a tone and expression you might give to someone who has just rammed into your car.

'Hi, yes, that's us,' I say.

'I am Derusha. Follow me. It's hard to find our ranch, especially in the dark,' she says.

I see her looking at the glow of red coming from my phone in the footwell. It's like I've already pissed her off.

Should I pick it up or leave it?

'You coming?' She says this as if she's been waiting all day.

I'd called the commune a few weeks ago to explain that we were documentary makers interested in the Twelve Tribes. I reassured them that we wouldn't film unless they were happy for us to and that we wanted to experience their way of life. I love the idea of Gonzo journalism and having grown up in a group that were wary of outsiders, I figured the only real way to get an inside look would be to live with them and build personal relationships. They had agreed to let us stay and said they would 'see' about the filming element.

What I haven't said is what I am really interested in is the kids.

* * *

'She seems nice,' Sofi says with a half-smile as we pull out of the gas station.

We are arriving at the Twelve Tribes during one of the most tumultuous weeks in their history. Synchronised raids have just happened at their communes in Germany – their children have been taken away. An undercover journalist named Wolfgang joined and lived for six months as a member of the Twelve Tribes (that's dedication). He installed secret cameras throughout the commune because he wanted to capture the abuse that he was certain was happening. His mission was to give it to the authorities and to do an exposé. Police stormed four communes in Germany and took 80 children away. We'd already made contact and had an agreement with this group before the raids happened. But, still, I am surprised that they are letting us stay.

Derusha's truck takes off quicker than we expect, flying down a pitch-black road. Mamacita lurches through the dark to catch up with her; there are no lights and no signs. We kick up dust, creating an almost cinematic haze illuminated by the truck lights. Trees overhang the road and feel like something out of a creepy kids' book; silhouettes of crawly, spikey, shadowy arms.

'Bleugh!' I say with a shiver. 'It's like the trees are trying to grab us.'

'Or maybe keep us away?' Sofi keeps her eyes on the road as she asks, 'Would you be able to find your way back out of here if we needed to?'

'Not sure,' I say.

I need to pay better attention to the road.

'No GPS?' she asks.

'Not a lick.'

We pull into the ranch. The hills cut an outline into the night sky – the stars are bright and beautiful, but also clear enough to signify we are far from a city. Far from civilisation. We step out of the truck into fresh, cold air. The mix of muddy farmlands and sharp animal manure stings my nostrils.

'Follow me,' Derusha says without turning to see if we do.

The sound of our feet crunching on the gravel is amplified by the quiet of the night as we crunch towards the glow of the commune. It reminds me of the gravel around my own home as a teenager, the one so loud you could hear it up from the top of the house if someone was outside. Almost like it was a homemade alarm system. We shadow Derusha closely to a small back building. She opens a wooden door on to a simple room with two sets of wooden bunk beds.

'This is where you will stay – with me,' she says.

We walk into yellowy light and dusty smells. She swings the door of a tall wooden cupboard open and points to long dresses and tabards.

'We all share clothes here. We appreciate you wearing, and only wearing, these dresses and coverings, please.'

She looks us up and down and says, 'Your clothes cannot be worn around the men, they are too tempting.'

I glance at Sofi, the two of us standing in oversize flannel shirts and baggy jeans, and wonder if this really is a look that could tempt you away from God.

A lamp catches Derusha's shape as she moves around the room, throwing shadows across the lemony walls, long, thin ones that climb up the ceiling, the kind that I imagine could break away from their host and take on their own life. The kind that could scare kids (OK, *me*). A shiver starts in my chest and ripples through my body.

Something isn't right with her.

There is paranoia taking up the air: is it my own fear projected onto these walls, or does it come from her?

Derusha smiles as she pulls her bed sheets back.

Or am I the untrustworthy one here under false pretences?

I settle down into bed, taking in the tiny dorm, its bunk beds, the open wardrobe with our uniforms for tomorrow, and it sinks in that we are *actually here*, in a religious community.

No soft-serve, no trial run. We are really here.

* * *

My tired body feels every lump in the mattress, the blankets are itchy, my nose tickles from the dust and a really familiar feeling envelops me. It is one of seclusion and being cut off from the world. Out in the middle of nowhere, in a commune surrounded by outlines of the hills and thousands of stars. It's a feeling that I am almost comfortable with.

I dream of fires, of ticking clocks, of feet that never stop running, of searching for someone whose face I can't see. In among this, I hear the sound of biblical horn – it's a soft and round sound. My eyes jolt open, the horn goes again. It's a shofar being blown, the Twelve Tribes alarm clock floating through the early morning light into our tiny dorm. It's their 'Reveille' song.

Derusha leads us down into a field for the first gathering. A tower of thick smoke cuts through the pink morning light, 40 people stand around a blazing fire. It's vivid and solemn. The singing starts, the gathering sways, children with eyes still sticky from sleep stand next to their mothers. Everyone is dressed alike, adorned in headdresses, fervent eyes. It's a place of peacefulness. We are in another world. This is truly beautiful.

What an amazing, opening scene to a documentary this would have made.

A man in gold-rimmed glasses and a low ponytail steps forward and says, 'The children are going to perform a song they have written this week about our brethren in Germany.'

Kids as young as three years old shuffle next to each other, sleepy-faced, long dresses, mini tabards. Their high-pitched voices sing a song of defiance against the German government. Stumbling over newly learned lyrics, as they shout the chorus their hands make tiny fists. Then gathering starts in earnest and it's about one topic only: the raids. The adults refer to the German government as Nazis. They say they would rather be put in jail than damned by God for not disciplining their children. It's raw and angry.

And then one man points to me and Sofi: 'These women are here from Germany and England. They want to stay and learn about us and our way of life. Maybe we can learn from them what kind of society can take a child from its mother and split up brothers and sisters from each other?'

This was my biggest fear as a child: my brothers and sisters being taken away, being separated. This was what made me terrified of the police and outsiders. The flames of the fire lick my face. I have too much material round my neck, the tabard feels like a noose. I look around the gathering, trying to make eye contact, hoping they can see *me*, not the authorities, or someone out to take their kids. I feel the blister of eyes on me, I feel anger, fear; I feel like I'm about to be put on the fire to burn.

Another man steps forward to speak; he clears his throat.

'I am going to do a reading from the White Rose' – he pauses and looks at the children – 'to explain the White Rose. They were a resistance group in Nazi Germany but their writings have never been more appropriate.'

Again, he pauses, again clears his throat and a powerful, unexpected booming voice emerges.

'Isn't it true that every honest German is ashamed of his government these days? Who among us has any concept of the dimensions of shame that will befall us and our children when one day the veil has fallen from our eyes and the most horrible of crimes – crimes that infinitely outdistance every human measure – reach the light of day?'

These words that were written about the Holocaust, about some of the most unspeakable crimes against humanity, are read out now around this fire, but with different meaning and purpose.

'We are the resistance and the Germans will give our children back, we will overcome this evil system and its government.' His eyes slice through the smoke as he says, 'I wonder if the Nazi's regime really ever ended.' His gaze stops on Sofi – it feels a little like the Twelve Tribes are declaring war.

I want to look at Sofi, reassure her, my mind racing with what she could be thinking, feeling, but I look straight ahead.

'Now, and I explain this for our visitors, this is where we humble ourselves and confess our sins, both the sins we have committed and those good deeds we left undone, golden opportunities lost.'

There is power in fire, there is power in ritual, there is catharsis in confession. And there is power in this moment. Children as young as three and four step forward to confess what they feel they should be 'broken' by Yashua (their name for the Messiah) for – their pride, talking back, having insubordinate thoughts. Some of them seem like they are on autopilot, some are nudged to the front by their parents. When we were young, we had our own handwritten versions of these called 'Open Heart Reports': every day, we had to confess and be punished. I remember having to make things up to confess as it was worse if you left it blank.

'I am thankful for being corrected,' one little boy says.

'I need to trust authority even when my flesh is weak and trying to criticise,' a girl of about ten joins in.

'My flesh hates being handled and I have a hard time to overcome but I am thankful that I can learn,' a boy of about eight says.

'I have to overcome my pride,' another says.

Some adults join in with their faults and their needing to be 'handled' but for me, every time a child steps up, it does not feel like catharsis – it feels like shame, the flames of the fire burning with humiliation of these kids.

The gathering closes and we walk up the hill to breakfast in silence. A hot apple cider drink called 'vinny' is handed out, tangy but tasty. One of the mothers stops and says with a smile, 'Do you feel like your government is fascist regime?' Sofi manages a weak smile back. I can only imagine how hard it must be for a liberal, alternative, outspoken woman to keep composed – it all feels so personal, so targeted towards her.

We discussed our 'code' at the start of the trip: if we want access and eventually the permission to unpack our cameras, our opinions don't really matter, but our code says we won't lie. I'm torn between not wanting to be a total fraud, but also knowing that if we are ever to film here, we need to be as innocuous and invisible as possible. It doesn't really matter what we think right now, what matters is building relationships so we can gain 'access'. We are here to observe, not to try and convince them of a different way of life, be objective.

The mother continues, 'Of course, we live a life some people don't agree with and we have to make sacrifices. I know that I will probably live to see my own son beheaded in the End of Days.' She says this with an almost expressionless, nonplussed face as she's ruffling the blonde hair of her five-year-old boy. As if she's just said, 'Jonny likes candy too' or something equally flippant.

I look at her little boy; he's not scared when his mother says he's destined to get his head chopped off. As if he's heard it all before and accepts his fate as one of the holy children. I know this feeling of acceptance all too well from my own childhood. Of course, we would be killed in wars, of course we'd never grow up to become adults: it was our purpose and our honour. Many times, I have seen tactics of disassociation used by kids and not just in groups like these. Children who have desensitised themselves to survive are everywhere:

Mom wasted, Dad angry, in-house family fighting. Kids are malleable and resilient – to a point.

Over the coming days, Sofi and I become fully integrated in the group. I wanted to experience their way of life and that's what we get: we are expected to attend every gathering. We work in the fields picking kale. We do shifts in the factory they have on the farm, making their kale-based, sell-out health smoothie, the 'Green Drink'.

Wake up at six
Gathering at 6:15am
Breakfast at 7:30am
Breakfast clean-up 8–8:30am
Work in fields 8:30am–12pm
Lunch 12–12:45pm
Work in fields 12:45–3pm
Dinner prep 3–6pm
Dinner 6–7pm
Gathering 7–8:30pm
Housework 8:30–11pm

The never-changing, churning routine turns the commune into a well-oiled but never resting machine. There are no breaks, no times to contemplate the day, to mull over the teachings from the gathering, no time to bicker, to bad-mouth, to goof off. Every tick of the clock is accounted for – if there were clocks here.

My cotton headscarf picks up the evidence of our day: the smell of smoke from the gathering in the morning is still with me at breakfast, the mud of the fields clings to it at lunch, sometimes it carries the dirt of the kale we pick, the smell of the boiling potato water from dinner prep.

This is a pretty normal formula for communes and communities; it's easier to control large numbers of people if everyone's time is scheduled, it makes you feel like you have purpose if you are constantly busy, plus, it makes it harder to think and question authority if you are always exhausted. 'Many hands make light work', 'Idle hands are the devil's work' . . . scriptures to live by.

All the while, we're trying to make friends, to get to know people as individuals, gain some trust – to get them to see us as people rather than 'outsiders'. But there is a cavern of mistrust between us, heightened because of the raids. The details of the raids and their aftermath are still coming out now. We have no time to stop and read the news or catch up on it and there is a part of me that feels that knowing *more* details might not be helpful.

Not yet.

The routine means it's not as easy as I would like to connect with the kids. And they are quiet and so very grown-up. They go about their days with an adult responsibility. Afra, who is six and feeds the goats every day, Calah, who is eight and weeds the gardens with the skill of an adult, Eliab, who is ten, who works the saw and the hammer with the scary confidence of a foreman. The 30 or so children here are an invaluable workforce.

Well-behaved and strangely grown-up kids are another thing I've witnessed in children who have suffered trauma. My friend's eight-year-old niece, who has seen far too much violence and is as trustworthy as an adult. My girlfriend, who grew up parenting her own mom because she had addiction issues, doing the grocery shopping, cleaning the house, giving her mom hangover cures and putting her to bed. Sometimes trauma can make kids appear 'good' – there is no room for them to misbehave or be children. When outsiders would meet us when we were kids, they would wonder why their own children weren't as *lovely* and well behaved as we were.

But the kids who are silent around their parents here, when we catch them alone, feeding the goats, or up on the hill weeding, we can steal a smile or a song out of them pretty quickly. Afra looks at me with inquisitive eyes, assessing trust levels, before a flash of the child that's being contained underneath comes out with a giggle. Playfulness in children is magic. It's found on impoverished council estates in London, giant trash dumps in Ghana and the farmlands of segregated religious groups. Somehow, even if it's in small amounts, kids still find ways to be kids. There is a magic in this, but it's bittersweet that the strength of children's joy prevails and sadness that it *has* to.

*   *   *

In one of the gatherings we are told about 'The Rod'. Their right to spank their children. Their full authority over the children is justified in a simple claim of possession: they were given to them by God. And no one, not the German legislature, has the right to cast doubt on this authority. And they have proof that you *have* to spank your children. They drag out printed 'evidence' that the children who are being raised in Sweden, where corporal punishment is banned, are a 'Generation of Monsters'.

'Children are growing up with damaged souls, unbearable burdens of guilt. All you have left when the spanking stops is hell breaking loose,' the gathering leader says before he finishes, 'What kind of hell? Sweden has the highest rape statistics in all of Europe.' The parents nod in agreement.

Do they feel they are stopping rape through corporal punishment?

We look for clues of 'The Rod' here. We have seen kids taken out of the room, often by solemn-looking adults – they are taken from meals, from field work, from the gatherings. Eliab motioned to the door: Calah being marched out, held by the hand, with heavy solemnness. I feel my own childish feet on that walk, the firm grip of a dominant adult hand, no kicking, no screaming, 'silent like a lamb to the slaughter'. But we never see anything, we never even hear a child's cry.

Each night, I ache for the promise of my lumpy bed, exhaustion in my bones as I stand at the sink and scrub out the mud from my fingernails. I notice the cuts multiplying on my hands daily that don't seem to heal, the water that comes off my face is a milky grey. My reflection seems to be changing rapidly – swollen eyes, tired skin, a bagginess to my features as if they have been prised off my skull a little.

Each morning, I awake to the sound of the shofar with an exhausted vigilance. A familiar feeling. I slip into the routine like an uncomfortable but well-worn boot – you know where the rubs are, where the blisters form, where the skin wears raw. You know its pain well and every day you jam your swollen foot back in.

Over the next few days, perhaps it's sharing a room, perhaps it's because we have shared shifts, I feel like we are growing closer to our roommate, Derusha. It's night-time – we sit on the floor in our room together, the low light pulls my heavy lids, each blink longer than the last, as we quietly fold linens, our final task before bed.

A comforting job that's done quietly.

Derusha breaks the silence: 'I was once a mother.'

The surprise of this wakes me up. I'm afraid to ask what 'once' means – I give her some space to speak.

'I raised two boys on this farm, was married to a man in this community.' She says this slowly, monotone, no inflections, no drama. 'He started to disagree with God's word, like how we raise our children.'

'What happened?' I ask.

'He spoke of leaving many times. I told him I would never leave, I woke up one morning and they were gone.'

I feel almost no emotion in her voice. Maybe she has compartmentalised this, maybe it's resignation, maybe that's how she gets through losing her kids. Her eyes hold mine for a second, then she looks down and continues folding.

'He turned his back on God,' she says, looking at the neat line she has just formed in the fabric.

'Did you ever see them again?' Sofi asks.

'Oh yes, a few weeks later, he came back. He said that my sons missed me and again tried to get me to forsake my faith. That was a real test from Yashua that day, but I did not waiver.'

She smiles.

I want to sympathise with her, I want to be objective, or give her some empathy, but I struggle. She's lost (in my eyes) everything for her faith – it seems she wears the loss like a badge of honour. I want to say to her, 'What if Yashua isn't coming back? What if everything they're telling you here is a figment of someone's imagination? What if, for one moment, you allow yourself to think that your husband was right?' Instead I say, 'Do your sons visit?'

'They got too contaminated by the world and started to influence the kids here to sin. So, they are no longer allowed to visit.'

'You must really miss them,' I say.

'They are no longer the boys I raised, they are of that world now.'

Now, this stings; I can't help but be triggered. In Derusha's face, I experience my parents' coldness. The part of me that as a teenager was shunned is stabbed, a white-hot needle into a wound decades old. There is also a part of me that longed for what Derusha's husband did for her kids. I daydreamed that scenario in so many different ways: being shaken awake in the middle of the night by a dad who wants to break me out.

He is the hero that little me was desperate for.

* * *

Our days morph into each other, exhaustion sets in and while I feel like we're making friends with some of the people here, the trust issues also start to deepen. We, as single women without children, are considered by the group to be the bottom rung. And even though Derusha is not my favourite person, seeing how she is treated and how her place must have changed since she became a 'widow', pains me. I keep reminding myself that she has a choice. But when the hours of a day are stolen from you and replaced with exhaustion, when it is reinforced twice a day that you are not good enough, when you announce your shame every morning, choices and options feel further and further away.

And the longer we're here, the more it feels like Sofi is starting to commit, perhaps subconsciously, small acts of rebellion. *Is her tabard getting tighter? Perhaps her shirt buttons are undone by accident?* My watchfulness for misdemeanour and trouble flips on like a floodlight. Maybe it's me, maybe I'm being overly sensitive?

Then, in the afternoon, as I carry a bucket of corn across the lawn to the kitchen, Sofi is taken aside by Derusha. Sofi's face registers what's being said with what feels like, even from here, a thousand 'fuck you's. My stomach drops.

'She told me that my tabard is too tight, that I am sexualising myself.' She points to her tabard: 'THIS? Sexy?'

I shake my head in disbelief as I continue towards the kitchen. I'm worried that it will look like we're talking about what just happened, I don't want to be seen co-conspiring. *For fuck's sake!* Why bother getting called out on something so stupid? We're not here to rebel, we're here to blend in. We're here to build trust. And with that, I feel our relationship, if we ever had one with Derusha, could be blown.

That night, I lie in my bottom bunk, my body limp, my back throbbing from the fieldwork, but my brain alive with a loop of noise. Am I stupid to think their distrust of us will change the more that we prove ourselves out in the fields, the more kale we pick, the more likely they will let us film? That the time spent in the kitchen will translate into time interviewing the kids. I tell myself that it will, *it must.*

Has a dishonesty crept up on me? Am I slipping into a world where no one says what they feel? I can't tell. The longer

I'm here and the more I'm sure that the kids are not in a good place, the more righteous I feel in my deceit. We smile, but we don't agree with what we see. We smile when we are treated like servants, we are passive when we feel like shouting. My mask of duplicity snaps in place with ease.

And when I look around at the disciples, who do I see? Their masks? Smiling zombies, placid covers for what they really think? Is there 'internal thought' anymore? Has the collective identity become so strong, it's wiped away the inner narrative or being. At times I have felt this with my parents: my questions fell on the ears of the collective, the answers are from the book, a feeling of everything being scripted. But perhaps that is the indoctrination of scripture.

Have we come at a time so sensitive that we will *never* get what we want? And I realise instead of being concerned by the raids and how potentially volatile this situation would be for us, it excited me in some way, it whet my appetite to get in among it, to see it from the other side first-hand. It gave me a sense of aliveness to know that this was afoot.

I still have an ambition, perhaps a false hope, of wanting them to like, or at least trust us so we can film here. But every day that passes, I feel less like a filmmaker, more a member of the Twelve Tribes.

* * *

The next morning, I walk back from the shower to see Sofi pulling her bag apart. A chaos of clothes, moisturisers, socks all over the dorm floor.

'I think they've taken . . . stolen my watch,' she says.

'It's probably in the truck,' I say. I think it's highly unlikely that it's been stolen – surely, members aren't even allowed to wear them?

She motions to the direction of the toilet. I follow her in and she turns on the tap. She whispers to me, 'I think they've been through my stuff. This is not the first time I've noticed, but this is the first time that I'm almost hundred per cent *sure*.'

I wonder if she's turned on the tap to drown out the sound of her voice.

I'll help her look for it, I say, and we head out to the van. I want her to calm down, I *need* her to calm down.

'They're never going to let us film here, you know,' she tells me.

Opening cupboards and bags, she says, 'Things are getting fucking worse by the day. And I'm pretty sure they've been listening to us in that room, maybe even recording us. If they have been, then we're fucked, for sure.'

While I want to tell her that's ridiculous, I mentally scan all of the conversations we have had in the room to see if anything might incriminate us. A deep-rooted survival tactic, auditing every moment to prepare a 'defence case', my mind in hyper-protective mode.

'Look at the state of them, Sofi,' I say, trying to soothe her. 'They don't even have can openers, let alone recording devices.' I hope she doesn't hear the desperation in my voice as I feel the situation slipping rapidly out of control. 'Also, look, we're going to be late for breakfast and that's going to look suspicious. Let's not get freaked out and make it worse, yeah?'

Up in the dining room, my eyes dart around, following Sofi's movements. Someone hands her a cup of vinny.

Did Sofi just fake a sip? Fuck! I really need to keep an eye on her.

Did she just pour the vinny into a plant?

Shit!

This is getting out of hand. *First, they're recording us and now they're poisoning us?* Rumours like this are rife about new religious movements – poisonings, surveillance, but it's not actually a common, done thing. It's sensationalism, isn't it? Not real life. A cup of vinny isn't the problem, the weapons of control are more psychological; the mental exhaustion, the shame, the repetition. Not brainwashing, but conditioning. These weapons are more powerful than what you could pop in a cup. Sofi was raised in a family system of free will. For her, this regime will feel endless, confusing; she must be exhausted. These are farmers we're dealing with, not high-tech spies with sound recording equipment. *Aren't they?*

As people start to move into the circle for the gathering, I lose sight of Sofi. The singing starts and my heart sinks as I realise she is definitely not here. Derusha must have noticed too as she leaves the room with a stomp.

Ten minutes later, Sofi walks in and what could just be a tired, fed-up face might also come across as angry and rude. *Jesus, Sofi!* I'm mad at her that it's gone this far – getting told off by members of the group for going missing, dressing wrong, causing issues. I shake my head.

There's one thing she's right about: we'll never get to film here now.

And now in this stuffy room, crammed full of people, claustrophobic with the smell of bodies and sweat, I start to feel that the situation has slipped out of control. I need to do something.

Anything. And I need to do it now. I wait for my moment and when the floor is opened up, I take my chance, wait for a lull, breathe in, stand up and step forward into the focus of the circle.

'Sofi and I, we have come here to learn about your group and we realise we have come at a time of great strife. We have heard about the pain that you feel, a pain that cannot be understood, unless you too have had a child taken from you.'

I look around the room, hoping to make some kind of connection; some faces stare down, some stare through me.

'We've also heard that you feel misunderstood and that if people could see your way of life, they would understand you. Because if it's not seen or experienced then it cannot be understood. So, I offer you this: if you want people to see you as you are, we can show them what we are seeing, living with you now. Maybe we are here, as filmmakers, during this time of strife, not by some great coincidence, but for a reason.'

Sofi squeezes my hand as I sit down, giving me warmth and encouragement, and as she does, the nerves that were somehow held back start flooding in.

*   *   *

After the gathering, I ask for an audience with Yosef, the leader of the commune. I get rejected, so I write an email to the Leaders of the group, suggesting we film them and give them the opportunity to be 'seen'; laying out our case, and hoping they can see serendipity in the timing of our visit. But as the day goes on and we hear nothing back, it really sinks in that it's gone too far. The way that they feel about us has been heightened by what's going on in the Press and by the fact that the children in Germany still haven't been returned to the Twelve Tribes. Perhaps we are a physical manifestation of their fears and their enemies.

We stand in a candle-lit barn for our final gathering. The heavy smell of wood hangs low, the darkness of the room surrounds the disciples, creating silhouettes that seem to move in slow motion. And I feel it all. I am not numb through my tricks of escaping my body or my mind, I am not thinking how this would look on film – I am present in the room, absorbing the words, the intentions and the emotional frequencies.

I start to feel a heavy ache.

Have I lost my empathy for Sofi and what this place could be doing to her? Have I gone so far into this wormhole that I forgot myself? In my survival skills of desensitising myself in this environment, have I desensitised myself to my friend? I felt that I could see so much *more* because my experience allowed me an insight, but perhaps it also gave me a blindness. And I know we have to go.

One of the men says, 'The slap in the face is what makes the follower obedient.'

Another says, 'The flesh gets in the way of the Lord.'

A mother gets up and says, 'Parents need to overcome the instinct of protecting the child. That is a selfishness that gets in the way of God's work.'

A little boy stands up and asks to be 'broken' – his eyes never leave the ground.

I wish I could escape my body now, but I can't. The tears that run down my face are red-hot, the ache in my throat is a ragged scream trying to claw its way out. I can't stop. I feel the pain and shame of every child that stands up. The air too dense to breathe, my chest feels like a prison.

I stumble out into the fresh air, filling my lungs with it, breathing out the heaviness of the gathering. Wiping away the tears that refuse to stop. I feel an arm around my shoulders.

'You ready to go, cherub?' Sofi says.

'Uh, huh,' I say, shaking.

Sofi closes the door of the van behind us and with the click of the handle, calm floods in.

'So . . .' She gets down on her knees and starts to wipe my face as if I'm a child that just did a muddy faceplant. 'They released the films of what happened in the German communes.'

'Really? Fuck! Have you seen them?' I ask.

'No, I've been here with you, dummy!'

'Shall we have a look?'

'Well, we're leaving, aren't we?'

'Yep.'

The internet struggles up in these hills, but finally, we suck enough up to pull up a video.

The little blonde-haired boy is about four years old. He whimpers as a middle-aged woman drags him down some stairs into a dimly lit cellar and orders him to bend over and touch the stone floor with his hands. Another little boy watches as the woman pulls down the first boy's pants and then draws out a willow cane.

'Say you are tired!' commands the woman in an emotionless voice. The swoosh of the willow cane strikes the screaming child three times.

The little boy refuses to say he is tired, so he is hit again and again – a total of ten times – until, in floods of tears, he finally says, 'I am tired.'

Within the space of a few hours, six adults are filmed in the cellar beating six children with a total of 83 strokes of the cane.

The video ends. We sit in silence. My fingers are pressed so tightly into my palms, my nails nearly draw blood, my back rigid with adrenaline, my jaw locked. The tears have stopped.

I am fucking angry.

'How many of those kids do you think we can fit in this truck?' I whisper through clenched teeth.

'Two things: we're not Child Services and corporal punishment is legal in the States. Horribly, what is happening here isn't illegal,' she says.

'It just feels fucking horrible to have seen that and just drive away,' I say.

'We don't have a choice,' she says.

I realise we are now exactly what they might have been paranoid of this whole time: two outsiders genuinely talking about kidnapping their kids. We need to go and we need to go now. I want to burst into that barn, scoop up those kids and run. But I am not a saviour, I am not a hero, I am a woman turning around and driving away.

Sofi stares straight ahead as Mamacita flies down the dark road away from the Twelve Tribes. The stretched-out arms of the trees that looked so ominous on the way in are still reaching towards the van, but there's no way they could hold us back.

'We'll be back here, you know? This isn't done,' I say.

She nods in the dark.

'Not by a fucking long shot!'

CHAPTER 7

A Whisper in the Dark: 5 Years Before

'I think I found an escape route!' Maria runs her fingers along the edge of a large, straight gap in the floorboards. 'It could be a trap door,' she adds.

'Maybe it's how the knights and ladies used to get away from their enemies?' I say.

We'd been told about the history of 'The Manor' by my dad – 'Five hundred years old,' he said, 'and would have had knights walking through these halls.'

I watch Maria pushing the wood, her olive-skinned hands trying to find a latch. Twelve years old, she is the bolder of our duo. We are a team, best friends (the first real friend I have ever had) and I know if this was a hatch into another world, she is the one I would want to go through it with.

The house is enormous. Not just because of the number of bedrooms, though there are 16 of them. It's the sheer scale of the place. Like it was constructed by medieval giants. The front door is twice the size of a normal door, with ornate metalwork. There are large dark panels on the walls, carved in deep wood. In most of the communal rooms (there are five of those, six if you count the kitchen), there are massive fireplaces. And it has huge grounds, with lawns, gardens and woods.

Acres and acres of green.

It's enormous, it's grand. And now it's ours. I have lived in some pretty weird places – tiny yellow caravans, bright pink houses in Johannesburg, horrible flats crammed full of people, I've even lived in a barn. But *this*, even by our standards, is something else.

I first met Maria when we moved from the Teen Home to the one before this one. The Birmingham Home had been disbanded, the Teen Camp dismantled, the kids sent to new places as 'renewed End Time soldiers'. It's been nearly a year since I left that place and I still feel it on me, The year in the Victor Camp was so vast and so encompassing and it went by so slowly. I know in reality it was an old house with wallpaper and carpets but it felt like it was made of concrete slabs. The outside was surrounded by fields and trees but it was as though I had weights on my legs wading through mud. It was full of kids my age and yet I felt completely alone. The place was filled with my silence, but it gave birth to loud voices in my head that started to argue with my sanity. And then strangely, we were gone: I was told we were moving in the morning and by the evening, we had left.

Once gone, it was almost as if moving to a new house meant that none of it had happened. That year snatched from us through the change of our physical surroundings. And yet, moving into a new home, I was still, in theory, on Silence Restriction.

On day one at the new commune, I saw this girl my age with black, frizzy hair, cleaning the floors. Hunched over a bucket with a wild look about her. When I walked into the room, she looked up and stared me dead in the eye. Eye contact is not allowed with someone on Silence Restriction so her eyes boring deep into mine were shocking, exciting and dangerous. It was Maria – and she was still on Silence Restriction too.

That night, I was told that Maria and I were supposed to share a bed. It's a strange thing, sharing a bed with someone you don't know and have never spoken to. Being that physically close to a person when you have felt so disconnected and alone for so long that you've wondered at times if you only exist in your head.

Maria was already bundled up in the top bunk. I climbed up timidly, pulled back the blanket just a little so it wouldn't come off her and slipped in. Maybe I wouldn't wake her.

'Hey!' she whispered into the dark.

'Hey!' I said back.

Hey! The first real word I had uttered in a year. So simple. A single syllable that means so little, but meant more than anything in the world.

And right there was my escape hatch back into humanity. Back to sanity. A whisper in the dark. For the first few weeks, we talked in secret after lights out. We talked about everything that we'd been forced to keep inside, the stuff we never dared say out loud; who we feared and who we hated, and even more dauntingly, what we now hoped and dreamed for. She told me she was put on Silence Restriction nearly a year ago – she'd fallen down the stairs and broken her collarbone. The home took it as a sign from God that she needed to be punished so they put her on the Victor programme.

For the first month or so, I would wake up early every day to check that she was still lying in the bed next to me, that she wasn't a figment of my imagination. Day by day, we became braver, until we decided that we should start to talk in public, just a little, to see if anyone noticed. And we were right: in this new home, without all the Leaders from the other home around us, no one noticed and we became visible again.

* * *

I look up at the atrium ceiling of our 500-year-old home.

This house has had many secrets and probably will have many more, I say to myself.

Maria opens the hatch in the floor. The creak of the wooden trap door starts to grow until it becomes a deafening squawk. When it opens, it reveals a basement below that's as big as the living room. It must stretch under this entire section of the house.

'This really could be an escape route,' I say, baffled that her guess was right.

'GIRLS!' My dad's voice rips through the old house.

We slam the trap door shut as he shouts, 'Don't you have some work to do?'

'Yes!' we say in unison as we run off.

His voice follows us up the stairs with, 'Don't make me split you two up again!'

We have been at The Manor for nearly two months.

It's early, dark and quiet. My eyes feel like the night has glued them shut. I nudge Maria. 'We gotta make breakfast . . .' Her hair looks like a bush that's been in a fight, her eyes tired, one of them leaking with sleep. She groans. I feel it through my whole body too, that heavy pull of never quite having enough sleep. But time is getting away from us already. I jump out of bed and pull my clothes on. We've been sharing a job running the kitchen for a while now. While I don't like these early morning starts and the bed is pretty tiny, even for two scrawny kids like us, I love being part of a duo. We are dependable, we work hard; we very rarely 'slack off' and for that (for now) we are allowed to be together.

They had split me and Maria up a few times before. Friendships are not really allowed – we know that they can get in the way of the Lord's work, they can be a distraction or a bad influence. You are allowed to feel connection, but not if it starts to overtake the group. It's the same with families. My brothers and sisters are all here (except the older ones, Chad and Kris), but we aren't in the family unit, all split across different age categories. You can be close, but you can't be *too* close, you can't put the needs of your family above the group. This rule is easy enough to get around: You just have to act like you don't care as much as you do in front of other people. You act a little colder, you don't talk too much to each other, you don't look like you're sharing jokes. It's pretty easy.

'C'mon,' I say, shoving a hairband in Maria's hand.

The house is dark and full of the sounds of sleep as we creak to our workstation. The stone kitchen floor is cold; I can feel it through my rubber shoes. I wriggle the ache out.

'Freezing!' I whisper.

'How many people are we now?' Maria asks as she pulls a big white barrel out from under a counter.

'As of yesterday? Sixty-three.'

She scoops out the oats, counting out each scoop, making sure we have the right amount. As I watch the small white flakes pour into a massive steel pan, I am so grateful that we finally ran out of the horse food from the Birmingham Home. Thinking about those brown flakes makes me gag.

'Next week, I think we'll have a full house so we'll have to start planning for that . . . about how we're going to make this food stretch to nearly 100 people,' she says.

'Stretch' is the word we use most in our kitchen – 'How can we make this stretch?', 'Put beans in it to stretch it out', 'Water it down, it will stretch it out'. We are constantly trying to do what Jesus did, feed 5,000 with five loaves and two fish. But instead of expecting a real miracle, we just figure out how to 'stretch it'.

Half an hour later, the shuffling into the wooden-panelled dining room for breakfast starts. Kids, Teens, adults, babies. Clammy hands held around the clusters of tables as someone blesses the meal. Then the race to eat begins, not only because of the scarcity of the food – there is never really enough, no matter how much we 'stretch' – but to get to devotions on time. We battle against time and the day has barely begun.

Teens hurriedly ram their last mouthfuls of watery porridge in as the clean-up crew pull their plates away to soak. The scraping sounds of dining-room chairs being dragged into the living room cuts through the plucking of acoustic guitars. We can always tell what time it is or where we are supposed to be through sound – guitars, prayer, hallelujahs, the bell for dinner. There is a sonic rhythm to our life. Our homes run with almost mechanical clockwork. There is no margin for 'lost time' or 'slacking off'. Maria and I run into the living room and find a seat on the floor. A few minutes after the scarcity of breakfast, chairs for devotions will also be gone.

How will we fit 100 people in here?

*   *   *

Uncle Andrew is the leader of this house. He stands at the head of the room, framed by the big old wooden fireplace behind him, holding a Bible and some papers. I believe that he is English originally, but he has kept his distance from us in ways that other Aunties and Uncles don't. Most regale us with stories of their 'lives before the Lord', where you can find out a little about them; some were 'the smartest boy in their school' like my dad. Maybe they were 'a runaway' like Auntie Phoebe. Auntie Lilly, Maria's mom, was a go-go dancer in a nightclub. While the adults tell us these stories to explain how shocking the outside world is, and how lucky we are to have been born into this community as the Chosen Ones, they also tell us to reveal the beauty, excitement and power of the day they were enlightened.

All I really know about Uncle Andrew is what I see standing in front of me, a tall man with a salt-and-pepper beard and a balding head. Perhaps his leadership explains the distance he keeps from us. Perhaps we wouldn't have as much respect for him if there wasn't a little mystery.

He waits for the gathering to be still and starts to pray: 'Lord, thank you for this house, for keeping us safe in these uncertain times. Please be with Auntie Pearl right now, and we ask that you put a stop to her mother and her evil ways, and stop her from hurting your children.'

Auntie Pearl has been in our prayers daily for the past three weeks. I think back to the day that it all started. I wasn't there, but had the story told to me so vividly multiple times I feel as if I was. The police raided one of our homes looking for Auntie Pearl's baby boy. They had a call from Auntie Pearl's mother, terrified that her grandchild was in great danger, maybe even dead. They smashed down the door and searched through every cupboard, suitcase and drawer – 'The police even looked under floorboards, like we had chopped the baby up and hidden him,' they said. No one could believe this had happened.

We had been running from the authorities and the Press for years and now a full raid?

The police found the baby safe. Of course, he was – we don't chop babies up. But now Pearl's mother had started a custody case against her, against all of us.

'Because this is bigger than Auntie Pearl', 'Because if the Judge believes it's not safe for her baby, then it's not safe for any of us,' I had told Maria, mimicking what I had overheard my parents say the night before.

So, because of this new court case, after all these years of living under the radar, or on the run, we are now in what they are calling an 'Open Home'. And it all makes sense: why this big house, why we live so close to the Systemites in this tiny village. My dad looked for this home for exactly this purpose: to be out in the open.

Uncle Andrew continues, 'We have a *new* mission.' He looks around the room without blinking, motivating us. 'It's not going to be easy, we are going to have to adjust to being in the public eye.' He points to his right eye dramatically, pausing, so we can take the importance of this moment in.

'Everyone here is going to have to learn how to behave in front of the Press. That trial run that we had in the last home with the *Guardian* journalist went well.'

I think back to meeting the journalist from the *Guardian* a few months ago. I can still remember his face, the white hair that framed his face, a very English accent; he was maybe the kindest man I have ever met. An adult who spoke to us differently, asked us what we wanted from life, what our dreams were . . .

'I want to explain Gideon and Rachel's role in all of this.'

Uncle Andrew interrupts my memories. He points to my parents, holding hands, presenting a united front. My dad changed his name again, from Jacob to Gideon – I am still getting used to it.

'Gideon and Rachel are the new public faces of our group, not just in the UK, but the whole of Europe. It's an important role.'

I look at my mom and dad: their identities seem to be shifting. As well as the name change, they are dressing differently. Mom has cut her hair into a bob, Dad has grown a bristly moustache that he plays with theatrically – sometimes he punctuates his sentences, or emphasises a point with it, as if it's a prop in a monologue. I wonder if these shifts are for the 'important role' they are playing.

'Gideon and Rachel's whole family will be a part of this too. Which will mean some changes.'

Maria pinches my arm, a pinch that says, *That means YOU.*

Uncle Andrew pauses and signals to my dad that he has permission to speak.

Dad clears his throat and says, 'We are both honoured and excited about this new, but challenging role.'

Mom doesn't say anything, she just smiles at my dad and then at the room earnestly.

Uncle Andrew goes on, 'Some of you need to be taught how to speak to the Press and we will start training pretty much immediately, because while they, Gideon and Rachel, are the public face, this house is now an open home.' He points his finger around the room slowly before adding, 'If a reporter comes in, they can talk to any of you.'

I pinch Maria back.

See, that means you too.

*   *   *

Later, I am summoned back to the living room.

Auntie Phoebe sits in the middle of the room. She has long hair, even for an Auntie – it falls halfway down her thigh, coarse and very black. Long hair like Phoebe's is like a medal of success: our leader Moses David loves long hair, it's the ultimate sign of femininity. Auntie Phoebe told she us grew up in Greece – I imagine her whipping that giant black braid around, wearing a tunic like Greeks from the biblical times. But today, she wears a long skirt, woollen tights, a cardigan and a turtle neck underneath – she must find it hard to keep warm.

I have been chosen for this for a few reasons, I think, but the most important one is they asked all the teen girls if they had had any 'sexual experiences' with adults and they sent the ones that said they had to other homes. Out of the public eye. We had a quiz in a media training session the other day and one of the girls said she had sex with her dad in front of every one. Her family was gone the next day.

That's not the right answer.

'Take a seat,' Auntie Phoebe says without looking up from her notes.

I grab one of the high-backed wooden chairs from the side of the room and drag it in front of her, perfectly placed so we are eye to eye. Like most of the women in the house, Auntie Phoebe acts in different ways depending on the situation. If there is an Uncle in the room, she can be subservient, but if she's alone, she's in charge, she's dominant. The women aren't passive here, not quite, it's more about knowing how to flip between what the need is. Their voices change, their mannerisms change. And right now, she is dominant, unmoving and serious.

Still she doesn't look up.

'So, you were quite good at this last time, if I remember. You were one of the ones that the *Guardian* journalist interviewed.'

I am surprised by this compliment. And that she remembers. Finally, she looks at me: 'This time, I am just going to ask you the questions, not give you any answers. Let's see how you do, shall we?'

I nod.

'OK, and try to act normal, relaxed.'

I nod again.

Her voice drops, the tone a little cooler: 'And remember, these journalists will be smiling and speaking to you nicely but they are trying to trick you and trying to harm us. So, don't be fooled by them. Keep up your guard and act relaxed.'

I nod again. She shifts into the role of journalist and puts on a formal voice: 'Why do you think your parents want to raise you like this?'

I breathe in, remembering to speak slowly but without too many pauses.

'My parents believe in religious freedom, that we have the right to worship God in whatever way we please. And it's not unusual for Christians to be persecuted like we are now, it's happened throughout all of the Bible and history.'

'Good,' she says. 'It would be better if you can give an example, we can also use these interviews to witness for the Lord.'

'Jesus himself was persecuted,' I say. 'They tied him to a cross and killed him. And he was the son of God.' I scan her face, hoping for validation, hoping she thinks this is a great example. But I can't tell if she is satisfied.

Then she asks, 'What would you say if they ask you why you don't go to "normal" school?' (She puts air quotes around the word 'normal'.)

I get a rush of excitement as I remember almost the exact wording that my dad uses: 'We have an education system here that not only honours the scholastic subjects, but also has Bible studies, which I hear are lacking in schools. Also, we get to be taught by people that we love and live with, and in small groups. Not classes of hundreds.'

'Say overcrowded classes, hundreds might seem far-fetched,' she corrects me.

I nod – the details are important, or it might show that you really have no idea what a school looks like.

'What will you say if they ask you about how much you work in the house?' she asks.

'It's good for children to have responsibility, it's a part of our learning and it helps us to develop.' It feels like she is expecting more, so I add, 'We love to help around the house.'

I shut out thoughts of early wake-up calls, the contrast between how cold that kitchen is in the morning and how hot it gets when you have to run an industrial oven. I shut out the criticism we get if we don't manage to make the food 'work' for the number of people. I just imagine myself watching my baby brother sleep. It's nice. Quiet. Cosy. I end on a dreamy note. 'We love to help looking after our brothers and sisters.'

'What will you say if they ask you how you are disciplined or even punished?'

'Our parents love us and the other adults here love us as if they are our parents. We are raised in love. I wish all children could feel as loved and looked after as we do. Even the ones in our homes who maybe grew up with just a mother have a whole household of people to look after them.'

These words tumble out of me on autopilot – memorised, rehearsed.

'Very good.'

She shifts in her chair, perhaps signifying that she is dialling the 'interview' up a few notches.

'What if they ask you about the flirty fishing? What if they say, "We hear that the mothers here used to be paid for sex by men to support the homes"?' she asks.

'I have never seen or heard of this. My mother and father have a loving relationship. They are a good example of a wonderful marriage,' I respond without hesitation.

She chides me. 'This needs more, it's a bit weak. Maybe say something about hoping you have "that" one day when you grow up.'

I nod.

Now she goes all out: 'What about the Davidito book? Have you read it?'

I think back to the photobook that was in every house that I grew up in. In the book, Davidito, Moses David's son, was being 'made love' to by the Aunties of the house. There were pages and pages of photographs. All the adults had cartoon faces on them and there was Davidito, naked in the middle, being fondled, being sexually caressed to put him to sleep. They called it 'Love Up Time'. And then I remember the day we burnt the book because people on the outside 'Wouldn't understand it'.

'We got rid of that years ago,' I say quietly.

'No, that is not the right answer,' she snaps.

The blow of disappointment and shame fills me. I got this far and now I've messed up. I come to my own defence in my head: *I don't think anyone has given me this answer yet, isn't it OK if we just don't have the book anymore?*

She interrupts my internal plea with an irritated tone. 'Just say that you don't know what they are talking about.'

OK, act innocent.

'Should I say, "What's that?"?' I ask.

'No, that will open them up to start telling *you* about it. Say you have never seen or heard of it,' she says.

So, we must lie. 'Deceivers Yet True' the Mo Letter told us.

But, they have said, the lies will protect us.

'The Davidito Book does not exist,' she says, wagging a finger at me.

CHAPTER 8

Tucson and the Cosmos: 15 Years After

The drive from California to Arizona is breathtaking. We kick up dust through the arid Martian scenes. A long drive can be a rinse for the soul, not just the physical distance or time, or ever-changing landscapes. It can be as simple as having to 'sit' with, or in, your thoughts. And we have plenty of time to 'sit': the 12-hour drive takes us four days; we're in no rush and neither is Mamacita.

When we first got out of the Twelve Tribes everything felt brand new, we were babies spellbound by the mundane. A *hello* from a petrol attendant, a cold sip of beer, the bite of a cigarette on the throat. A talk through the night about how lucky we are. Holding each other as we walk on the beach, a run screaming into a cold ocean. All of it seems extraordinary. While what we experienced wasn't what we wanted, and didn't have the outcome we'd hoped for, coming out of it renewed my gratitude for my life and how far it has come. Catharsis. The freedoms that I am allowed, the right to say what I want, to wear my well-worn, second-hand clothes instead of a shared wardrobe of head scarves and tabards.

'Fuck that fucking tabard!' Sofi said as she pulled a bobbly thrift shop T-shirt over her head.

Now, as we ride through Joshua Tree, I share the front seat with my sense of loss from the Twelve Tribes, riding with the memories of it, of *them*. I miss the kids we made friends with. The sting of that last night is still sharp. Mixed up in all this are the feelings of guilt I have at leaving them behind. My hands are bound – I know I can't do anything, but that doesn't abate how guilty I feel.

I need this drive, I need to see so far into the distance that it hurts, to realise that I am a small being on a huge planet that has been here long before me and this trip. I need the perspective. Does it help to feel small? Does that allow me to have not done anything? Does the perspective erase responsibility and guilt?

I need to 'sit' in it.

'How much longer to the motel?' Sofi asks.

''Bout an hour,' I say.

'Talk to me about Gabriel,' she says.

We're on our way to Tucson. To the 'Global Community Communications Alliance', a group led by a man called Gabriel of Urantia. After the yogic monks and the fundamentalists we've just left, I'm thirsty for something different.

'Let's dive into the world of Divine Cosmology,' I say, pulling my research out. 'Gabriel's cosmology is based on a mix of religious teachings; a bit of alien channelling, Mormonism, Hopi tradition and *The Urantia Book*.'

I'd never heard of *The Urantia Book* before. Apparently, it's quite a hit, with its own curious backstory. It was written sometime between 1924 and 1955, and its authors are named as 'numerous celestial beings'.

'So, no one author?' Sofi asks.

'High-deity authorities and super mortal personalities . . . So, not of this world. Maybe aliens, ghosts, angels, who knows? It's a lot to take in, even the Bible had physical authors.'

Thirty-five of them to be precise.

I perch a foot on the dashboard, turn the music down low and start to read the book to Sofi. *The Urantia Book* is a baffle that tries to explain a multitude of topics: the origin and meaning of life, mankind's place in the universe, the relationship between God and people and the life of Jesus.

Simple stuff.

Sofi looks over at the giant stack of printed papers.

'The book is long,' she says.

'Unsurprisingly.'

'And complicated,' she adds.

'What I do like is that it tries to fuse together physics, science, cosmology and religion,' I offer. I've never really understood religions that don't update with scientific progress. It just seems a little daft not to modernise when you can. Imagine my shock when I found out at The Dog and Gun pub quiz that the world was *more* than 6,000 years old.

We could get tied up in this giant volume for days. I come to the realisation that it's like trying to read all 66 books in the Bible so you can understand the Children of God.

A fruitless, complex task that really wouldn't get you any closer to the mind-bending teachings of David Berg.

* * *

We pull into our motel. It's brilliantly cheap, wonderfully tacky and right in the middle of a stunning stretch of desert. I'd booked it because the website said 'Jacuzzi'.

'We hundred per cent deserve *that*,' Sofi said.

The dusky pink, Adobe-style units look out onto the mountains and what we *hope* will be a good sweep of desert sky to stargaze. I check us in and grab a six-pack from the tiny store – this cosmic cult exploration might take a little while.

'This is perfect,' Sofi says, grabbing one of the chairs.

After cracking open a beer, I throw my head back as the fresh cold bite hits the back of my throat. I close my eyes, the sun strokes my face. The smell of chlorine and sun screen mix together – it pulls me back into multitudes of holidays.

I sit up and a drip of condensation hits my papers, reminding me to get on with it.

'If you're going to set up a cosmic cult, Sedona is the perfect place to do it,' I say.

Sedona is described as a cathedral without walls because of its glorious red vortexes. Some claim spiritual energy is at its highest point in these vortexes and you can tap into the frequencies of the universe. And it's where three million tourists a year come in search of spiritual renewal.

'Which is a tonne of potential recruits, if you think about it,' I say.

Sofi nods, her eyes closed. Like a Texan lizard, she lies back on the hot pink plastic recliner, absorbing the desert sun.

But, as well as the vortexes, Sedona harbours cosmic magic: it's one of America's most popular destinations for spotting UFOs. Every night, UFO hunters go out equipped with night vision glasses, binoculars and telescopes. There are a staggering number of reported sightings of everything from orbs and portals to aliens, all within the high desert sky.

'I've always loved the idea of aliens and UFOs,' I say.

'I mean, why not?' Sofi says.

'Yeah, why not believe in the magic of it? It's not like we've ever started any wars over people "believing in UFOs",' I say.

'Unless, of course, that's still to come.' She laughs.

* * *

Gabriel has written three other books: *The Cosmic Family, Volume 1*, *The Cosmic Family, Volume 2* and *The Divine New Order: A Cosmic Shift in Consciousness*. These books are meant as a follow-up to *The Urantia Book* and aim to provide 'real answers' for the crises our world faces, explaining ways in which every soul can genuinely contribute to healing their own lives and our planet.

Sounds both rational and progressive.

A little bit more left field are his beliefs in reincarnation, which Gabriel calls 'repersonalisation' or 'souls who have lived before as starseed'. According to him, most 'starseed' had their very first life on another planet, in another universe. Gabriel believes he himself is starseed with several repersonalisations: he was a Jedi knight, Confucius, Lao Tzu, Buddha, Moses, Abraham, Alexander the Great, the Apostle Peter, King Arthur, Saint Francis of Assisi, Mozart, William Wallace (after the movie *Braveheart* came out), George Washington, Abraham Lincoln, Joseph Smith Geronimo, Chief Joseph and many, many others.

I pull up a YouTube video of Gabriel saying, 'I'm either insane or egotistically mad, or I am who I say I am.'

What a brilliant statement.

'Classique,' Sofi says.

In this video, Gabriel looks like a classic ageing new-age hippie – tie-dye smocks, grey hair and beard, beads and crystals round the neck, archetypal (clichéd) headband. Sometimes he even carries a staff like a Shepherd – a metaphor for a Leader in many a group, including my own.

'Woah, look at that!' Sofi says, pointing upwards.

The sun is beginning to set on our motel. First, it explodes with reds, oranges and hot pinks, then the deep blue of night follows. We sit and watch in awe. Each passing moment reveals more glowing pinpricks in the universe's fabric. I get lost in the Milky Way, my head swirling from the beer, the day's heat and galactic gratitude.

One of the past lives Gabriel has had is who he was immediately *before* 'Gabriel of Urantia' – which was Anthony Delevin from Pittsburgh. Anthony had stints as a Catholic priest, a Protestant pastor and a musician. He claims to have invented the genre 'CosmoPop' and recorded an album called *Love Unicorn*.

'Wait, is that online?' Sofi interrupts me.

We search, and while this brilliantly titled album isn't online, his newer music is all over YouTube. We lose ourselves in the cyber rabbit hole. Just two girls sitting in their bras and pants in a car-park Jacuzzi, on the edge of the galaxy, following the digital footprint of a cult leader.

By 1989, he co-founded the Aquarian Concept Community and was calling himself Gabriel of Urantia.

'Amazingly at this time, he had also been bequeathed with the story of the universe from the universe itself. How brilliantly convenient!' I say.

'Or perhaps egotistically mad,' Sofi says, imitating Gabriel's accent.

'Gabriel is a mouthpiece to celestial beings and can channel alien transmissions. He was given this message by an alien: "I am the commander of a fleet of three thousand spacecraft that will participate in the evacuation of the planet when the change point comes". The ET went on, "You are needed to help us prepare for this evacuation. It will not be an easy task. You will be called a fraud and a deceiver . . ."'

'No shit! He's covering all bases there,' Sofi laughs.

'Ha! My parents used to say, "If you are being persecuted by society, you know you doing the right thing!" A failsafe get-out clause . . .'

'It's clever, mad . . . But clever.'

'I'll tell you what's mad: Gabriel of Urantia . . . whatever . . . is somewhere right now, under this same magnificent sky that we are under . . .' I say dreamily. 'Maybe channelling an alien or two.'

*   *   *

The group recruits new followers in a few different ways. One is through their tour company that takes you on a spiritual tour of the vortexes, through their WWOOF'ing; a farm training programme where you gain room and board for working the fields, via their deli in Tucson.

Yep, another deli.

'Once you have been recruited, full membership means you give over everything you have – land, savings, everything – to the group and live within the commune. If that's too much for you, you can also join them for a weekend for $500 or get a personalised alien transmission for $1,000.'

'One K for an alien transmission, from someone who has been both Buddha AND Alexander the Great? Sounds cheap to me . . . Hand me that towel?' Sofi says.

The desert temperature has dropped, the cold has got to me too.

Sofi dries herself, breathing in short, sharp, quick breaths as if she has picked up something hot. Her wet skin is tanned, smooth, reflecting the neon lights of the motel that have just been switched on. Pinks and greens mixed with wet flesh create an other-worldly scene on her body. I see a flicker of images: Gabriel, the Cosmos and the future that awaits us.

She catches me staring at her.

'So, what's the plan?'

'I reckon we just call them and ask if we can join, like we have before,' I say, my voice fuelled by beer and bravado.

'Sounds simple,' she says.

Then I get a pull on my stomach, a twinge of the Twelve Tribes in my belly.

A large black dog patters over and lies on the tarmac near us. He stretches out and rolls on his back, legs splayed.

'Cuuuuute!' Sofi says.

Perhaps she's missing her dog and maybe her life, back home. The dog meets her gaze, holds it lovingly for a second, then cocks a leg and starts licking his balls enthusiastically.

'Mmm . . . lovely!' she says.

'What *IS* for dinner?' I laugh.

* * *

We arrive in Tucson the next day. It's buzzing, erupting with artists and musicians, vintage stores and quirks and hipsters on every corner. The fashion is effortlessly cool – Stetsons teamed with Doc Martens, crisp shirts and battered jeans. Old-school Americana with Beatnik and bohemian details.

We are pulled into an art exhibition by the sight of fresh culture, fashion kids and free booze. Within minutes, we are being chatted up by a photographer who wants to do a shoot in the desert with us the next day. He is selling it hard when a voice from behind interrupts:

'Eric, you pervert! Trying to get another unsuspecting out-of-towner on a shoot?'

The voice comes from a guy in a cowboy hat and the confidence to wear double denim. He grabs two drinks from a passing waitress and hands them to us without missing a beat.

'I'm Cliff, welcome to Tucson.'

Cliff works his way round the exhibition, sprinkling charming stories about each person we meet, presenting us with a sparkle: 'These girls are documentary makers, isn't that fantastic?' He radiates graceful coolness, warmth and sarcasm.

'Who *was* that guy?' Sofi asks, pointing to the photographer from earlier.

Cliff laughs: 'Ah, that's Eric Kroll. He's photographed a few faces – Debbie Harry, Madonna, people like that.'

'Ha! Good job Bexy didn't know about that a minute ago . . . She would have ended up in a sand dune with her knickers down.'

She's joking. But she's probably right.

* * *

176

Cliff takes us to a bar that feels like stepping into the carriage of an old train. We walk past old-school indoor telephone booths, leather chairs and dark wood. It smells like cigars in here – not cigar smoke, but the smell of one when you hold it up against your nose. Unrecognisable Blues songs strut through the air as I order drinks.

'Are you with Cliff?' the barman asks. 'These are on the house.'

At the table I am enveloped in the glow of Cliff's life story; we hear about the music he played in the seventies, how he ran for mayor in full drag with a mop bucket, promising to 'clean up the city'. He was a part of scenes I am obsessed with (and only learned about in the last few years): the seventies New York Punk scene, the Factory, he was mates with Johnny Thunders, David Bowie, Angie Bowie (who lives in Tucson now) and he once went on tour with the New York Dolls. His life feels like a movie plot.

He offers us somewhere to park our van, says he'll show us around the town and make sure we're taken care of.

* * *

The next few days in Tucson are colourful and musical, saturated with sunsets and local street art. We spend nights hanging out with artists, going to gigs on front porches, looking through Cliff's photo albums stuffed with the greats of the 1970s. We take long, philosophical walks with Sadie, his gorgeous dog. We almost forget about Gabriel.

Almost.

We're up at Cliff's house. We've just done a little film shoot in his back garden (the desert) and we're fixing dinner in his kitchen. By this point, Cliff knows what our plans are and he's done a little digging of his own, talking to locals and people who know people who lived at the commune. And the picture we have of the cosmic group starts to change.

Cliff tells us that the families that live there have their kids taken from them and put under the charge of other adults. That Gabriel practises polygamy but no one else is allowed to. That Gabriel has had sexual allegations raised against him by former members of the commune. He uses his transmissions from aliens to suggest that attractive women should leave their partners for him as they have 'already been with Gabriel in a past cosmic life'.

'That's handy,' I say.

'Also, apparently, he thinks he can heal you with his penis,' Cliff says.

'Aha, that old chestnut!' Sofi says, nearly spitting a mouthful of water out.

'If I had a nickel . . .' I laugh as I continue to chop onions, unfazed.

Cliff continues, 'It *is* funny, sure, but he apparently also has a really bad temper and I don't know, I just worry about you going in there . . . The other thing is, he's just recently been fucked over by a couple of journalists, so I don't think you'll get in as "filmmakers".'

I lie in bed that night, staring up at the beige ceiling of the van, listening to the gentle rhythm of Sofi's night breath as she sleeps, thinking about Cliff's warning. Cliff is a great guy and I can see that he is trying to help – this is coming from a good place, he's not trying to sabotage us.

But while Cliff is wonderful, he doesn't really know me or what I'm capable of, or what I can handle. I've handled scary. I've handled worse, I'm sure of it. A cosmic failed pop star doesn't frighten me. I go back and forth, but I know there is only one way that I want to play this out: I am going to go into the group under the radar. I'll get in through their WWOOFING programme and see what happens.

As the idea forms, I feel a rush of adrenaline run through me. I'm going off-piste, I'm going rogue. There is no way I'm going to sleep now. I hush the small voice in me that's murmuring about danger, trauma and risk. Switch *her* off.

She doesn't know what she is talking about – if we listened to her, we'd never get anything done.

* * *

The next morning, I contact the group through their website, saying that Sofi and I want to learn how to farm. I schedule a Skype interview with Gabriel's daughter, Dharma, who wants to know more about us. The call with Dharma is in two hours. I get myself ready – prepping, waiting, rehearsing what I'm going to say, what likely questions there will be, what curve-balls could get thrown, playing the conversation out in my head, over and over.

The sound of the Skype ringtone pierces my thoughts and jolts me upright, even though I have already been waiting at my screen for ten minutes.

Ever punctual.

Dharma's pixelated face appears on screen and then comes into focus. Her long, dark hair parts around her face, framing a wide smile that wears no make-up.

'Hello there,' I say.

I look through the digital window from my world into hers. My screen is filthy. Dust. Dirt. A greasy thumbprint. Blurring the image in front of me and maybe warping the one she sees in front of her. Her questions come out of a thin smile:

Where are you from?
Why Tucson?
Why Urantia?

I sink into the familiar stickiness of trickery. My well-known world of spun identities, the ones that saved me as a child and the ones that helped me survive when I first left. Like breathing in an entity. On autopilot, another one of 'me' takes over the conversation.

But is this entity here to help me now? Is it here to protect or harm?

Dharma ends the call by saying she'll get back to me in a few days with an answer. I start to feel the thick hot sense of validation. A rush to head, clouding out the *pointless* chatter saying this is a bad idea.

I have won! And it feels brilliant. I am on the verge of getting in.

'Ha!' I spit out wildly.

* * *

The sun sets on Tucson, the heat of the day pulled out like a sharply inhaled breath. Tonight, the change feels dramatic. Sofi and I sip beers outside a bar as the sun sets. We gather more amber-stained glasses, our sips turn to glugs, our conversation becomes more liquid, loud, rapid. Words spill out, uncontrolled, gushing onto the street that we stand on. A swirl of so many issues: Why are we still here? What did *that* mean? Why are we going to Urantia? This isn't a FUCKING HOLIDAY!

The dam that has been holding in months of tension and fear has burst.

I wipe my eyes, registering that people are watching. *Are they concerned? Excited? Entertained?* I force a laugh through gritted teeth. *We're joking*, it says. And then see Sofi's shadow moving down the street. I squint through the lights, their blurry golden arms blending into each other.

Where is she headed?

Ah, fuck it!

The hot smell of sweat and beer hits me as I walk up to the bar alone. Thuddy sounds go straight to my head. I throw a tequila down, it explodes in my throat and almost shoots straight back up. Someone tugs at my shirt and I turn to see a girl's face so close up to mine, I can taste the rotten fruitiness of her breath.

'Do you know, you look like that British girl from *GIRLS*?' she shouts.

Fuck off!

I smile.

I push past her into the bathroom, rub the tequila dribble off my lips. I sting from the clumsy comparison of a character from a TV show. It's not the first time I've heard it, but tonight it hits a different spot. My reflection looks back at me: '*That British girl*'. I see a drunk girl with tattoos, wearing a pilgrim hat, standing alone, shit-faced.

Walking cliché.

I pull my hair back, I pull at the skin under my eyes.

What the fuck am I even doing here?

As I sway back to the truck, my belligerence turns to Sofi.

Is she sabotaging me? Maybe she never even wanted to make this film? Maybe she thinks we are just wasting time.

Maybe she's right.

* * *

Back in the truck, I'm barely able to take my shoes off before I pass out.

The sun is aggressive, pushing its way into my bed. There is an emptiness in the spot where Sofi's warm body should be. And then, as my hangover fully kicks in, so too does the bleak realisation that today is my birthday.

Of course, alone today. Of course, on your birthday.

This is perfect.

Abandonment wrenches through me. A hole in my gut, an unhealed wound picked at, but with a hangover's magnifier, the scab has been ripped rather than picked.

'Hey, you!'

My sister Kate's voice is warm on the phone. I'm primed for a moan about what's happened – I can always count on Kate for sympathy and to take my side.

To understand Kate's essence is pure care. I am loath to compare her with our own mother, but I can't help but do so. It's from Kate that I saw my first real, true example of what a mother should, or could be. And it shook me. Concerned, empathetic, watchful, caring, loving, lioness. It was the love in the little things she did for her kids: put their socks on the radiator in the morning when they were teeny so their feet would be toasty warm, planning their birthdays meticulously, allowing them to attend Bible School that summer they begged her, even though it made her scared and sick. And then the big things: I saw her have *nothing* so they could have pocket money, shoes, parties. I wondered where she had learned this kind of care. Did she have such a perfect example of how she didn't want to raise her kids through my parents that just by doing the opposite she could 'mother'? I won't pretend I wasn't jealous – I was. Who wouldn't want their socks warmed for them?

Little brats!

Kate's tones flow through my phone, soothing, calming, *perfect*. Just the mothering I crave. I choose to concentrate on the abandonment 'on my birthday' part of the story and she gives me sympathy. I tell her that I'm going into this next group alone if I have to – my stoicism and bravery beaming to the forefront – and then conversation turns to Gabriel.

'Hang on,' Kate says. 'This guy has a bad reputation and you're trying to sneak into his group?'

I feel her sympathy turning to disbelief. Kate is empathetic, sure, but she sees through my bullshit like glass. I'm about to get a telling-off.

'He could just be a sad dude in a purple cloak, who thinks he can channel aliens,' I say.

'Well, in that case, *why* is it so important for you to get in? Why take risks? Especially alone?' she says.

'Kate . . .' I whinge.

'Sofi might have a point, Bex.'

'Ugh!' I say.

An adult argument.

'You sound a little reckless,' she says.

'Kate . . .' I whine again.

'Listen, I don't want you anywhere near that guy, OK?'

This is not how I want this to play out – I need her back on side, telling me how brave and great I am.

I'm raw, needy and still hungover.

* * *

I walk into town. *How did I end up here, in Tucson, abandoned and alone on my birthday?* My self-pity is ripe. And without really thinking about it, I end up walking into the Avalon café, the recruitment centre for the Urantians.

I had no plans to come in here on our visit, I wander in completely by accident. The smell of coffee and warm bread welcomes me. I look up at the specials board: super food bowls, falafel wraps, tofu tacos. *Maybe I should buy myself some birthday cake.* Drawing the victim card yet another time. The staff are young, dressed with cosmic cool vibes – big earrings, floaty tops, delicate wrist tattoos, Buddhist beads round their necks. I breathe in a heavy dose of sweet, warm air.

Sofi would love this place.

I scan the café for a seat and there, in the corner, 250 miles away from where he should be in Sedona, sits Gabriel.

Gabriel is framed in a perfect beam of sunlight from the window above him. It feels as if it's planned. His purple psychedelic top that would be 'out there' anywhere else is at home here; his beard and hair glow white in the holy afternoon sun. He is smaller than I imagined.

This is my chance.

This is the time to meet him.

I lock eyes with him, on autopilot as I move across the café.

'Hi Gabriel. My name is Bexy.'

He takes my hand in his. His fingers split in the middle with my hand wedged between them, pudgy digits making a strange vice around mine. Like I'm holding the hands of a cold waxwork – I haven't held a hand that gave me this kind of feeling since I met the leader of the Scientologists in the UK.

'Nice to meet you.'

I am surprised by the high-pitched squeak that comes out of him – he didn't sound like that on YouTube.

'I have been speaking to your daughter,' I say.

He nods.

'I am hoping to come and stay with you in Urantia.'

'Maybe I'll see you there,' he squeaks.

I take that as an invitation and as my cue to leave. The sounds of the street hit me – cars, wind, chatter, bringing me back into my body. I make it round the corner before I clutch my belly, bent over, with one hand gagging the hysteria in my throat.

This is a sign.

I am on the right track.

I am ON THE RIGHT TRACK!

Breathe, Cameron, breathe. I have to remember every word he said, every movement, so that I can get it right when I tell Sofi. This 'divine' serendipitous happening is bursting out of me as I run down the street. A hot swell of happiness, pride, valida-tion is growing and filling my body. My need to do something and to prove myself is so potent, I am high off it and it drowns out everything else.

* * *

A few hours later, I answer my phone before the first ring has time to finish.

It must be Sofi.

'Hey, is that Bexy?'

It's Dharma – even better.

'Hi Bexy, I am calling to tell you it's not good news,' she says.

The high rushes out of me like a blown-out match.

'So yeah, we're not going to be having you here at Avalon.'

The walls of the truck start to collapse inward.

'Now or ever.'

Her cold tone and icy decisiveness are startling. I barely recognise the woman I spoke to yesterday. The hand that holds the phone starts to shake.

'My father told me that he met you. And he saw the same thing in you that I saw when we spoke.'

My throat is too thick to speak. I don't have to ask what they saw, she is relishing telling me: 'You are empty and void. We see you, Bexy. Your life is meaningless.'

I feel my finger in the corduroy of the front seat. Scratching letters. Scratching what I wish I could say.

Scratching a way out.

'You think you have friends who care about you, but they see exactly what we see, an empty, empty pit of a person. Do you think that they care about you, those people that you have in your life?'

Images of my friends appear, but they are just out of reach, losing focus with every word she says, fading into darkness.

Why are they in my life?

'You think you are living, but you have no idea what that really means and I don't think you ever really will.'

Dharma's words wrap around my throat, choking my defence. I feel further than ever from my strength, as if there's a pane of thick glass between the part of me who wants to scream, 'You have NO idea who I am!' I can almost see *her*, the strong one shouting from behind the glass. Mouthing these words. Banging her fists on the pane.

'Do you ever stop and think to yourself that you are not good enough? That's your conscience, trying to tell you something, because you are *not* good enough.'

The grown-up part of me knows why she is doing this. She's using classic techniques that I have heard my whole life. Phrases designed to break a person. Designed to make you feel meaningless. That tug at the darkest parts of ourselves, the ones that, when we are lost, we believe to be true.

I am worthless.
I am meaningless.
I am nothing.

And even though I know what she's doing, it still works. The adult me fades. I feel empty, worthless and hollow – exactly how she wants me to feel.

Because maybe she is right.

She finishes on, 'I will pray for you.'

I slump back into the corduroy of the seat.

* * *

A lamp-post switches on, its bright white light instantly surrounded by tiny flies. Manically they buzz, slamming and smashing their heads into the glass. These idiots believe that they are flying towards the sun. But they are just hurting themselves, repeatedly crashing until they collapse.

Stupid, mindless creatures.

Dry-eyed, numb with defeat, the smell of gas in my nostrils, the faint sounds of people in the distance, I sit watching the flies die, one by one.

Never learning their lesson.

The door pops open and Sofi pulls herself in. The familiar smell of her fills the truck and breaks the dark spell.

'Hi,' I say in a quiet, low husk of a voice.

'Well, what fresh hell has happened here?' she asks.

I feel she knows this has nothing to do with the words we spilt the night before.

I look at her and press 'Play' on my voice memo. Dharma's voice comes out, crisp and clear, cold. I wince. We sit through it, her voice filling our space for a second time. Sofi takes my hand. And then it ends.

'Nasty cunt!' Sofi whispers.

My hand covers my mouth, catching a laugh. Tiredness and relief wash over me – Sofi, my lifeline of realness. I tell her the backstory on Gabriel in the café and the lead-up to the phone call.

'Someone has been busy,' she says.

I reach out for her warm hands. 'Maybe it's time to go home,' I say. We're nearly out of money, this was the last-chance tavern. She looks at me, nodding, knowing. I feel this idea filling her with both comfort and sadness, like it is me.

'Look,' I say, pulling out my battered notepad, 'I made this list while I was on the flight over here of all the things that could go wrong.'

My finger points to a water-stained page scrawled with my handwriting.

She reads it, trying to imitate my voice, giving it a sing-song melody:

What could go wrong on our trip around America joining cults?
We don't film anything and come back empty-handed.
We run out of money.
Me and Sofi fall out and never speak again.
One of us has a meltdown/break down/goes mental
One of us wants to stay in one of the cults or abandons the other.
The trip is pointless and a waste of time.
Everyone thinks I'm mad/an idiot for doing it.

We are both silent for a second. And then erupt, uncontrollably, with laughter so forceful it's hard to breathe.

'Everything on your dumb list has happened,' she says through her laughter.

I gasp for air, wiping the tears from my face.

'Don't worry, I will speak to you again, we've got to get this giant truck back to LA,' she continues. Then she looks at me with one eyebrow raised, as if about to crack a joke and says, 'Hey, Idiot! Happy Birthday.'

CHAPTER 9

What Do We Want? 4 Years Before

This might be the day everything changes.

The atmosphere in the house has a sombre electricity running through it, even at this time of the morning when all should be asleep. Rumours run wild through the home. Someone said that it happened in Paris, someone else said it was Argentina, someone else said Spain. All I know for sure is that there has been a massive raid on our group. Somewhere in the world.

My bare feet pad down the 500-year-old staircase as I follow the sounds of people, cars and commotion to the bottom of the house. The crunch of gravel tells me it's coming from the front driveway. I push open the doors to the dining room and creep through the dark. The floors are cold on my toes. I leave the lights off so no one knows I'm here, and find a spot to watch through the window. My fingertips grip the pane; I crouch down to keep hidden. I can see my dad standing outside the front door, silhouetted by a floodlight shining into the dark of this feared morning. People are pushing microphones towards him; he is illuminated for split seconds at a time by cameras that flash like lightning. There are reporters' cars and vans in the driveway and spilling out onto the road leading into the village. I can't make out what he's saying to them, but whatever has happened today, it's huge.

* * *

'The time is NOW! This is the time of our great persecution,' Uncle Andrew booms in this morning's devotions.

Everyone sits upright, everyone is present. Even my brother Joel is listening.

Uncle Andrew's eyes burn and barely blink. 'Last night and this morning, there were raids. The devil's army, policemen, stormed our homes and stole our children.'

His words punch the air out of the room.

'It happened in France.'

He pauses.

'It happened in Argentina.'

The room is quieter still.

'And it happened in Spain.'

I get the feeling he is pleased with his dramatic tone. I don't dare look around, but I don't need to. I can taste the devastation, the rage and righteous indignation filling the walls of this overly packed living room. Breathing it in bites like hot metal on the back of my throat.

My mind runs at full speed: Just one raid in the UK, for just one baby boy, changed our lives overnight. And now three countries have been raided? All organised? All at the same time? This really is the beginning of The Great Persecution that we have been waiting for, the beginning of the End Time. The Bible's prophecies are coming to pass and nothing will be the same again.

My mom and dad are not here, this is their time to be on the frontline. They have said that this is their 'calling', their purpose; that they are needed now more than ever.

Uncle Andrew continues, 'The Family, Grandpa and Mama-Maria have never needed this home more than now. We have such an important role to play. Is that clear? No goofing off, no talking back, keep to your schedules. Stay "in the Lord". Understood? We must pray for our brothers and sisters and the children that have been taken from us.'

His prayer fades as my mind flies through the windows of the living room to hunt down the locations of the raids. I can see it all, vibrant, and hyper real. I'm in Paris, it's early morning light and soldiers in round helmets wearing green camouflage appear in the low mist, like the pages of one of Moses David's comic books coming alive. Brutal men drag screaming children out by their hair, yanking them from their mothers' teats. The mothers wail like at the Wall of Jerusalem, breasts out, hair drenched with sweat, shouting, 'NO, NO, NO! Not my baby!' The fathers in handcuffs, on their knees, solemnly accepting their fate.

It's midnight in Argentina, the mothers and fathers sing 'The Cry of Revolution' as they are rounded up in the court-yard of the home. Stoic and ever-enduring. They are stripped naked, like in our End Time Stories, led out to an ice lake and made to renounce Moses David.

'Renounce him and we will set you free!' the solider shouts, pointing a gun at their heads.

And one by one, they drop in the lake, frozen. Their heads unbowed. A fatal decision to stand by their faith and receive the highest accolade: martyrdom.

Anything could have happened. And it might be us next.

'Hallelujah, thank you, Lord, Hallelujah, thank you, Lord,' the sound of tongues disrupts my daydream. I squeeze Maria's hand with excitement, my eyes burning through closed lids, thrilled by the idea of catastrophe.

*   *   *

Uncle Andrew wasn't lying, we needed to be prepared and alert; 30 different press outlets come to the house in the first 48 hours. They are everywhere, always accompanied by one of the adults, normally in teams of three or four; someone holding paperwork, someone with a stick and a microphone on it, someone else with a video camera, sometimes with lights too. But among all these people with their teams and technical accessories, my parents are the stars of the show.

Mom and Dad look different. They hold themselves differently; they have been given different clothes to wear, they have had even shorter haircuts to appear more like 'them'. The way they both speak feels more assured. I hear them use more complex vocabulary. They cut out all the words, phrases and acronyms we use; they could both 'pass' for 'them'. The changeovers between their interviews happen at a high speed; rooms with different camera crews in them, my parents sit in the middle. They always look a little bit unnatural in these setups, the chairs a bit too close together, or a little bit too close to the middle of the room, not where you would normally sit.

Lights on, everyone in their places, now look 'normal'.

I wonder if I look different too: I stand in my parents' room in front of their full-length mirror; I look at the shirt and skirt they have given me to wear, bit baggy on these scrawny limbs, but they feel almost brand new. I touch my hair, poke some of the frizz back into the half-up, half-down style I am wearing, a 'do' that normally isn't allowed. As I run my hands down the stiff cotton of my new shirt, I wonder if I pass for one of 'them' like my parents do.

I wonder if I'll have to give it back when this is over.

The questions are as expected; a lot of the time it feels like the reporters were given the same set that we were. There are no real surprises, everything is like we rehearsed.

'Are the children unsafe here?'

I hear my dad say, 'Our children are happy, healthy, well-educated kids.'

'There are allegations of sexual abuse, what do you say to that?'

'In all my 20 years in the Children of God, I have never once seen a single incident of child abuse.'

'Will the Children of God disband now that they have had their children taken away?'

'This isn't the first time that Christians have been perse-cuted for their beliefs and it won't be the last. We will fight to get our children back to their loving parents, where they belong.'

My parents seem so quick, their answers so sharp. Even my mom, who I haven't seen speak out that much in my life comes across as eloquent and self-assured. They work as a team; Dad undeniably takes the lead as she confirms everything he says, nodding empathically. Sometimes she answers questions on her own. Among all this wild change, my parents really are perfect for this vital job.

The whirlwind of journalists lasts for about a week. Now the Press have left and the house has settled and we get back to our routine. Our clothes have returned to normal. The crisp white shirt is gone, my hair in the same low ponytail at the nape of my neck. The days are back to cooking, cleaning and devotions.

Maria and I prepare lunch. The menu is liver and potatoes. Liver is one of my least favourite things both to make and eat because I know what it looks like when we prepare it: covered in lesions and puss-filled boils. We get our meat for free from markets and abattoirs in local towns and cities nearby. The adults tell butchers and market traders that we are a voluntary service organisation, they take out a folder full of photos that show pictures of orphanages, or kids in Africa or Asia. We have lived like this for as long as I can remember: whatever gets the job done and puts food on the table. They have repeat donors that they go back to every week. Which is helpful, but it means that the stuff we get is normally out of date, occasionally completely off. The barn where we are headed to is where we keep the food we are given – including the dreaded liver. No matter how we cook the stuff, I never want to eat it.

We pull our shoes on and grab jackets from the rack. No one really owns any of these, we just wear what we need to when we need to. My arms slip into the sleeves of a big man's jacket that falls below my knees.

Our shoes crunch on the pebbles of the driveway, the freezing air cuts the back of my throat as I breathe in. But the cold is not the only thing waiting for us outside. Gangs of teenagers have been hanging out at our front gate for the last few weeks. Ever since the news broke that this little village with only 300 residents has 100 of 'us' here. That's quite a high ratio of 'us' to 'them'. After the Press left, the teenagers remained. Like a water stain after the glass is gone. A memento. And our journey to 'liver-town' crosses the eyeline of where they stand.

I squint into the wind and pull my coat tighter. We're nearly at the barn door. And then a bellow from the gates:

'OI, SEX CULT GIRLS!'

I shoot Maria a look as her hand grabs mine.

'OI, SEX CULT GIRLS, OVER HERE!'

A mocking roar.

I'm about to break into a run when I feel Maria pull my hand back a little.

Don't show them fear, I read from her pull-back.

Yes, she's right.

'OI, SEX CULT GIRLS! GIVE US A BLOW JOB!'

I push the barn door and as we fall inside, we burst out laughing; Quiet but almost painful giggles.

'Did you see them?' I ask, gasping for air.

'Yes, I had a little look out the corner of my eye,' she says.

'How old do you think they are?'

'A few years older than us? Maybe 14, 15?' she says.

Her smile feels knowing.

'Do you think they're dangerous?' I ask.

'I don't think so . . . do you? They are gross, though. Blow job, hahaha!'

Blow jobs are all over the Mo Letters so we know exactly what these boys were asking for.

'I liked their jackets,' I say as I swing the door of the chest freezer open.

'Yeah . . .'

I feel her eyes on me, then watch her looking down at her own clothes. We both wear black plimsolls, the rubber kind, without socks. Long, woollen jumpers fall over cotton baggy leggings, finished off with great big man-sized jackets. Maria's jumper hangs over the breasts that puberty brought her recently, then swamps the rest of her tiny frame. I'm now 12, but still stupidly skinny and small. I smooth the jumper down that hangs over my knees like a large woollen sock.

'They must have nothing better to do than sit at our gate,' Maria says, jumping on top of one of other chest freezers to pull out the frozen bags of meat.

'Maybe we are the most interesting thing going on.'

I agree with her.

'And maybe *they* don't have to cut the boils off out-of-date liver,' she adds.

'They must be bored,' I say.

'Ariel was telling me the other day that Systemite teenagers get something called "pocket money",' she continues.

'What's that?' I ask.

'It's money their parents give them every week,' she explains.

'Wow! What for?' I ask.

'I don't know,' she says.

'Wow!' I say again, not really sure how to process this. 'Just to have?'

'Yeah,' she says.

'Gotcha,' I say, grabbing the bags of frozen liver.

We stand at the barn door, facing the cold. I look down at the bloodied see-through polyethylene skins in our hands. It could look like we're dragging body parts from the barn to the house.

This will make us look even more weird.
Maria looks at me: 'Ready, sex cult girl?'
I laugh nervously, big breath in.
'Ready,' I say.

* * *

The raids finished with that one big bang, but the court case continues. And it feels like it's never-ending. We pray for our solicitors and we pray against the enemy's solicitors. We pray for Pearl. We pray against her mother for trying to steal her grandson. We pray that the judge is lenient. We pray and we pray and we pray.

It is the biggest part of our lives.

But besides the changes that have happened, the openness of the home, the talking to the Press, the court case itself feels abstract. It's everywhere, in every conversation, devotions and prayer, but not actually a part of our lives. We don't ever see the solicitors, I am not going to court.

My dad told us, 'Of all the children they have tested, not one has said that they have been abused and not one has even had a bruise on them.'

But we have never seen any tests of any kind. I don't get tested to see if I have been educated. None of the children here have been tested for sexual abuse, no authorities come to our home.

So far, our prayers have been unanswered. In all three countries that were raided by the authorities, the children still haven't been given back.

And then, one day in devotions, Uncle Andrew stands in front of us, issuing a battle cry: 'We will not hide in the shadows any more.' His voice becomes louder, chest puffing up. 'This week, we shall go to the embassies of France, Argentina and Spain. And we will demonstrate. And we will demand that they, "Let our children go".'

Oh, wow.

Demonstrations – our parents are so, so proud of the demonstrations they did back when the Children of God started, when they wore sack cloth and ashes on their faces and shouted, 'WOE' in the streets. When they were really in a 'Revolution for Jesus'. And now we are allowed to do it. This is our time to go into the limelight. Fulfil our purpose. I shiver with excitement.

Uncle Andrew continues, 'This is a very dangerous thing that we are about to do. We are going to ask all the homes in the UK to come to the Argentine Embassy in London . . .'

I can barely contain my delight: we will get to see *London*.

'I am going to warn you, while we have had signs from the Lord that this is the time for us to come out into the light and show our strength and our willingness to fight, we ALSO need to be aware that this dangerous enemy's armies could use this as their chance to take ALL of us. To imprison everyone. There will be skeleton crews at the homes with the children, precautions in case we are taken captive by the enemy's armies.'

We have read about the enemy's armies our whole lives and now we will be in front of them. I think about Heaven's Girl, when she was captured by the End Time army. *Heaven's Girl* is an illustrated series about the adventures of a Children of God teen in the Armageddon. She wears leather sandals, has a long braid down to her waist and a see-through mini dress that her erect nipples poke through in every drawing. *Heaven's Girl* is a handbook of both what to expect and how to behave and act in the End of Days.

There are over 20 *Heaven's Girl* comics in the series. I think about the one where she is captured by the End Time soldiers. Ten burly men in camouflage seize, handcuff and shove her into the back of a van. One soldier says, 'Hold her down, let's rape her.' Heaven's Girl responds with, 'You don't have to rape me. In fact, if you uncuff me, I can love you easier.' I remember thinking what a clever ruse it was to get them to uncuff her. But she wasn't trying to get away: the comic shows her having sex with all ten soldiers. The moral of the story was how important it is to 'show God's love' to the soldiers. I flicked through the comic, disappointed that *yet again* the moral of the story is between Heaven's Girl's legs – I would love it if Heaven's Girl would trick the enemy, just once.

* * *

The morning of the demonstrations, we wake up earlier than usual, buzzing with excitement. Our room feels so different as we get dressed. There's a sense of purpose, a pure exhilaration that we are doing something so special and potentially dangerous. Pulling on the sleeves of a second-hand denim jacket I have been given to wear, I run my finger across the tiny writing on the edge of its golden buttons. They shine as I pull them through the slotted mouths cut into the blue fabric. I never thought I could have something this 'worldly' – I keep touching the stiff material, rubbing it between my fingers, hoping I never forget how it feels.

How things have changed.

Up until about six months ago, when we travelled, the van's windows would be covered with bin liners; some kids said they were blindfolded when moving from location to location. But today, we sit in the back of the vans on actual seats – some even have seat belts – and start our trip down to London. I hold Maria's hand and look out of the windows, taking in the greens and browns, hills and trees of where we live, which changes to motorway and finally, to the standstill traffic of the capital. We pass by old buildings, giant statues of lions and men on horses, fountains and huge gates to enormous parks – worlds away from the Manor House.

We pass by what is without a doubt the biggest mansion I could ever have imagined existing. Maybe the biggest mansion in the world, with giant gates in front of it. I whisper to Maria, 'That's the kind of place a king would live.'

As we pile out of the van, stretching and shaking out the hours of travel, an Uncle comes up to me and tells me excitedly that he knew my mom and dad at university and then the Bromley factory.

'You knew them when they were Systemites?' I ask, interested.

'Yes. I borrowed your dad's toolkit, and he came looking for it and never left, and then your mom came looking for *him* and never left.' I feel he is very pleased with himself. 'It's all down to me,' he adds proudly with a wink.

Was I supposed to thank him? I wonder as he walks off.

We start to assemble around the giant white columns of the Argentine Embassy. My sister Kate moves towards the back of the crowd; she is hanging out with a Teen boy who moved to our home recently. I'm pretty sure they are secretly holding hands. Maria looks over at them and then raises an eyebrow at me. I nod knowingly, pleased that we have *both* figured out what's going on.

'Let's get to the front,' Maria says.

'Yes, that's where the action will be,' I say, pleased that my voice sounds so brave.

My dad has a loudspeaker and once we are all gathered – there must be hundreds of us – he starts to shout, 'WHAT DO WE WANT?'

We all shout, 'Our children back!'

My dad's voice again: 'When do we want it?'

'NOW,' everyone shouts.

Our voices echo across this street in London, tourists stop and watch us, traffic slows down, all eyes are on our demonstration. We hold placards that spell out our screamed demands. We have brought empty prams, which we line up at the front to show our children are missing. In between bouts of shouting, we sing rousing songs. I look at Maria, holding a placard we made, singing a song called 'Let Our People Go', and it feels like a battle cry. Photographers and Press arrive and take photos of my mom and dad and then work their way down our demonstration line. The sound of car horns, shouting and singing is electrifying.

Then police show up.

Maria grabs my hand – 'Look, Romans,' she says. 'Romans' is our code word for police from the Bible.

'Oh, woah! Romans,' I repeat.

And as these men in black carrying truncheons approach, thoughts race through me: *Will this be when we get arrested? Is this our time to be shoved in the back of vans like Heaven's Girl?*

Then two of the police start to direct traffic around us as another tells my dad to 'Please keep the kids behind the barriers so they are safe.'

The demonstration lasts all day – we shout until we lose our voices, till our arms ache from the weight of the placards. We shout until the words we say lose their meaning.

But the devil's armies never come.

*   *   *

The demonstrations happened weeks ago, but they are still our only real topic of conversation. We came home to an anticlimactic low of normality. That was the closest we have felt to our fulfilling our destiny so we live in that day for weeks, feeding off it. Describing and re-describing every building that we saw, the traffic jams, the reporters, the Romans turning up, what the tourists were wearing. Sometimes we even break into a jokey 'What do we want?'/'Our children back!'

Maria and I prep lunch, deep in another conversation about the demonstrations. The kitchen echoes with our excited chat and the smell of mud hits me as I pull out a brown paper sack of potatoes. Then a weird sound interrupts us:

'Giiiiiiideeeeooooooooooon!' it howls.

We both stop: it's my dad's name.

'Giiiiiiideeeeooooooooooon!' it taunts again.

Maria's eyes widen, her eyebrows shoot straight up. I scan the potential answers to what it could be – it's not the Press, that's not how they act; it can't be a raid, they happen early morning and it's lunchtime . . .

'Giiiiiiideeeeooooooooooon!' – a sing-song mixture of voices.

It must be those kids at the gate.

Then a sharp *BANG* cuts through from outside. Mixed raised voices tumble through, then shouting. The back door slams. A high-pitched nasty scream rips through the house. We drop our potatoes and bolt towards the scullery doors, making it onto the stone steps to see my dad staggering inside, covered in blood. Auntie Phoebe screams again.

Blood pours down his face; it rivers down his cheeks, pools on his shirt and jacket.

'Oh my God!' Maria whispers.

'Dad, are you OK?' I ask.

'It's fine. It's FINE! Get me a wet cloth NOW.'

My heart pounding, I run. I grab a tea towel from the kitchen and shove it under the tap – it's got to be those kids outside.

They must have beat him up.

I pause, then think, *I wonder what he did to them?*

Dad's anger is quick and dangerous and I have seen it so many times.

Maybe that's not even my dad's blood.

'What happened?' I ask as I hand him the cloth. He looks at me through eyelids that are swelling rapidly. It's so rare to see him in a vulnerable state, I'm shocked to feel a tear running down my face.

He straightens up and starts to dab the blood away.

'What happened is we are being persecuted, like we knew we would be. Those teenagers are not saved by the Lord and are evil because of it. They mocked me like the children mocked the prophet Elisha and we all know what happened to them, don't we?'

Maria and I know exactly what he's talking about. In the Book of Kings, some children mocked the prophet Elisha and he cursed them; they were torn apart by female bears sent as a revenge act from God. It's a grisly, gory story.

Bloody images rush my brain; the teens at the front gate in a gruesome mess, with heaven-sent angry bears, tearing their limbs off. A blood-spattered, detached arm hits the driveway, still wearing the sleeve of the jacket I coveted so much.

This might get ugly.

As my dad cleans the wound, I notice his nose is split on the bridge. It's a deep gash. When the blood is wiped away, it's not as bad as it first looked. But the swelling has started to spread.

He's going to have black eyes. Poor Dad.

'Alright, you've seen enough. Back to the kitchen, girls. NOW!' he growls.

We walk back to the kitchen and Maria looks over at me: 'Wow!' she mouths.

My hand shakes as I pick up my peeler and sit back next to the muddy pile.

'You OK?' she asks.

'It's just weird, seeing my dad like that,' I say.

'Yeah, it's weird.'

Confident Gideon, he is never weak.

'Still think those guys *aren't* dangerous?' she asks.

The question hangs in the air as we scrape the potato skins into the bin. My dad is never vulnerable, he never shows anything but authority, anger, intelligence – all of which he weaponises. As the potatoes reveal their underbellies through tough, muddy jackets, I start to think about all the times I have *wanted* to see my dad beaten up, covered in blood, injured or even dead. I glance at my nails, thick with mud now, black from my work, and I feel strangely guilty. It doesn't feel how I wanted it to. The number of times I have thought how much better we, and more importantly 'she', my mom, would be if he wasn't in our lives.

I think back to the first time I tried to kill him – I would have been about five years old. I tried to poison him with things I found out in the garden in Africa. My nails looked the same then from digging, black as they are now. I made him his morning tea and watched him drink it, imagining him dropping dead at my feet, turning me into an instant hero. Instead he said, 'What the hell is this grass doing at the bottom of my drink?'

So disappointing. I hoped at the very least if the tea wasn't deadly poison, it would work to take me back in time. Or forward. *Anywhere but here*, I thought as I threw back my head and gulped back the last drop of leafy liquid.

And things weren't even that bad back then.

'I didn't know how lucky I was when I was five,' I mutter.

'What?' Maria says, bringing me back.

'Nothing,' I say.

CHAPTER 10

They've Won. She's Gone: 3 Years Before

'She's getting thinner,' Maria says as she looks over at Kate's tiny body.

'I know, she should be showing by now,' I say.

We stand at Kate's bedside in the 'Girls' Room'. A dorm crammed with far too many girls. Girls who sleep on the floor, girls on the top bunks, girls on beds on wheels that roll out from under bottom bunks and girls 'doubling up' like Maria and I do. This ocean of girls recently started getting their periods in waves that have all linked up like tides to the moon and when that happens, it's like a tsunami of moodiness, anger and aches flood through our room.

It's not really what I imagined coming of age to feel like.

But Kate is no longer part of synchronised flow: She is pregnant. She's 16. She fell in love with that teen boy who we saw her with at the demonstrations. He is 16 too. Not an unusual age to get married or pregnant here, especially as there is not much time before the End Time.

She lies in the foetal position in a single bed by the window, which is the one privilege we girls can give her in the hopes of giving her some space and making this easier. The massive window that frames her bed makes her look almost childlike. Her groans are almost inaudible. She hasn't really had the strength to walk in months, but they still keep forcing her into the workforce, putting her name on the schedule. She can't eat anything we make for her. Even the smell of our cooking makes her wretch. The minute she can, she comes back up here and curls up.

'There really is nothing that she can eat,' I say, shaking my head.

My mom got pregnant the same time as Kate, this will be her twelfth baby. Contraception is strictly forbidden, considered to be a sin against God. So here, pregnancy is like air, we normally don't even notice it, women are always pregnant, breastfeeding or miscarrying.

Funny to think their babies will be the same age.

'I have never seen anyone this skinny this many months in. She must be at least five or six months pregnant,' I say.

'Kate, what do you feel like eating? What do you think you could hold down?' Maria asks her softly.

'Maybe something sour. Can you guys close that door so that smell doesn't come in.' She's balancing trying not to breathe in or puke out. I roll up a towel and push it into the bottom of the door, hoping that stops the smell of boiling meat enveloping her.

* * *

'What have we got that's sour?' I ask Maria.

'We have one lemon. Oh, we have a crab apple tree, they're sour,' she says, ever resourceful.

My hand wraps around Maria's arm as I whisper, 'We need a plan, she can't go on like this.'

'Last time, they said no special treatment. They won't change their minds,' she mutters under her breath. 'Let's think about it.'

We've already made a case to the home about Kate's health.

But the answer's clear in my mind and I'm going to have to do something I haven't done since I was four years old to make it work. That night, I wait until the adults have their meeting. I look through the windows in the dining-room doors: my mom and dad sit next to each other, faces solemn or maybe bored.

Now's my chance.

My feet fly up the stairs, two at a time. I tiptoe down the hallway and creak a door open, poking my head through: no one is around.

It's safe . . . so far.

My feet know all the noisiest boards in this hallway. I skip soundlessly. All these rooms are adjoined. I slip through the next door: again, empty. I breathe for the first time since I started this run.

I stand in the middle of my parents' room, I *know* there is money in here somewhere. Chest of drawers, bedside tables, bags in the bottom of the cupboard . . . It could be anywhere, my dad always has some. I start to look carefully through drawers, lifting papers, making sure I keep everything in the same order that it was in. Blood rushes to my face as I think about the last time I did this: in Johannesburg, when I stole the flirty fishing money from Auntie Beverly.

I was four years old and prowling the halls during quiet time. I walked up to Auntie Beverly's doorway. I had been in her room many times before, but since that morning's 'big news', I wanted to see if the room felt different. *This* was the room where the 'top' hooker for Jesus in Africa sleeps. As I crept inside, I held my breath. I ran my hand along her bedsheets, noticing the rough balls on the cotton from wear.

This is where all the Lord's work happens.

On the nightstand were piles of money, all neatly stacked up in lines.

Cash for Jesus.

I didn't know exactly why money was important, just that it was. Grabbing fistfuls of the paper notes, I jammed them into my knickers. This act was filled with so much adrenaline, I could hear my heartbeat in my head like a thousand cymbals crashing.

I snuck back to my room, shut the door and pretended to nap to cover my tracks. And then I heard the words I wait all day for: it's 'Get Out Time'. 'Get Out Time' was the time after 'Quiet Time' – our hour outside, when we would run to the forest for our wars, practise being soldiers for the End Time. But today is nearly 40 degrees, sizzling hot and all eyes will be on the pool that this house, like so many houses in South Africa, has. The call of 'Get Out Time' is like a call of the sergeant, or the snap of the hypnotist's fingers – it pulls me to attention and nothing else matters. I ran through the house, through the living room where the glass doors lead out onto the promise of cold, wet freshness.

I sprinted past the shapes of my mom and my sisters and then took a flying leap through the air towards the pool. Water rushed in, replacing the sounds of the kids, the garden and the African day. My whole body cooled from the sticky heat in an instant. Looking up, the sunlight and garden became mini shapes of different colours above me, shattered, peaceful and beautiful. But then, floating in the pool among these shapes is the stolen 'Hooker-for-Jesus money'. It's all around me, gracefully suspended. But my brain snaps into immediate fear, knowing what this scene will mean for me. I wanted to stay down there forever, I never wanted my floating body to reach that surface. But a large hand reached in, the sounds of the garden flooded in with the heat, and I am taught *exactly* how important money is to my dad – it always has been.

That robbery did not turn out well for me. And getting caught now would be even worse.

It doesn't take too long to find a leather purse with three notes and a few coins in it. I'm not sure what will be the most suspicious if it goes missing. I take one of the notes – I don't want to have to do this again for a while.

I quickly get into bed to cover my tracks. The stolen note imprints itself on my tightly fisted hand. I wonder how long the imprint of this sin will last on me. As soon as the light is out, I stuff it between my mattress and a wooden slat. Phase one is over. I pull my covers over my face, my heart still pounding.

I will not sleep tonight, I have sinned.

But I do. And I sleep well.

*   *   *

I spend the next day waiting for my moment. And it's *now*.

I slip out the back door, my eyes focused on the bottom of the garden. I avoid the paths – they are covered in gravel. The sound of smashing footsteps can be heard from far away, like a natural alarm system.

I'll take the long way round through the fields.

The wet grass squeaks beneath my feet, the cold air hits my face and fills my lungs as I run. And as the cold hits me, so does the realisation that this is the first time in my life I have ever left home by myself. I have dreamed of doing this since I was a child. Running until my insides were filled with the outside, every step putting more and more distance between me and *them*. When I was small, I used to draw maps of what I thought the surrounding areas looked like – I'd pack up my belongings and wait for lights out. Then I'd sit on the floor, desperately trying to stay awake long enough to make my escape while the adults slept. Only to wake up with the morning light, still gripping a plastic bag containing socks, a T-shirt and a crumpled drawing of 'the outside' in my hand.

Waking up to yet another failed escape.

So, this run has been a long time coming. My pace is fuelled by both fear and freedom.

My feet speed down the path that leads to the middle of the village.

Slow your breathing down.

I steady my legs as I walk up to the small convenience store. Sparks seem to be flying through my thighs. I've been in a shop before, but never alone. I slip inside, the creased money balled up in my hand as I am enveloped in the warmth and delicious smells of the shop – a mix of fresh fruit and sweets.

'Mornin'.' The shopkeeper's voice ignites my nerves.

A pleasant smile sits on his shaved face. He looks clean, like maybe he showers every day. I become very aware of what I must look like to him, a frizzy-haired, panting, sweaty kid in 'other people's' clothes. He *must* know where I'm from. Everyone in the village knows about the 'Sex Cult'. But his face doesn't change, as if this is the most ordinary thing in the world.

Slow your breathing down.

'Mornin',' I respond shakily, cracking a damp smile and hoping to mimic his calmness.

Act like this is ordinary for you too.

'You need help with anything?' he asks, touching his flat cap.

'I'm looking for sour stuff,' I say, my American-ish accent standing out like a beacon against this English shop.

'Well . . .' He smiles. 'Let's have a look, shall we?'

He patiently points out the things that are sour in his shop: 'Bitter lemonade is sour,' he says, holding a plastic bottle. 'Lemon drizzle is sour,' he says, pointing to a cake. Then he shows me a jar of tiny pickled cucumbers, some packets of vinegar flavoured crisps, some sour sweets and of course, lemons. He never asks why I need the sourness, he just shows the items as if I am an alien seeing British food for the first time – and maybe I am.

I grab everything except for the sweets, uncrumple the money and hand it over. He looks at me with soft eyes and says, 'You can pay me the rest next time you come in, don't you worry.'

Now it's just for the trip back.

* * *

It's late that night in the Girls' Room. The lights are out and the hum of sleep is already taking over the space. Cutting through the dark are the angry whispers of Kate and her best friend, Ariel. Kate devoured the food from the shop, and managed to keep it down, so perhaps that's why she's got the strength to talk. Even through her sickness, I have seen her grow more and more angry; under her tired weakness, there's an inner strength that's seething. I remember this fiery side from when she was really young, then there were the years of her trying to blend in. But she is 16, pregnant and perhaps sees our lives from a different angle – as a mother.

'What did they think was going to happen?' she whispers.

'I know, I know,' Ariel says (Ariel is Kate's 'Maria', her soulmate).

'Did they not think about what would happen, that they would get away with what they have done to us? Did they not think about what would happen when we got older and started leaving?' Kate's voice cuts through the night.

'Shuuush!' Ariel says kindly.

My fists bunch up my sheets, I'm nervous the other girls can hear them. I wish they would be quiet. And just keep safe. I wish they would just keep this stuff to themselves. But I know that it's true too.

There had to be consequences.

'Yeah, did they think all of us would just forget? Just make the home "open" and that just erases everything that's been done before?' Ariel says.

'Maybe they thought no one would ever leave,' Kate says.

'Well, from what I've heard, people ARE leaving. The "End Time" hasn't happened, so now what?' Ariel says.

'I know they are leaving, but how? Where are they going? How are they surviving?' Kate asks. As she says this, I can hear it in her voice: the need and want to get out of here too. And fear runs through me that before too long, I may lose my sister.

'I don't know, maybe they have families that can take them in,' Ariel says and then she takes a breath before adding, 'But I do know that there are some of them who are testifying in court.'

'Who?' Kate asks.

'Remember Saphira?' Ariel says.

I think of all the things that happened to her – how they made her stay in isolation for months, how they beat her, her arm that nearly rotted off when she got burned, the stuff that she told me she went through as a child with her stepdad that made me feel like I was the luckiest alive with my own easy childhood.

'And she's not the only one,' Ariel adds.

My body goes rigid. I worry that the pounding in my chest is loud enough to give me away, to alert them that I am awake and listening.

Teens rebelling and testifying against us.

This is huge. Should I be scared that they will tell our secrets and testify – the very thing we are being trained to stop? Should I be excited that this could all come tumbling down soon? Should I be afraid that my parents could be put in jail? Should I be excited about the possibility that if they do, I could have a life 'out there'?

It feels like there's a wave of change coming. On top of this big news I have also heard about small rebellions happening in different homes. That some of the Teens are gaining a newfound boldness. And this scares me. We aren't far enough away from 'how things were' or how we pretend they never were. Rumours fly around; whispers of Teens drinking, kissing. I heard about a girl wearing jeans with rips, some style their hair like the Systemites. It's bold. And it's stupid. This type of behaviour would have been completely unheard of just six months ago. Music is one of the system's powerful ways to get the devil's messages to the masses' brains and so is completely forbidden. If you play pop songs backwards, you can hear hidden messages that come directly from Satan so while it might sound like light, fun, playful music, it could be telling you to take drugs, kill other kids, or commit suicide.

I lay in bed and worry that things are going to go back to how they were in the 'Teen Home'. It's been such a short amount of time that we have had these perceived freedoms. We have to 'look' like we are of the world here, but we can't 'be of the world'. With everything that's going on, the court case, living in an open home might give us the idea that there is freedom in our house. But a door slightly ajar does not always mean 'a way out'. And the 'freedoms' we are given are given with a purpose – to give the perception of freedom to journalists and the authorities. These freedoms are not for us, they are for them.

I thrash through a night violent with visions; of being trapped in a glass box where Maria, Kate, Ariel and my siblings are on the other side. Perhaps they can see me, but as I bang on the glass, no one turns. I scream from behind the transparent cage and no one notices. The air in the box is running out, but I can't smash through it.

I wake up, my throat raw from an empty scream.

Later that day, with the dream still playing loops in my mind, I am filled with nervous energy that I can't shake. *A bad, bad feeling.* I open the door to the kitchen to start work, I jump as a hand reaches out from the pantry and pulls me in roughly.

'Shhhhhhhhh!'

I am face to face with Maria, her eyes wide and a finger on her lips.

I furrow my brow.

I haven't said anything.

'Look.' She pulls out a cassette tape from her pocket.

'Put that away, Maria!'

I don't have to ask her what's on it – it's not our music, which is clearly labelled and so familiar. I look at the tape in her hands; I feel it could harm her, like it could burn into her skin, poison her through its plastic jacket.

'You can't walk around with that on you. You have to hide it somewhere,' I whisper.

I grab her hand, afraid for her. I want to protect her, but I feel like the walls are closing in on us in this tiny room and there might be nothing I can do to stop the inevitable.

'I know, I know,' she says, pulling her hand away, trying to sound relaxed.

'Where are you going to keep it?'

I want assurances.

'In the attic. I promise you, I'll hide it with the cassette player,' she says.

* * *

Later that day, I head to the office. I've been training in office administration for a little while. I'm getting the hang of it. I used to think of the fax machine as some bizarre, bleeping machine from outer space, now I can almost do it with my eyes closed. I have to send out rebuttals and press releases to lists of numbers my dad gives me. He says the newspapers only print stuff when it is 'sensationalist' but we have to 'play our part' to get our message out.

I press my finger into the plastic numbers, enjoying how they beep, then wait for the screeching sound, which means the message is going through the wires in the wall, through cables across the sky and ending up in the office of a newspaper somewhere.

Over the squealing of the fax, My dad's distinctive voice growls through from the next room. He is with another one of the teenage girls, and they are prepping for the UK court case.

'Have you read through it?' he asks.

'Yes,' she says.

'Enough to remember it?' he asks.

The question feels like a threat.

'Yes,' she replies.

'Enough that if you are in a courtroom, full of Systemites, full of the enemies of the Lord, and you are questioned, you will *remember* it?' His tone is one I know well – cold and intimidating.

'Yes,' she answers in the same small voice.

'Would you be able to remember this affidavit in front of a judge?' he probes further.

I know what affidavits are – I found out last week. A testimony, sworn and signed, they tell the story of our life here. They are 'integral' to getting our story *right* in front of the judge.

'Yes.' She is even quieter now.

'Good, so sign it.'

'Sign it?' She sounds confused.

'Write your name here, in this box,' he explains.

Over the last week, quite a few Teens have had to sign affidavits. Barely anyone is going 'into' court, but their testimonies are. I wonder who wrote her affidavit for her, what it says and how hard it was to memorise. I wonder if they call Saphira a liar. Someone, perhaps my mom, or my dad, will have written their stories for them so they sound 'just right' for the court, so that we can keep our way of life safe.

* * *

They've caught Maria. I knew this was going to happen; I knew she wouldn't be careful enough. I knew she would get seen, or heard, or told on by someone. It's only been a few days since she has had the tape but there are BellWethers (spies) everywhere. It was only a matter of time.

And now they have the tape and they have her.

I can only imagine what's happening to her. She's receiving her punishment upstairs. They may have stopped the beatings since we moved into an 'Open Home' but if there is one thing we can be sure of, when it comes to our punishments, the adults have always been creative.

They will want to know where she got it from, who else knows about it; they will want a list of names from her. But, Maria never cracks. She would never tell on another person – she is loyal to a fault. Tough as nails, she would take a beating any day rather than let someone else get one. She is the toughest girl I know.

I wait for her in our room. She comes in red in the face, her eyes puffy, but I can still feel the edge of pride prickling off her. I am desperate to ask her what happened and how she is, but

I know that I should keep my distance from her for the time being. Till it's safe. For both of us.

For her punishment, they have put her on a Temporary Silence – she is not allowed to talk for a week. She's been given extra chapters of the Bible to memorise that she will be tested on, she has been given extra chores and her first 'official warning'. The rest of the punishments don't worry me, but this last bit, I haven't heard of before. Nobody explains to Maria what it means and that's what scares me.

The countdown has begun. The Day of Judgement is on the horizon.

*   *   *

We feel the tension in the house building with every second that brings the court judgment day closer. We have been in this legal battle for two years. This whole home, our whole lives, have been set up for this. Our entire lives revolve around this abstract but very real entity. We have the worldly clothes, the schoolbooks they bought, so we can appear educated; my dad teaching us how to perfect English accents so that we can sound 'normal'.

We exist, in this state, in this house, because of it. But hanging over us is the chance that we could lose.

The adults say that it will only happen if the Lord wants it too. But they also say that if we do lose, it will be because of those backsliding, evil Teens. When the adults talk about them, it is with venom: they are possessed by demons, they are a part of Satan's army. Because of *them*, our entire way of life as God's children could collapse. We are warned that if we go off-track, or go against the group, we risk becoming like them. Like vampires, we will no longer be ourselves, be our parents' children, be sisters, be brothers. If we stray, we no longer deserve their love or to be a part of our families.

'Do you want to be tortured with loud music for days and nights on end? That's what they did in Waco.'

Waco is the horror that feels the most probable. When Waco happened, it was all the adults talked about. The religious commune that was burnt to the ground by the American government. We have been told everything, every detail. It was the scary story that brought to life and proved everything we were told about the Antichrist, the government and their men. We had even been shown the footage of the group in flames.

'Those children burned to death in their beds. This is what those backsliding Teens could do to you,' my dad shouted across the living room.

The end of the court case is coming, and danger could be too.

*   *   *

The Day of Judgement comes. Maria and I are in the Girls' Room. We have spent all day going back and forth over what the outcome could be, and what it could mean for us, if our lives flip on their axis by the time night falls.

'Hallelujah! PRAISE THE LORD, HALLELUJAH! THANK YOU, JESUS! THANK YOU, LORD!'

The sound of joy flies up the stairs.

'HALLELUJAH! THANK YOU, JESUS! THANK YOU, LORD! PRAISE THE LORD! THIS IS AMAZING NEWS.

THANK YOU, JESUS. WE LOVE YOU, LORD. PRAISE BE THE LORD!'

The clapping seems to take flight and becomes contagious through the house, going from room to room. We can hear the sound of footsteps running down the stairs towards the voices – it *must* be good news.

Maria looks at me grimly: 'Sounds like they've won,' she says.

I shake my head. 'No, listen.' I point downstairs. 'You mean, we've won!'

With a chilling truth in her voice, she whispers, 'No. *They've* won.'

The celebrations continue the next day, the adults revelling in the full story of our victory.

Maria and I climb down into the dark, grey, concrete, musty cellar to get wine for the celebrations for the adults that night. This is the cellar we found on the first day here. It's what we sometimes call our 'escape plan' because of all the tunnels it has out of this old house.

'There is so much wine,' I say, looking around the huge underground room.

Why, when we have so little food, do we have all this wine?

As she pulls out a couple of bottles for the adults, Maria says, 'You know that some of the Teens get the key and steal it, don't you?'

'I mean, yeah, of course,' I say, worried where she is going with this.

She looks at me. 'I think we should take a beer, just to try it.'

'Maria . . .' I say.

'Not a bottle of wine,' she says.

I hate to disagree with Maria, we rarely do, but also, she is on an 'official' warning. I'm desperate for no more bad things to happen, especially to her. She sends a pleading look.

'C'mon,' she says.

'OK, let's do it,' I agree.

* * *

A few weeks later, we find out my younger brothers have been keeping a secret. Josh found an old television in one of the outhouses and gave it to my brother Sam to fix. Sam has been obsessed with taking electrical things apart and putting them back together since he was a little boy. It's a gift. He started with small things like plugs, then worked on things as complicated as a hairdryer. He got the television to work and the two of them have been sneaking off in secret and watching it.

Maria is mid-debate with them.

'Come on, Josh, let us come and watch it with you,' Maria says.

I have never known anyone as persuasive as her.

'It's too dangerous for all of us to go together, we'll get caught,' he says, not looking up because he knows if he does, he'll break.

I agree with him in theory, but I also really want to see the TV.

'How about if we do a trade?' Maria starts to bargain. 'You let us watch your TV and we'll let you have a sip of one of the beers we have.'

'Maria!' I bark at her.

God, this is exactly how we will get caught.

Before long, the barter has been agreed. I start to fill with a mix of fear, nerves and excitement. It's risky and stupid, and could get us in a lot of trouble but I don't want to miss out.

We follow the boys up a ladder into the attic. Josh grabs my hand and pulls me up into the musty, woody room. The room is full of old boxes, suitcases and other innocent crap. Sam pulls back the tarpaulin and there it is: a tiny black-and-white TV, its sides covered in dust. But the screen is clean and ready to go.

'Put it on then,' Maria says.

She finds a perch on some boxes, I find a spot on the floor. Josh turns the telly on, while Sam stands next to it, a coat hanger sticking out the back, adjusting it until an Australian TV show comes on. The show is full of people who are our age and teenagers in their school uniforms, going to and from a café. We laugh at their accents and the things they say to each other. Everything sounds strange and silly. Most people in the Family who come from Australia still have American-style accents, so these ones are pretty alien to us. Josh and Sam have seen this show before and are getting pretty good at mimicking them. Maria pulls the beer out and snaps it open. I hold the can in my hand, trace the roundness of its tinny silver top and then I take my first-ever sip of beer.

'Not sure I like it,' I say.

Josh burps, 'NOT SURE I LIKE IT' all in one go. And we start to snigger. We pass it around, having a sip each as if we are at communion. Straight after that TV show, another Australian show comes on. I start to feel a little bit dizzy, things feel funnier, it's a nice feeling. The things I normally think about feel further away, the group is a little further away too, and the threat of being caught is also a little dimmer. Maria pulls another beer out, pulls back the ring on the top to crack it. SWOOOOOSH! It explodes. Beer goes everywhere.

'NOOOOOO!' Maria screams.

I shout, 'SHHHHHUSH!'

The boys are both bent over, laughing. Then, suddenly, the boys stop laughing. Josh's face goes pale. And we turn to see Uncle Juan, Maria's dad, at the top of the ladder with a face full of shock.

Josh and I throw the cans under the tarp. Sam turns off the TV, we hurry to hide our shame, as if it will help, as if it will wipe away the image of the four kids Uncle Juan has seen drinking beer and watching an illegal television. We watch out the dusty attic window as Maria chases her dad through the courtyard, shouting, 'Daddy, stop! Stop! STOP!'

'What do we do?' Josh says.

'Everyone split up, go brush your teeth, get somewhere visible, read a Mo Letter in the living room or your bed,' I say.

Josh looks at me: 'How is that going to help?'

'Maybe Maria can talk Uncle Juan round,' I say.

*   *   *

Uncle Juan is without a doubt our favourite, most lenient, loving and caring uncle in the house. It is a stretch, but maybe Maria could persuade her dad not to tell. Maybe if she promised we would never do anything like this again, he would just let us off. Just this once.

Up in the Girls' Room, I wait. I wait for my punishment, my 'official warning' for my isolation. An hour goes by, but there's still no sign of Maria. Dinner comes and goes. Still no Maria. I'm really worried now. Maybe they have forgotten what they said about this home being an 'Open Home', maybe they don't care that they have told everyone that things have changed. In fact, when I think about how recent it all was I start to shake. Just because we have burnt the 'Mo Letters' doesn't mean they never existed. And if they could change things to look like this *for* this court case, couldn't it just as easily go back to how it was now that it's over?

Anything could happen.

It's dark when I get called upstairs. I walk into a solemn, heavy air. My parents sit with Auntie Phoebe and Uncle Andrew in their bedroom.

'We have some very troubling news for you,' Uncle Andrew starts.

I look around the room: Maria is not here. What have they done with her?

'Maria is leaving us,' Phoebe says.

What? Where is she going? Where are they sending her?

But I say nothing – I know that's not why I'm here, to ask questions.

'She has decided that she would rather live with her auntie in Spain, that living here is too challenging for her. And we agree. It's with a heavy heart that she is going to go, but we think it's right. And her recent behaviour has shown us that she has become too worldly. One rotten apple . . .' Uncle Andrew's words fade into nothingness.

I can't believe that she is getting *out*, that they are *allowing* it. I'm happy for her. Devastated for me. And I can't believe I'm losing my friend.

I start to retrace how we got here. If only I'd told her 'no' in the basement, put my foot down, been stronger. If only I'd never let her take the beers.

Uncle Andrew is still talking: 'This is happening immediately. Uncle Juan is going to go with her to get her settled in. She is still by the world's standards "underage" so we feel it's right. We wanted to tell you face to face, because we also want you to see this as a warning: we don't accept worldliness here and we feel that this will also benefit you . . .'

Again, I slip away into my mind. What is life going to be like without her? Every day without her. Every meal without her. *Everything* without her. But then it hits me: she is going to be *free*.

So maybe that moment in the basement was her own 'escape route', her strange, and dark, unexpected escape route out of here.

And then it all happens quickly.

She sits on the floor in the Girls' Room, a few things in front of her, small clothes rolled up next to a plastic bag.

She looks up.

'You know that I don't want to leave you, don't you?' she tells me and as she says it, the proud, tough Maria breaks, her voice cracks.

I kneel down beside her, put my hand on hers.

'I know, but I also don't want you to stay here.'

'You will be next. I promise this isn't forever, and when you're out, we will live together, just like we planned.'

She smiles as she says this, her chin trembling.

'It's fine, I will be fine. I will be better knowing you are out there,' I say.

'You're the only thing I'm going to miss,' she says.

We put her rolled-up clothes in the plastic bag. Such a small amount of belongings to leave with, but if she could have left it all, I know she would have. And while there is so much I want to tell her, anything that I want to say to her she knows already. We have shared everything: a bed, our fears, our dreams and our nightmares.

Everything.

And before I can even take in what's happening, she's gone.

A Hollywood Goodbye: 15 Years After

Neon lights, palm trees and a warm breeze . . . Sofi and I have made it to Hollywood.

We have driven the truck all the way to this bizarre, super-ficial, magical town. Before our flight home, we have a few days and want to see people we know, find a spot to leave the truck and spend a few nights at a friend's house here.

It's sunset and some of Sofi's friends pick us up in a convertible. They pull up, music pumping into the street. A rowdy entrance. We drive through the streets, soaking up the electric atmosphere and traffic pollution, taking in the palm-lined roads. If I close my eyes, the bass fills my whole body. It's all so alien, like we just stepped through a portal into a sun-drenched, perfect-bodied, roller-skating, alternate universe.

We're heading to a bar in East Hollywood. I almost don't recognise Sofi – she has transformed from tabard-farmhand-flannel-shirt-wearing tomboy to cool blonde. Red lipstick, her bleached hair whips around her laughing face. She could be en route to an afterparty. She catches me looking at her and gives me a wink. My vision is blurred by my own newly washed hair, my clothes are my own; I smell clean as I taste unfamiliar gloss on my lips. I am reminded of my other life back home in London, one that I will be back in soon enough. A life where the idea of picking kale, early morning 'gatherings' and chasing cosmic penis healers will haze into the past.

We drink in the stories Sofi's friends tell us. One guy is from Berlin, an entrepreneur who runs clubs. The other guy is a semi 'face' in LA. He has a radio show, but more interesting than who he is or who he knows in this town, is his life before he 'made it'.

'I used to clean strip clubs,' he announces from the front seat.

'Wow!' I say.

One word suppressing a million questions.

It's weird to think about a strip club being cleaned. Such a mundane task in a place that promises fantasy, sex, glitz and the chance of being rubbed off by a girl perhaps paying her way through college. I imagine him in his rubber gloves, vacuuming up the seediness of the night before.

Of course, strip clubs need cleaning.

I shake my head.

'I used a really, *really*, strong disinfectant on the poles,' he adds proudly, as if telling us the secret to his millions.

I nod from the backseat.

'You gotta or they end up smelling like hot dog brine.'

'I can imagine,' Sofi says flatly.

Clearly, this is a guy who knows what he is talking about. The American Dream: from cleaning strip poles to radio host.

Anything can happen here.

As we pull into the car park of the bar, I get a message from a musician I know in LA: 'Maybe see you later. See how my session goes. x' The nonchalance stings. I feel my need for val-idation through human contact rising like bile. I'm nauseous. It's a demand I fight every day. But it's easier to control when I'm busy, or perhaps being dangerous, or maybe just out of harm's way in a field of spinach. I have dedicated far too much of my life to chasing this familiar indifference.

'Margaritas?' I say, my smile like a hyphen.

We walk into the dimly lit bar and I'm toying with the idea of a round of shots.

That will help.

As we move through the achingly cool crowd, I see a guy standing at the back alone, partially lit by a spotlight, clutching a drink. And, as if someone has pressed 'Pause' on this scene, the room goes silent. All I can hear is my own heartbeat.

His face reminds me so much of someone from my past that I am slammed back into a corrugated barn, nearly 25 years ago.

I am standing on a tyre. About 10 feet wide, it must belong to a tractor or a combine harvester. On the other side of the tyre, facing me, is Maria.

I feel the cold inside my thin clothes, but my face is burning red-hot. Eli stands above me. At 17 years old, he looks *almost* like a man. He is the size of one and he has the power and authority of an 'Uncle'. He calls the shots, he is in charge, but there is still the padding of childhood in his cheeks.

We stand in this warehouse at the back of the commune. Concrete floors and corrugated iron, the smell of farm and hay in the air. The eight or nine kids around me are shouting. Eli has told them to. While, at first glance, it might look like they're frenzied, excited or complicit, everyone is playing a part.

No one wants to be here, in this circle, except for Eli.

Eli explains the 'rules'. Maria and I have to fight each other. This tyre is our ring, the kids are the spectators.

I feared that Eli had noticed our growing friendship, I sensed that he didn't like it, as if two ten-year-olds getting close was a threat to the group. In a commune of this size, we had hoped we'd slip through the net, but *he* noticed.

'And the fight will go on until one of you can't get up anymore.' Eli's voice pierces through my thoughts.

I feel my blood like it's trying to escape my body, pushing its way through my skin. I look at Maria and I'm terrified. She has become my whole world in such a short space of time. In just a few weeks, she saved me. And now I have to fight her. *Hurt her.*

Eli is shouting, whipping up the tiny spectators like a twisted emperor of Rome standing on the sidelines, watching a Christian being fed to a lion. But *we* are the lions, *we* are the Christians, and we are children.

Ten years old.

And while the words that come out of Eli's mouth are full of rage, there is a wetness in his eyes. They are filled with excitement. He licks his lips. The stink of pleasure emanates off him, watching and demanding the destruction of a young friendship. I can almost taste his thirst. Maybe he is more excited by the power he holds by controlling and puppeteering this violence. Maybe by this point inflicting pain with his own hands has become boring.

He should be one of *us*, but he has been turned: he is one of *them*.

Maybe growing up here has made it impossible for him not to turn out this way. Maybe what has happened to him – the horrors, the beatings, the abuse – means that he could never be anything else. Maybe he had no one in his corner to say 'that's not OK'. No older brother to tell him 'what they are doing to you is not right'. These things he comes up with for us aren't a part of Grandpa's teachings, they are his own machinations. And so maybe the violence and twistedness that they raised him in has become embedded. A part of his blood. His Being. And it is spitting out of him now, scorching through his pupils, producing the dribble on his lips.

I look at her, straight at her. *My friend.* And as I lock eyes with her, the yells around me start to quieten down, the sounds fade to mute and everything except for her face goes out of focus. The voice in my head screams, 'I don't want to do this' and hers says back, 'We have to. It doesn't mean we don't love each other. So just DO IT!'

It would be pointless to cry, to try and stop it, or to weakly pretend. That will not satisfy the animal in Eli.

I look at her. I feel a rush of rage go through me and my inner voice says calmly, 'Then let's do this.'

The sounds come rushing back in and we start to fight. It's hyperreal and we move in slow motion:

I fall.

She falls.

She pulls me back up to push me back over.

I feel the burn of the concrete floor rip through my fingers.

The slam of my body into hers.

My skin tears.

I hit the ground and as I do so, Eli spits in my face. The spit is ripe and it burns hot and cold at the same time.

I taste blood as she grabs my hand, holding me, supporting me, but pulling me back into the fight . . .

The sounds of this LA bar come back into focus. *Have I been staring at this stranger, this man in the back for minutes? Or was it just a second?* He locks eyes with me.

'Bexy, is that you?' Eli says.

I see the faces of my childhood nemeses frequently. I've seen Uncle Jude sitting in a café in Stoke Newington, I've seen Uncle Jonathan walk past me on the other side of the street in Arizona. In these visions, the imprint of a face appears on an unassuming and innocent person and I'm thrown back into a moment from the past that feels more real than the ground I stand on.

But never has it been this real.

'*Fuck*, I thought that was you!' he says.

There are over 1,500 bars in Los Angeles, yet here he is, in this one.

My skin prickles. I take in the man he is now. The chubbiness of youth is gone. He has thin hair and a slight physique. A man that I wouldn't look twice at in any other context, but I was so afraid of as a kid. The things he did in the name of *them*. The things I fantasised about saying to him if I ever saw him again as a grown-up, an equal. And here we are. The universe and serendipity are giving me that chance. The chance to grab him by the scruff of that weak neck and shout in his face:

Did it make you feel a man,
All that shit you did to little girls?
Do you feel like a fucking man now?

But I can't summon the rage, the righteous indignation doesn't come. I see a sad, flaccid husk of a man before me. He has no strength and no power over me. All I feel is pity.

'Can I buy you a drink?' he says.

'No, thanks, I'm good.'

'I'm sorry,' he adds.

'I know,' I say.

And I really do.

*　*　*

The next day, I wake up disoriented, my mouth dry, the slow wooziness of alcohol still in my blood. My face is buried in a musky armpit. I reach out to hold some of the warm skin I am tangled in.

'Morning, idiot.'

'Morning,' I croak.

Content, blissed and validated, I wake up next to my friend.

'What a night!' Sofi says.

'Still in shock. What died in my mouth?' I ask.

'It didn't die, it crawled into mine for its last breath . . . it died there.'

'Don't blame it, who wouldn't want to die in your mouth?' I say matter of fact.

'That is the *loveliest* thing you have ever said.' She laughs, turning over in bed. 'What are the chances that we would run into him there? Those assholes have a lot to answer for – how many other people could be walking around, doing who knows what to people? They're kind of the perfect ingredients for creating psychopaths. Pass me that water?'

'Yeah.'

She sits up, takes a gulp. I flop my head in her lap, my brain starting to throb a little. I'm grateful I'm still quite drunk.

Hell to pay later.

'But how many weird things have happened on this trip?' she adds.

Morning light comes through the window. We sit in silence, our breathing in synch, as we watch particles of illuminated dust.

'The light – beautiful, isn't it?' Sofi whispers.

'Uh-huh,' I say.

She strokes my hair and says, 'I can't believe that you turned out OK.'

'I did?' I say.

'No. Course not, you're batshit . . .'

I laugh.

'Is everyone in your family OK?' she asks and I feel a real tenderness and concern cut through the boozy haze.

'Mostly,' I say.

'What happened with Kris?' she asks.

* * *

Seeing Eli last night kicked off a whole conversation about the kids who had 'turned'. We spent hours at the bar, talking in depth about Guard syndrome, about kids who mirrored the adults' behaviour to survive. About how I wasn't sure if Kris had been taken over by the group and become one of them, or whether he had joined their forces to protect me.

Was there more going on than I, a confused ten-year-old, was aware of?

'Ah, Kris is amazing,' I say.

'Thank God!'

'I was confused, but there is no doubt in my mind now that he did what he did to look out for me. That's just him and his nature.'

When Kris had been forced to become a low-ranking shepherd in the Victor Programme, he had tried to use their system to protect us. And it had worked, to a point. But he was also brutally used by the group. During the court case against the Children of God, 'The Victor Programme' came under scrutiny. The group shipped the leaders that were culpable out of the country to keep them safe, and made lower-ranking shepherds like Kris take the stand. Kris thought he was there to explain the regime from the perspective of a 15-year-old, but when he was cross-examined, he realised his affidavit had been rewritten. And he was questioned as if he, now 18, had had some sort of responsibility for the Victor Programme and the abuse that had happened in it, when in fact he was a victim of it.

'That's disgusting,' Sofi says.

'I didn't even know about it at the time, he was their "patsy" in court, and he was a just a teenager when it all happened.'

'Did your parents know about this?' she asks.

'They were a core part of the strategy team for the court case, so it may have been their idea.'

I move on, and start to tell her about the last 15 years where Kris became the father figure of our family. Our protector. The older brother that sacrificed himself for us.

And sacrificed so much, in so many ways.

He looked out for Kate when she was pregnant; he helped her find her first house. He was amazing with her kids, always round her house to fix things, to make Sunday dinner, to watch cartoons at the crack of dawn with his niece and nephew.

He was a guide for me when I left; he helped me write my first CV, gave me a boost to go to night school and learn secretarial skills, wrote music with me, brought me down to his home in London for weekends on boozy punch and (protectively) freaked out when I started taking recreational drugs.

He sorted my brothers out. He moved them into his own house, put deposits down on flats for them, gave them advice, got drunk with them, showed them his bizarre and often dark takes on movies, screenplays and popular culture.

I tell her about how Kris and I went to South Africa to see our little brothers and sisters who were still in the group and too young to leave. We stayed for two weeks, filmed interviews with them in secret, to use as evidence if we needed to get them out. I was 21 then and he was in his late twenties. We got back and Kris felt he had no choice but to move to South Africa to keep a watchful eye over our brothers and sisters.

Not an easy move – South Africa is not an easy place to live.

He gave up his life with us and his home and his job. I know that him being there, on the scene, never too far away, gave my brothers and sisters a sense of security, normalcy and a guardian on their corner. My parents only allowed supervised visits, he was in a constant contact battle with them. A daily, weekly, all-encompassing battle to look after his siblings.

He stayed in South Africa for ten years, waiting for the kids to reach an age when they could leave, and sending them home to us, where they could be housed, where we could put them through school, in a support network that we can now afford to provide.

'What a hero,' she says.

'I know, he is the brave one for sure.'

'I don't know, you can be pretty brave too.'

As she says this, she catches a tear racing down my cheek with her thumb.

Again, we stare into the light. Our thoughts merge and swirl around in the air above the bed we lie in, our shared experience dancing in the dusty light. Days spent in fields, the yogic monks, the stinky meth cook, the children of the Twelve Tribes, the extra-terrestrial skies of Arizona, where we became like one. Our hearts full with the miles we have driven, the beds we have shared, the home we created in our truck.

'Do you think we will look back on this trip when we are older and think we were fucking nuts?' I ask.

'Nah, we will think we were cool.'

CHAPTER 12

In Black and White: 3 Years Before

Every day is like a sick surprise. For months after Maria leaves, every morning is the same. I feel OK the first second I wake up, but just for one second. Somehow my sleep has erased the fact that she's gone. Then, it hits me all at once, like someone sitting on my chest. Winding me. How can it sting this much, every, single, day? And why does sleep give me that cruel second of peace before daylight slams home the truth?

I wake up in my bed alone.

I lie and look at the ceiling; I feel like I have to physically push the weight off myself to get up in the dark to make break-fast, pull those pots of oats out for the thousandth time, find a seat on the floor of the living room for yet another devotions session. It feels empty. The hole of 'her' takes over the whole of me. I am in the same place, the same rooms, but everything in my world is different.

I can't talk about it, admit my ache to anyone. We were never meant to have that kind of friendship – there would be no empathy for me missing her, just judgement. Once someone is gone, we have to act as if they never existed. If they're *lucky*, they are erased; if not, they are spoken about with spite and scorn. They are shunned, possessed by the devil, they are back-sliders, they are no longer one of us.

The idea I have to forsake her, our friendship and the memory of it, grows from a thought into a hatred and a spite inside me. It develops into a disgust for my surroundings: the devotions, the Aunties, the Uncles, the group itself.

And this is why no friendships are allowed. Because the seeds of doubt blossom from experiencing unconditional love. They grow when you can share questions, when someone witnesses and recognises injustice with you. They flourish from the freedom, even if in secret, of sharing rage, pain and fury. I am not as weak as I was when I was ten and this world convinced me of my own madness.

When I couldn't grip on to my siblings anymore for my sanity, Maria was my person, the one who could see the very deep crack in this world they created, the one who could recognise the insanity that lay behind it. It was Maria and my love for her that convinced me that the madness was not in my head.

It was in theirs.

* * *

The office is small and dark, tiny windows barely allow natural light onto the numerous desks crammed into the space. When the adults work here, the florescent lights are always on. I keep them off. This is where I prefer to be. Out of the way. Alone. I sit on the beige carpet, papers spread out in front of me, my afternoon's work. I have worked in the office long enough for my parents to trust that I will 'just get on with it'. The paperwork is simple: Collate. Staple. File. Every day is the same.

The only thing that has changed since Maria has gone is that my parents have made a new outsider friend, someone we would call 'A Big Fish' or 'A King'. He has said that he will help our home record some of our family music using his equipment, so every now and then me and two other girls go with him to sing our family songs on tape. Short breaks out of the house. Short breaks from this.

The work in the office is mundane. And it doesn't take long for me to get distracted. But I know I can make up the time if I need to. The office has computers, a phone, the fax and piles and piles of papers in filing cabinets. I open the top cabinet; the smell of ink and toner is not unpleasant as I run my finger across the different coloured carboard dividers. The second cabinet clatters open when I pull its silver handle, there are a few folders lined up. My finger stops on a dark blue leather folder with a label that says 'Press Clippings'. It's clear that someone has taken some time and care with this. I sit on the floor behind a desk, hidden from the door, should anyone use it.

I thumb open the leather folder and flip through the first few pages without pausing; every page has cut-outs of news articles stuck onto it. Pieces of see-through tape hold together *their* history of us. As I flick through, I realise there are hundreds. Sometimes three or four stuck on a single page, sometimes there are articles so long, they are cut up over a few pages.

Big bold black titles shout at me from grey backgrounds:

'Sex Cult in Tiny Village'
'Crazed Cult Leader Abuses Children'
'Orgies and Prostitution for Christ'

Black-and-white photos accompany the articles. Many of them are of my parents. I look at my mom and dad's faces, smiling in different places in the house, sometimes outside; their 'worldly' haircuts, blazers, my dad's 'prop' moustache, my mom's wide smile.

My dad's face sits next to text that reads:

The group's leader is 41-year-old former fireman Gideon Scott, self-styled 'House Shepherd' of the British branch of the Children of God, which shares the same leader, David Berg. Mr Scott, whose wife Rachel is a psychologist, has 11 children. He said yesterday: 'We have nothing to hide. We threw open the house in accordance with what Jesus has said.'

Mom's not a psychologist, is she? I know she went to university but I thought she dropped out. Maybe it sounds better to say she is one. My dad goes on in the article:

'We are a normal Christian group, and there are many millions of Christians whose beliefs are as real and as full as ours. We allow free love between consenting adults, and our children can have sex if they are over 16, but not with mature adults. I don't believe in contraception, I suppose that's why I have 11 kids – and as far as I know, they are all mine.'

I flip the pages onto an article titled 'Hookers for Jesus':

> Soon after the cult's inception it moved to Britain, where the practice of attracting new recruits by seduction earned its proselytizers the name 'Hookers for Jesus'. The cult was accused of kidnapping and brainwashing young people, denying them contact with their families while they were indoctrinated. More recently, it has been associated with allegations of sexual abuse, and several state authorities in Australia had begun to investigate.

'Brainwashing,' I mouth the word. It's interesting, my parents talk about it all the time. *How do you wash a brain*? Mine feels full, too full, not clean and washed. My finger pauses on an article describing the kids during the raids. A scene I have imagined so many times.

> The police commissioner in charge of the operation was taken aback by the children's condition. 'They seemed like Martians, autistic,' he said. 'They were living in compartmented cells and answered questions like automatons. Whenever one of them tried to say something, another would look at him and he would fall silent, terrified.'
>
> *Autistic Martians, ha, Maria would love that.*
>
> I start to imagine what we do look like from the outside; I think about how we police ourselves, and

each other, even the kids. It's how it has always been. Do we really come across as Autistic Martians in comparison to kids 'out there', the kids outside the gate for example, who are given free money and spend their time shouting at us? Are we robotic versions of those children?

The shutters have flown up, I have been given a peek through a window from their world into ours; it's in black and white in front of me. How *they* see us. My finger follows lines and lines of memorised answers in print on the page: 'no abuse', 'never happened', 'happy lives'.

The black-and-white words that my parents spoke, words that I have been so proud of them for, for their quickness, their wit, their razor-sharp answers. I was so proud that they were chosen to protect our generation of kids. Even when I knew they were lying, they had lied to protect us.

They were protecting *us*, right?

I can't put the book down, I can't stop my finger racing through the articles, each one revealing more. I speed through a journalist talking about confiscated videos with sexual content: 'There are amateur videos said to be taken by members of a religious sect that calls itself the Family of Love. The video tapes, shown by television stations in Argentina, depict nude girls, some no older than eight, dancing in provocative poses. Officials in Argentina say pornographic videos and literature were confiscated in raids on seven homes run by the sect. Court sources say some of the tapes depict sex between children and adults, one between a father and daughter.'

I didn't know that they confiscated anything in the raids. My parents hadn't told us anything about this. But, as I read, a memory rushes front and centre from South Africa, of me as a five-year-old watching these films that had been made for Moses David by the young girls. We were told they were beautiful, expressions of love. I remember the day some of the Aunties and young girls filmed them in our home. We weren't allowed to walk past a certain window, in case we were 'in the background'. I could hear the music playing loud from the room that the camera was set up in. Me and Joel found a spot to watch. I could just about see their outlines through the net curtains. They stripped off their clothes erotically, slowly, gyrating to the music. Joel and I mimicked the dancing from our hidden spot, rubbing ourselves mockingly and laughing silently.

The title on the next page reads:

DAVID BERG ABUSES OWN GRANDDAUGHTER

'. . . His granddaughter has accused him of starting sexual practices with her when she was five . . .'

I have lived every day of my breathing life in this group and even for me, with my knowledge from the inside of this world, to read this feels shocking. It's not news to me, but I am reading it in a *new way*. Like seeing your face reflected in a mirror from behind, your features are reversed. You have seen your face one way your whole life, and now you look at it and you don't recognise it, everything seems to slip off sideways. I had read Moses David's writings about his sexual fantasies with his granddaughter Mene, but somehow this knowledge just faded into the full tapestry of what we experienced and were taught. Just a small part of it. It didn't even stand out. Now these words leap off the page and I feel a little sick, sick that it only registers as truly messed-up when I read it in this dim, beige office from a book of clippings.

I turn the page again. My hand shakes, wondering what I'll see on the other side. My sharp intake of breath cuts through the dim room. A photo screams from the centre. It's a few years old, black and white and grainy, but it's definitely me. I touch the edge of it and a grey smudge appears on my fingertip, revealing just how real it is, so real it leaps off the page and puts a mark on me. It was taken on the day we went to London for the demonstrations. I stand outside the Argentine Embassy, wearing that denim jacket they gave me that I loved so much, my childish face contorted from shouting with raw enthusiasm.

I didn't realise that I looked like that. My hair flies out of its low ponytail, frizz frames my face. I look so much smaller than the people around me. Smaller than I imagined. I look like a child. I didn't feel like one on the day that this was taken – I felt grown-up, I've felt like an adult for years.

I don't recognise myself.

The headline reads, 'CHILDREN OF GOD FIGHT BACK'.

In my tiny, outstretched arms, like a shepherd's staff, is a placard painted with large words by my amateur brush.

It reads, 'Let our Children Go'.

CHAPTER 13

Forgive Nothing: 16 Years After

My parents have gone.

My eyes focus on the rug in the middle of the floor. Plants are woven into the tapestry, their leaves reaching out to each other. I stare so hard they flicker, start to move towards each other, like shivering, trembling arms, reaching for comfort, but they can't touch, they are just a little out of reach.

I sit in my living room in London. I've been back from the trip for six months, almost settled back into London life. But the last 24 hours have changed everything.

I have just interviewed my parents.

I feel nothing. I don't feel angry, I don't feel sad.

I am numb.

'Here you go . . .' Paz walks in with a glass of water. I have known him for eight years. He is a producer, he is my sounding board, he is a good friend. And perhaps he thought that he would be walking into a victory party. And here I am almost catatonic.

'Thanks' – the word dries my mouth out as I say it.

Yesterday, I was meant to fly back out to the States, but the group I was going to stay with cancelled my visit. Disappointed, confused, I sat in my kitchen, wondering what my next move should be. And as I sat there, a call came through from an unknown number. It was my dad. *We are in the UK* and *we want to see you*. Was this a sign? Was this supposed to be my next move? Maybe it was all along.

To go back to the source.

Now, just half an hour after they have left, I am shutting down. Everything is shrinking, like what happened in this room happened at the end of a tunnel, or a telescope pointed the wrong way around. In a tiny peephole. My brain is trying to protect itself, minimise the feelings of shame and failure that are on the periphery, their nasty shadows creeping in from the corners.

Everyone told me that meeting up with my parents was going to be hard.

Everyone told me facing them after all these years would mess up my brain.

Everyone said it would throw me back a step or two.

Be careful.

But the stories I told myself, about my strength and capability, were louder than 'everyone else'. All I needed to do was get them on camera. Everything else I could take care of. I am an experienced interviewer – they can't affect me now like they did when I was a kid.

'So . . .? Did you give them hell?' Paz asks.

I wonder if he's joking.

I take a gulp of water. 'I don't think so, I don't know,' I tell him, confused.

'Shall I have a look?' he says, walking towards the camera still sitting in its tripod, the witness in the room, still pointing at the couch they sat on.

'No, no, no,' I say.

Fuck. It's that bad.

I want to believe that what just happened didn't happen. If Paz watches it, it will confirm that it did.

Paz looks at me, worried. 'OK, OK . . . I won't watch. You need a stronger drink than that. What else you got here?'

My voice comes out thin and weak. 'I really thought I would feel different from this. Like a release maybe . . . I feel gross.'

I can still smell their presence, even their clothes, the Old Spice my dad wears, and yet, did it really happen?

It did.

* * *

My mom and dad sat on my couch, two figures lit up with a warm glow from fairy lights on the floor. Mom was wearing a long skirt and white top, Dad in a button-up shirt and cardigan. They both look old. Art and photographs cover every surface. There is barely an empty space on the walls and floors in this tiny living room, the bits and bobs I have around that make 'my home'.

It's weird to have them sitting among my things.

I'd set up for the interview. Fixing up my tripods, checking my memory cards and sound equipment. My dad still sports his moustache, but his hair is now fully grey. Mom's hair that has always been black is now blonde – strange to see her like this, it's hard to connect her with the mom I had growing up.

It's probably a maintenance thing, to hide the age coming through.

They talk about the diet they are on at the moment – 'The Hollywood Diet'. I hear my dad say the words 'Carb Cycling'. Bizarre that two cultists should care enough about their weight to do a fad diet with the word 'Hollywood' in it. It seems carnal, worldly, not very godly.

Plain weird, I think.

'I'll sit there, and you two sit here,' I say to no one in particular, anxiously fiddling with the tech around the room.

'Are you using one camera or two?' my dad said in an authoritative voice.

I take a step towards them, trying to take up some space and move into 'filmmaker' mode.

'There'll be things that we'll talk about in this interview that will be relevant to you and things that are going to be more relevant to other people.' I looked at them among the fairy lights, the portrait I painted of my grandma, the photographs of years of life I have had without them. How would I approach the list of injustices from my childhood, that in this room, seem a lifetime ago? How would I balance the needs of the kid from *then*, and the adult I am today?

As I finished setting up, I heard myself say, 'That's lovely!' Like a 1950s housewife bringing out a steaming hot pie for her guests, rather than a woman about to confront her parents. I sat down opposite them and put a gentle foot forward.

'I suppose a good place to start is asking you how much you know about this film that I'm making?' I say.

My mom straightens her top, smiles and says, 'Well, we don't know very much about it. We know that you've been visiting some religious communities, but we'd really love to hear more details. Exactly which ones you've been to and what it was like? What was your experience there?'

I answer, listing groups and dates, and then realise that the interview has been turned around on me. I am describing the Twelve Tribes, giving them a brief history of Ananda, rambling on autopilot. I try to turn it around to us: 'My focus has been the children. The questions I've been asking families are all around the idea of raising your kids in groups, where you don't necessarily know what the outcome will be, if you know what I mean.'

Do I think I'm being clever?

It's a weak start.

My mom smiled sweetly and said, 'It does make sense but I think you will find that the adults there certainly do know how it's going to turn out. They believe that the children will stay pure and separate from the world. That's what their hope is, that's what their desire is, that's the end result they want. So, they're probably very disappointed if their kids start leaving and it's not perhaps what they expected in the beginning at all. I think they probably want their families to stay together, within the group.'

They. The children. Them. The group.

We skirt around our history, using other people's stories to talk about our own, without 'outing' ourselves, like a thinly veiled 'asking for a friend'. Disconnected, once, twice removed.

'Yeah,' I continue. 'It's a complicated one, because obviously for me . . . I've got . . . you know . . . We've got our huge family and we've got our own history, and we're kind of dealing with the fallout of this situation now.' Where am I going with this? I'm not asking about their culpability, or even talking about their accountability as the only people in 'our family' who held any power.

Then, again, I water down the point by talking about 'other people' – the Twelve Tribes.

'So, I was talking to families who had young kids and the parents are very sure that these kids aren't going to leave. More than likely it's because they haven't hit puberty yet and they haven't started to become rebellious. And while our story isn't everyone's story, I'm a bit like, "Well, they might stay. But prepare for the eventuality of them leaving as well."'

'I think I agree with you,' Mom says.

Does she?

'I think we had unrealistic expectations and they probably do as well. Because you feel, as an adult, that you've found something so wonderful that you want to give your life to. So, you want your children to do the same.'

How normal this all sounds – 'something so wonderful' – like a calling, like getting into yoga, or clean living, maybe insisting your kids are vegetarian. It's plain and simple. As she says it, I can feel myself getting pulled into *their* version of our history.

'Everyone has to make their own choices,' she continues, 'and we were hoping that the children would make the same choice as us. Everyone has to find their own faith, whatever that is. We ourselves – in the time period we're talking about, 1968, 1971, when we first joined – we hated the fact that we were supposed to fit in a mould. And yet, we were trying to do that ourselves, with our own children. And why?'

My dad answers her question. 'Because we thought we had a better mould.' He takes a long pause. As if he has a bigger audience than the one in this room. Maybe it's the audience in the camera he is talking to. 'I look at my parents and their motivation was, be financially secure. Have a nice marriage. Have a house. Have a car. And that your kids would carry that on, but do a bit better than you did. And my motivation was that I wanted to make the world a better place. And in the same way, I saw my children's lives being better than my own. It was because they would fulfil that mission better than I did, of making the world a better place.'

Again. It all seems so simple. We lived that life to make the world a better place. Everything that happened to us kids was with that motivation.

And now that he has the floor, he starts to divert with histories of other religions and with stories of other people's families, of nuns who live on the west side of Hyde Park, of Muslim ways of life. He talks for a full 20 minutes while I sit there silent.

What the fuck is going on?

We dance around each other, in a world that isn't real, where no one speaks the truth, where everything is a different colour or shade than it should be, a picture made up of so many untruths that it creates a totally different scene – but it happens piece by piece so you don't notice till you stand back and think, *What the hell is that?*

I get caught up in their revision of the truth, so much so that my own memories seem like the lies, my past seems unreal. Would these two old people sitting in my flat in London actually join a cult? Would they have let those things happen to us, to me? My very real past becomes more blurred with every word. It's a thick heavy mist that I have to fight my way out of.

I choke on the bullshit, theirs and my own. I need to pull this back into some kind of truth. I talk about some kids I know from the Twelve Tribes, whose dad left for *them* and how that made me feel. That he was the hero I dreamed of as a child, and that his wife, Derusha, didn't leave with them. I asked Derusha, as she sat there, childless, if she would do anything differently and she had said, 'No.' I tell my parents, 'I find it difficult to understand a person that wouldn't do anything differently, if that makes sense.'

Is this really my attempt at asking if they have any regrets? Can't I do better than this?

I have done, I know I can – but not with them, it seems.

My mom says, 'There's things that we definitely would have done differently and that we really regret.'

I ask, 'When I was younger, did you agree with the decisions that were being made about us at that time?' I know what I'm talking about, they know what I'm talking about, but no one comes out and says it.

Mom says, 'Things were only bad for one year.'

They have convinced themselves and are now trying to convince me.

My dad says, 'There were some decisions we didn't agree with, but then you have to make a decision, "Well, do I disagree with this enough that I'm prepared to walk?" Am I prepared to think, "OK, I don't necessarily agree but maybe other people know better than I do?"'

I know he knows what I'm talking about because he says, 'They tried it out in the Philippines and they told us it worked, so we just got on with it.'

What they 'just got on with' was the Victor Camps. *Beating their own kids. The silence restrictions.*

I need to push them. Shout. Scream. But, somehow, they still have a power over me that reduces me to being a little girl.

And what did that little girl do to survive? She was quiet. She tried to please them because she knew the transactional nature of their love, she had to earn it. She knew that to be good and keep quiet was to have a kind of safeness. Be invisible.

And here I am, slipping into that role.

We are circling the point, getting closer to the truth, but on the edge of it, my mom starts to cry. I watch her, wet-eyed, quivering chin, and I feel a hollowness to the tears. Like watching someone emulating emotion and perhaps creating a diversion.

My dad interjects with, 'It's a sad situation for a family, but in actual fact, every family goes through hurt, every family goes through all sorts of different situations, developments and changes. Divorce can fracture a family. And it can take a long time for that to heal. So, the religious community is one example of a family which can be under tension. But so many families are under tension all over the world.'

Again, it's a deflection. And again, I do *nothing* to bring it back.

'But our biggest heartbreak, what keeps us awake in the night and what we often discuss, is how can we be a complete family? That is extremely important to us, extremely important, and that's something that we want to spend more time working on,' my mom says.

I know that she has felt this. A few months back, she sent me an email out of the blue with some garbled lines, talking about how she dreamed that she had died and none of us came to her funeral.

It was an email I hadn't answered.

I ask, 'What would be the first steps in that?'

'I think one of the steps we have taken – I like to think we have, anyway – is to be accepting of each one of you, where you're at right now,' my dad says.

Are we getting somewhere? Was that about him, or was it about us? It doesn't feel right.

I ask about them being the media spokespeople and how they feel about that now. They tell me there are things that they regret about that too. My dad says, 'We should not have exposed you to that, or allowed you to be a part of it.'

'How do you mean?' I ask, thrown by his admission of guilt.

He pauses, then says, 'We should have thought about the long-term effects of there being photographs of you in the papers.'

I am confused. This is the last thing in the world that I give a shit about. On the ledger of the things that they have done, of the things that have been damaging for us to be involved in, *this* is what he would have done differently? We were taught to lie to the cameras. We were media-trained. We peddled their bullshit until it felt like it was our truth.

'You were really good,' my mum says, cutting into my thoughts.

'Huh?' I say, shaken by praise that feels filthy.

Praise that makes me culpable in the cover-up too.

'You were *really* good at it,' my dad agrees.

* * *

I sit here now, with a whisky in my hand. Paz is quiet. Running over the things that they said. And how I got here. What had I convinced myself of? That I was a brave, brave warrior, that I was going on this quest, joining groups as some sort of saviour; that I could get the 'truth' out, that I could save children? That I was powerful and strong? And that maybe in doing so I could save myself?

I was a woman who had faced her fears, left a cult, created a new life. And yet my parents still have a power over me. And admitting that makes me sick. The fallout of this war covers me in a slick of deep loathing.

I looked at the two people who made me. Wanting them to look like fork-tongued, alien lizards, or at the very least, weirdo cult Leaders and instead I saw my parents.

Normal. Old. Harmless? Why do they look so fucking ordinary?

The unseen battle in that room was the fight between the moments of their betrayal stacked on top of each other. But hadn't they fed me? Hadn't they clothed me? What of all the times I had been cradled in my mom's arms? And most of all: *Hadn't they made me?*

It's the struggle between the tenderness I had been given – even if it was never enough – and the cruelty that I had suffered because of their neglect, or worse, at their hand. I see the tricks that they used and I saw how I myself had become a trickster – 'I was really good at it'. I saw their pumped-up confidence and faux sincerity. And it made me sick because it was like looking in a mirror at everything I hated in myself, and everything that I was afraid of made me who I really am. Because after all, I am half of each of them.

Their imprint. Their blood. Their child.

I have spent the last 15 years trying to become someone else, as far away from what they made as possible, trying to hide from this truth: That I am closer to *these* people than I want to think. I gave myself tool after tool – a new accent, different hair, a new name, an identity in the shape of a career, the joker, the carer, the people pleaser, the ambitious one – but under it all, was I still *that* child? And was I even now, so many years later, under their control?

'Mmmmmm,' Paz says.

How long have I been silently staring for?

He looks like he is biting his tongue.

'What?' I ask, defensively.

'Well, nothing, we'll talk about it another time. I think you just need another drink and a good night's sleep.'

'No, you started, so go on,' I say.

'Well, I never believed you when you said that you had forgiven your parents,' he says.

'What?' I almost shout the word.

'Sorry, I know you believed it. I know you thought it was done and dusted, and that you could do this trip and be objective, and that you could have this showdown with them. But I didn't buy it.'

'I have though, I have. I did it years ago, I told you about it when I did it. I had to do it, so I could get over it.'

'That's the thing, you're not over it. Look at you, you're angry. It's so obvious, hasn't any one told you? You haven't forgiven *shit*! You are lying to yourself if you think you have.' He says this in a voice filled with nothing but concern for me – there is no dig in it, nothing to gain.

'I *am* over it,' I say and realise how ridiculous I sound.

'If you believe that, you won't allow yourself to feel what you are feeling. If you don't allow yourself to feel what happened tonight and the shit it brings up for you – this could get really dark for you.'

'If you came round here just to educate me on the fact that I am pathetic, weak and stupid and stuck in the past, then you might as well fuck off,' I say.

'I didn't say any of those things, Bexy,' he says.

'Shit, I'm sorry. Sorry, I don't mean to take it out on you.'

I *am* sorry, I mean it.

'It's OK, I get it. Drink this,' he says as he pours me another whisky.

I take a big gulp and it burns; I nearly choke. Why whisky to calm nerves? Why not something gentler, why not a glass of milk? I look into the icy-brown liquid, swirling round with the half-truths, my weaknesses, my past.

'I'm really angry,' I say.

Paz sits next to me and puts his hand on mine.

'When you have been that betrayed by your parents, I don't know if you'll ever be able to *not* feel angry. It's fucking dis-gusting.' I nod, and lean my head on his shoulder and he says, 'If I was here, I would have knocked your dad out. You know that, don't you?'

I nod again. His kindness makes my eyes leak. I take another sip and then push my palms deep into the sockets of my eyes as if I can block out what is now so obvious.

'I am angry at myself, to be honest. Just having them back, in my fucking house, makes me feel gross and makes me cruel to myself. Why did I give them a platform? I shouldn't be doing this, I shouldn't be a filmmaker, I shouldn't be doing this project – it is pointless. And talking to my parents is pointless. What was I expecting to get out of it?'

He tries to placate me: 'Step away from it and have a look. In some ways it's helping your process and your own personal journey of actually coming to understand and basically come to terms with and being at peace with your past and your childhood. Even if this film *never* comes out, it's still an important part of your life.'

I know what he's saying makes sense, but I'm in no position to listen to good advice.

Not now.

'There's not . . . there's pretty much not a day that goes by when I haven't thought to myself, Why am I doing this? *Why am I doing this?* Am I mad?'

I had convinced myself I had grown out of what they had done to me into a strong fighter. In spite of them, I had taken on the world. I had a mission and a purpose. With every commune that I joined, I was undoing the wrongs of the past. I had convinced myself that I was over my childhood, that I had forgiven my parents and that I was enlightened.

I was *fucking* enlightened.

And it hits me, while I am repulsed by them, while I will never forgive them for some of the things they have done, while I see them as pathological liars and the gaslighters, there is a part of me, that child, that still wants them to love me; that still feels completely unworthy of love. That I will never be good enough unless I have it. And it's unattainable. And there is a part of me that still wonders, under all this that I have created: *Were they right? Am I evil?*

I wonder if everything I have ever done since I left was to prove them wrong. This thing that's been instilled in me since my exorcism and before. Am I actually a good person, or do

I act like one so people will love me? Am I ambitious, or do I on some level think that this will make the world think that I'm worth something, *anything*? What was this whole journey for? Just some giant bullshit expedition to make me feel better about myself? Nothing to do with the kids I met, or the truth? And if I can't, on this very basic level, sit in front of the people that in my heart, and in my head, I know are the perpetrators, and be brave enough to call them out for it, then what's the point? It's all been for nothing.

I am not brave, I am not a warrior.

I feel like I can't breathe, And I can't actually bring myself to say any of the things that I'm feeling; that I'm hollow, empty, beyond wrung out, that I have never felt more disconnected from myself, of who I think I am and who I want to be. And worst of all, I feel like I'm doing her, that little girl who went through all that, a disservice.

I can't stand up for myself against *them*.

I can't even stand up for *her*.

CHAPTER 14

The Disappearance of Martin and Linda: 1972

My parents met on the psychiatric ward in a hospital in Leicester.

Mom was one of three children, born in 1952. Her family lived in Derbyshire. She was the head girl of her school, a county athlete, a vegan and a regular churchgoer. She was also the first female to win the university scholarship she was awarded. Her brothers say she sailed through everything, blissfully capable and almost unthinking in her ability to pass exams, win scholarships and attain goals, like being the head girl. It was accepted by everyone in the family that Linda had still believed in Santa until she was 16. Which kind of breaks my heart. Whether that was the truth, a running joke or just an apocryphal story, like many family fables, it illustrates a truth about her – naïve, ethereal, unworldly, cerebral to the point of being out of touch. She was the middle child. Middle class. Pinnacle of hope and expectation for her parents and herself.

My dad, on the other hand, came from a broken family in the south of England, a fishing town in Kent. Martin's father was a violent drunk, but his mother was a member of the Salvation Army and the heart of her small community. He was considered (even if mainly by himself) to be the smartest boy in his school – from a poor background, he went to a posh school on a scholarship, which accounts for his 'Queen's English' accent. From what I know, my dad became a father by the age of 15 and had been drinking for three years by that time. I remember my grandmother telling me as a teenager how happy she was that my dad had 'found the Lord' because he'd been a 'fall-down drunk' by the age of 12.

They came from vastly different backgrounds and grew up in different counties, but their paths crossed eventually: in a psychiatric ward in Leicestershire.

*   *   *

Over the years, I have found that many people have a specific image about the people who join cults. They might have escaped from a ward somewhere, they're unstable, homeless, addicts or on the spectrum. Perhaps this gives them comfort, that there is a separation between 'us' and 'them', that there is something they can pinpoint which makes them different. That 'we' could never do 'that'. Perhaps it keeps us safe. It builds a barrier between us and the crazies in white robes singing, chanting or muttering to unseen gods. But these *nutters* could be closer to *us* than you think.

Undramatically, my parents were in the psychiatric hospital not as patients, but because they were both studying medicine at De Montfort University. My mom was in her first year of training as a psychologist and my dad was training to be a psychiatric nurse. Which is far more confusing to many than if they had met in hospital gowns, bare-buttocked, over a plastic cup full of jelly bean coloured meds. He had arrived there via scholarships through grammar schools. She probably had this route mapped out for her from an early age, both of them looking for a purpose outside of themselves. He was a wild one, while she was eagerly doing what was expected of her, making her family proud.

The way my father told it to us when we were kids, he was magnetised by her naïvety and 'good girl' persona. I get the idea now that he perhaps saw her as a challenge, something perhaps to break – a story I always felt had a slick of oily smugness to it. But perhaps he was just genuinely proud that he ended up with someone so far out of his league. He was a long-haired, motor-cycle-loving lothario. I have seen photographs of him during this time – leather jackets, ginger locks, super skinny, angular face, and I find it hard to believe that Mom, with her green eyes and hourglass figure, the raven-haired vegan, would have wanted anything to do with this bad boy with a destructive streak. But sometimes the heart wants what it *shouldn't* have.

He asked her out on a date. Her roommates warned of his indelicate reputation with other women at the university, which she ignored. He was charismatic and witty, a wordsmith who could talk himself into or out of any situation. And so, their first date happened, at an Italian restaurant, where he turned up drunk, immediately disappointing my mother's idea of who he was and what the night could have held – although perhaps she was mainly disappointed in herself. During dinner, it came to pass that he'd 'lost' his wallet (he hadn't). And as she paid the bill, she promised herself that this was the end of the road for them (it wasn't).

But maybe there was still something in her, something fighting to break away from 'everybody's' expectations of her. That perfect unalterable future. The good girl, with good grades, who was meant to do *so* well. So, a few months after this first, depressing date, when Martin (my dad's name 'before') suggested to Linda (my mom's name 'then') that they take his motorcycle across Europe on a road trip during their summer break, as friends. She said yes.

On a crisp morning, saddled up on a vintage bike, they headed towards Calais.

It was only about an hour or two into France that misfortune hit and the bike broke down. I imagine the two of them on the side of the road arguing about Martin's crappy clapped-out choice of vehicle and lack of foresight, or their political differences while desperately trying to hitchhike to anywhere but here.

And this is where the story that I have heard from both my parents on so many different occasions takes a turn for me. It's always told with a sense of romance and hilarity from both sides, because it's all a bit of fun. But for us hearing it as kids, it didn't feel *as* fun, even as a child who couldn't grasp the meaning of everything. The feeling that I got in my gut was that this bit of fun was a revealing of what was to come for my mother, the level of respect that my dad showed for women and the lessons he was teaching us about how they could be traded or sold.

Linda and Martin were picked up by a married couple in a sports car. Grateful for the lift, they drove another 50 or so miles before they stopped for something to eat. Linda didn't speak much French. Martin had enough conversational skills to get by and the stilted exchange quickly morphed into the husband trying to 'purchase' Linda from Martin for the night. The deal was my dad would get something in the region of 100 euros in today's money and a night with the guy's wife. And this random guy, who was over 30 years her senior, could have his way with my mom. When my parents tell this story, they laugh about it. *My dad's cheeky way. Naughty boy.* My mom's 'prudish' attitude to this transaction. *Frigid flower.* My dad usually ending on 'that was a lot of money back then, I could have bought an . . .', my mom giggling dutifully at the punchline she's heard at least 100 times. But, at the time, Mom decided, yet again, that this was the end for her and this appalling man: she was not his property to be sold.

At least, *not yet.*

Fast forward six months after she had called time on the friendship, to the morning that Linda discovered that Martin has gone missing from university, when he went to London to retrieve his toolkit from a friend who borrowed it and never came back (remember, *that* guy from the demonstrations). The whispers floating down the halls of De Montfort were that he had gotten entangled with some sort of group, some were calling it a religious cult, in south London.

Even though Linda wasn't a good friend of Martin's, she was a good girl and she had heard about these types of groups before and what they could do to a person, how they could misrepresent God or the scripture, and how they could poison naïve minds. She felt compelled to go to London and rescue this idiot boy who had lost his way. It wasn't the first time that Martin had done something stupid.

The next parts of the story are a blur of different accounts – my dad's, my mom's, my grandparents' – and like every story, each has its truth, fiction and agenda. I have tried to tell it as true as I can; some bits I feel I can tell as if I was there. Others are cobbled together from things my grandad told me in my twenties, while looking at photographs of a daughter that perhaps never really came home.

When Linda walked into the factory in Bromley, she found around 200 young people singing joyfully inside this high-ceilinged industrial home; sweaty, arms flung in the air, hugging each other. She says it was more than being happy, it was elation, liberation, enlightenment. She'd expected to find dull-eyed, brainwashed, mantra-chanting morons. Instead, this was the most alive she had ever seen humans be: bright, light and welcoming. Perhaps she tried to keep her cool among the fresh-faced hippies that were surrounding her, hugging her and telling her that this is *exactly where she should be.*

Perhaps this factory was full of kids who were not so much looking to follow Jesus, but for a place to belong. And from what they have said, that's exactly how it felt. The Children of God accepted them unconditionally and offered them something many had never known before: a home where they were loved and accepted, and where they were given purpose and enlightenment.

Eventually, she found Martin in the crowd and instead of the hard, witty, cynical man that she'd known, she was met with a softened gaze and a warm heart. She was baffled. They sat as she tried to persuade him to come back to university, told him that this wasn't where he *should* be. And he told her that he had never felt so right about anything in his life. Not only was this his home, but it could be hers too. He didn't come across as brainwashed, and quite the opposite, he seemed more in control and sure of what he wanted and his purpose than he had ever been before.

He had forsaken all.

Five hours later, Linda had joined. And this might seem sudden, but conversion rates were that quick. Sometimes it took one conversation to change someone's mind. A prayer that gave them peace, a feeling of contentment. She felt the warmth of God fill her with a simple prayer, asking Him to come into her heart, forgive her sins and give her eternal life. She told us she walked in to rescue my dad and ended up getting saved – she wasn't brainwashed, or waterboarded, there was no hypnosis, just the feeling of God filling her and making her brand new.

Now, one day in, not only was she a 'Babe for Christ' (a new member), but she was given her first test as to whether or not she could free herself of the shackles of her previous life. The test came in the form of having to cook a pig's head – which as a vegan, would prove that she truly was one of them. Having never even 'boiled an egg', she cooked the pig's head to prove herself to her new family. And with this rebirth, she changed her name to Rachel (which means 'sheep' – I only found that out recently, but it seems worth mentioning).

Within 24 hours, my dad (whose name was now Jacob) had a prophecy: if Linda's name was changed to Rachel, he should take her as his wife. He didn't share this prophecy with anyone until she walked up, reborn, rebranded. Already completely integrated into the group and not one to disagree with a prophecy from on high, Rachel put her faith in my father and this message from the Lord and agreed, for better or bizarre, to the marital union that would bear 12 children and last to this very day.

Back in Derbyshire, my grandparents were alerted to Mom's disappearance by staff at the university, saying they hadn't seen Linda in a few weeks. They drove down to De

Montfort University. I can imagine them at her dorm – eerily, everything in its place except for their daughter. All of her belongings exactly as they should be: her photographs laid out on her bedside table, her hairbrush still holding strands of her hair in its bristles. The girls she lived with said they weren't sure where she had gone but suggested that perhaps it had something to do with Martin. This was the first time my grandparents would have heard of him – the man who they would later feel stole their child and indoctrinated her, the man who took 'Linda' away from them forever.

The police were pretty unsympathetic about a girl going missing from university for a few days, potentially with a boyfriend. Still, they filed the missing person report and waited.

A few weeks down the line, she still hadn't returned to her studies, and even more worrying, not a single one of her friends had heard from her. Friends that she would speak to almost daily before she disappeared. This just wasn't anything like her. Then my grandad somehow tracked her down, perhaps because of whispers and rumours at Linda's university about a factory in Bromley.

Imagining my grandad going into the factory in search of his daughter breaks my heart. He was one of the kindest, most patient people I have ever met and I saw the pain of what happened when she joined the group first-hand. Even years later, he still mourned the daughter that he lost, the one he had such a close relationship with. He demanded to see her, he said he wouldn't leave until they had produced her. They told him that he could see her on one condition: a Leader was to sit in the room with them and they had to speak 'through' the Leader. I imagine my grandad pleading with his daughter to come home and then his words mimicked by a Leader verbatim, but filtered through the mouth of a believer to make them safe (or reduce their power). Imagine a man who fought a war against totalitarianism having to sit in a room and speak to his daughter through the equivalent of what he saw as a commissar or gauleiter. The Leaders might have had a hippie aesthetic, long hair and Flower Power, but what he saw was his daughter under the full control and power of a regime.

My grandad went home without her.

*   *   *

'Rachel' was sent on a mission to Holland, on a double-decker bus with the words 'REVOLUTION FOR JESUS' written across it. Holland was a hotspot for the counterculture and so for new recruits. My grandparents sent Jeremiah, my mom's brother, to Utrecht to track her down. They told him, whatever you do, even if you can't bring her back, take a photograph of her so that we know she's alright: they wanted proof of life.

The photograph that he took of her rests in my hand now. Her hair is long and wavy, the bustle of Utrecht is all around her. She's wearing a full-length brown dress with large orange flowers all over it, she has the biggest beautiful smile on her face, she is so, so young. She's radiant. And she's about eight months pregnant.

*   *   *

When I look at photographs of the Bromley factory and I see these beautiful, young bohemians with their arms in the air, guitars strapped to them, leaping around jubilantly, it looks pretty fucking cool. It looks like a scene straight out of a film. I have always been obsessed with Andy Warhol's Factory, the stomping ground of The Velvet Underground, the home of Candy Darling, and a spot where drugs, poetry and misfits melded together. So, to be attracted to the factory in Bromley, bursting with youth and new ideas, is something I can understand.

Imagine that in just one night, or with just one decision, the things that you have been worried about your whole life vanish.

What will I do when I grow up? That's now decided. Will my life have meaning? Sorted, you have the greatest purpose in the world. Will I be able to provide for my family? You have a new family now, and you are provided for. And as for the life you left behind, not only is there no place for it now, but you are *better* than them. You have had your eyes opened, you can actually pity them. And you have a community surrounding and supporting you.

Within this one decision, so many of our deepest human needs are satisfied: belonging, community, purpose, meaning. And taken away are all the things that so many of us worry about and fear. It's a pretty delicious idea. I mean, I can't be bothered to pay my rent or do my taxes, more often than not I am due in court for forgetting a gas bill that needs to be paid. And purpose and meaning, those are things I *constantly* worry about.

What's the price of this catch-all agreement? Simply handing over your free will, identity, time and all ties and connections to your previous life.

A price that my parents were willing to pay.

CHAPTER 15

Technicolour Dream Coats and Lord of the Dance

'Where are you guys?'

Paz's voice comes through the phone strong and clear, like he's sitting in the truck, looking out on the highway with me.

'Indiana, it's beautiful,' I say.

I look at my reflection in the wing mirror, run a hand over skin that's been touched by a month in the American sun. It feels unbelievable to be on the road again. Out of London. Away from my 'real job'. Out of my two-bedroom flat. This highway makes me feel free.

'How are the guys doing?' Paz asks.

Georgia is in the back asleep and Seb's at the wheel. My new team. Georgia is young and made of stern stuff. She's the assistant producer – she does the research and takes care of all logistics. She's eager to soak up every minute of this adventure. And Seb is our camera guy, who has worked for Amnesty International, worked on documentaries in South America and seen his fair share of shoots. Both are in their early- to mid-twenties. They're keen and hard-working. Sofi is back in Berlin, taking on a new challenge of what she calls 'Social work + Techno', studying to be a systemic therapist with a sideline of DJ'ing – the kind of combination I love her for.

'They are good, really good,' I say.

Georgia grew up on a farm; she's often pigeonholed because of her posh accent, but she's got both darkness and depth to her. Dry-humoured, she's also fiercely intelligent and often hilarious. She lived alone in Columbia just before she started this job but had to come home to England to face family tragedy. She is strong, with a willpower and ambition that will see us through many a tough spot on this trip.

Seb is calm, handsome and kind. The kind of face you ask for directions. Half-French, he sports a tight afro. He is softly spoken, teetotal, conscientious. Because of his time with Amnesty International, he has been trained by the SAS for things like being kidnapped, torture and isolation. Things that he told me might come in handy during his interview. But on this trip, he is teaching me the art of switching off – by watching mindless rom-coms about working girls 'done good' and sitcoms featuring friends who live in quirky lofts.

'Nothing gets you out of a dark shoot or a bad day like a shitty rom-com,' he told me.

As much as I hate it, he's right.

'Paz, you know we have three days of *just* driving, don't you? You probably don't need to do our "safety calls" every day,' I say.

'We said every day so let's do every day,' he responds firmly.

To be honest, I *want* to talk to him every day, but the people pleaser in me worries about taking up his time.

'OK then, there's not much to tell. We're on our way down to Kentucky, we'll be there in a few hours.'

'Yee-haw!' Paz's northern British accent changes to a southern drawl. 'You know, it's illegal to have Religious Reptiles in Kentucky!'

Paz is a vault of bizarre information.

'Religious Reptiles?' I ask.

'It's been illegal to breed reptiles for religious reasons since the 1940s,' he says.

'Ah, you mean like the Serpent Handlers of the Holiness Movement,' I say, realising that maybe I'm becoming one of those weird vaults too, but on one subject: religious eccentricity.

Hands appear out of the clouds ahead. Slick snakes held by closed-eyed men, dangle slithering over the road on our horizon. I feel a surge in my belly.

We are going back *in*.

This has been a long time coming. Two years, in fact, since the last trip. And while it's felt like forever, it has been the right amount of time for me to sort myself out. Interviewing my parents had an effect on me that I wasn't expecting and so a two-year hiatus, while long, had been necessary.

Since the aftermath of the last trip, the physical, emotional and financial effects, Paz insisted on helping to produce this shoot. So instead of the gung-ho, gonzo-style shoot I did with Sofi, we have a solid plan, a schedule and most importantly, we've spent a year negotiating permission to film in the groups we are staying in. Between us, we have come up with strategies to keep us sane and safe on the road. We have codewords we send to Paz if something goes wrong, we have a satellite phone and every day, without fail, we call home for a check-up.

I have taken the last two years, as they say, to 'work' on myself. Sledgehammer-to-the-foundations type of work, with everything that I thought I had figured out, stripped back and laid bare. If this was a movie, you would get a montage of me going back to therapy, back to film school, out on commercial shoots, making documentaries, researching this trip, doing deep therapeutic work on trauma, grief and abandonment, honing my skills and revving back up to get to where we are now. Like a scene in *Rocky* or *The Karate Kid*. This time, I feel more prepared, I feel strong and I feel like I understand more of my purpose and reason for this journey.

I feel ready.

And these two years have given me more clarity on *who* I am doing this for. At first, I may have been making this journey for the adult that needed validation or answers. Now I know that I am *also* doing it for the child that was silenced.

*   *   *

The last month on the road has been hard work, but it's been wholesome, productive and fascinating too. We have just left a group called Rose Creek, a community that lives in a compound in the forests of Tennessee. They are essentially devout Christians who choose to live in fellowship in a cluster of homes off the grid. Rose Creek originally had loose ties with the Twelve Tribes and started their movement quite late in comparison to most of the groups I have studied or visited – the late-1980s, two decades after that initial boom of NRMs (New Religious Movements) and cults.

This group of about 200 or so followers used to be pretty 'out there'. At one time they wore bright kimonos that were an adaptation of Joseph's 'coat of many colours'. Locals would see them strolling through the poultry aisle at Walmart in their technicolor dreamcoats, carrying samurai swords. They even went through a phase of wearing medieval outfits, decking themselves in coats of armour and velvet dresses. But now, on the external (fashion), at least they have normalised – they wear regular clothes, live on farmland, keep horses, cows and hens, and have a small creek where the kids can swim.

They could just be a regular intentional community.

But when we dug a little deeper, researching this place, we heard rumours of mind control, brainwashing and child labour. I wanted to know more about a group that had been through that many twists and turns, that many identities, in such a short space of time: how do they manage the parents' desire for religious freedom and the delicate balance of raising kids? What drew them to their suits of armour and colourful kimonos?

We drive down a wooded path to a large white single-storey building. I step out the truck into sticky Tennessee heat, the buzz of mosquitos and crickets and the sound of people singing. There is no cross adorning the building, but this is clearly their place of worship. We are here for 'The Gathering'.

A pang of nerves hits me as we walk in – it's hot and crowded and feels even hotter with at least 100 eyes on us. My first impressions: shirt feels suffocating. The space is big but modest, with foldable chairs, plastic cups, sunlight and fluorescent bulbs battling against each other. The leader of the group, Nathaniel, introduces us and we are met with instant hugs from the kids and welcome smiles from the adults.

I look around at the singing crowd and notice how many different kinds of folks are here. A lot of groups thrive off collective identity – dress codes and homogenisation. Here, some people look church-ready: there's a family of rockers, some old folks from Chicago who look like they took a wrong turn on their way to Costco and a tonne of kids. Some are clean-cut, some covered in mud, wearing farm clothes, while others look like they are on a day trip from an Amish community.

The gathering goes on for almost three hours. People share their problems, songs are sung and then, surprisingly, they break into Hebrew-style dancing at the end. It seems a little out of place. Some kids didn't get the memo about the Hebrew choreography and flail about like puppets with broken strings. As the gathering ends and the crowd of adults around us dissipates, a couple of curious children hang around us like dogs round a dinner table.

'Hi,' I say.

A little girl takes this as her cue and pushes a picture into my hand that she has drawn as a gift.

'Did you enjoy the gathering today?' she asks me sweetly. Her name is Chaya, she is funny, articulate and very open.

'Yes,' I say politely. 'You guys have some great music.'

She smiles as she says, 'Well, if you ask me what *I* think about the gathering, I'd say BORING!'

I laugh, taken back by her bluntness. I see Georgia and Seb hold in giggles.

Perhaps pleased with her foreign audience, she goes on, 'Bring snacks. Plenty of things to do, colouring pencils, papers, because you are going to have to listen to people talk and you have to pay attention.' She puts her hands on her hips, looks me right in the eye and says, 'It's HOURS long, you know?'

I am nodding.

Yes, I know. I one hundred per cent know – *I just sat through it, kid.*

I love her already.

After the gathering, Nathaniel gives us a brief tour so we can get our bearings. He then splits us up and sends us to different houses on the compound, not so much houses as elaborate mobile homes. But you would never be able to tell once you're inside, they are spacious, beautifully decorated, with all mod cons. I move into Nathaniel's house – he is a charismatic and charming guy, a father, and one of the first members of this group.

I have a single bed made up with pink bedding. A small room tucked behind a laundry area, it's maybe the closest thing I have ever had to a child's bedroom. It's strangely comforting, having this little childlike space of my very own. For a moment, it doesn't feel like I'm standing in the midst of what some have called a dangerous mind-controlling cult, or even a gentle farming village. For a minute it feels like I don't have a single responsibility in the world – no team to lead, no film to make, there's nothing but me and this single pink bed. This thought is like taking a Xanax; I crash into the bed with my clothes on and fall into a deep sleep.

* * *

The next day, Nathaniel drives me around in his golf cart, explaining the commune in a deep, low, brilliant southern drawl. Every word he says sounds like the narration of a movie: 'This land was all barren when we got here.' Of course Nathaniel would say 'barren'. It's wonderfully *dramatic*, it's what the narrator of a movie *would* say.

We wake up at 5am to film the morning harvests, run out into the fields with the children to catch rogue pigs, feed horses and chickens. Over berry picking, we hear stories of where the kids plan to 'end up'. Some children want to stay on this farm, some have dreams of going to university and others just don't know yet.

Chaya sticks to me like molasses. We get lost in the woods, we go to a drawing class together and I find out from her what it means to grow up in Rose Creek. I learn how she feels about God – 'He has a cloak and a big moustache and a purple staff', what it's like to watch your mother giving birth in the living room – 'exciting, but gooey and slushy', and what happened when the authorities came to take the children away. She has opinions on everything, she's sharp and honest. One day, she even tells me why her parents came to Rose Creek in the first place: 'Mom and Dad joined because they were struggling with drugs and alcohol,' she says, matter-of-fact. Chaya's parents moved here perhaps to find their people, or structure and safety – this is a place where they can let their children run free.

Another family we spend time with used to be Mennonites before they joined Rose Creek: Mennonites are 'pure people', not permitted to sing, play music or even have flowers in their house (flowers are considered 'too proud'). They have 11 children and they came to Rose Creek in search of more freedom, while still having a belief system and community. In the Mennonites, they felt 'spiritually squashed'. I hear stories about how the mom had to hide her colourful quilts in case she was shunned and the first time her children heard music at Rose Creek, they didn't know what it was – they held their hands over their ears and cried.

I wonder who was playing guitar that day.

I look at these two families, the alternative rockers from Florida and the former Mennonites, and wonder if there is anywhere else in the world that they would live on the same soil. Would they have ever crossed paths or given each other the time of day? And yet here they are, sharing a life in the forest, their children growing up together. If the American psychologist Abraham Maslow was right about our hierarchy of basic human needs, this place takes care of a lot of them: they are fulfilling their potential by following God. They have their needs of belonging taken care of, they are one big family, loved in the name of Jesus. They are safe and secure in this compound and through working together, they have their physiological needs taken care of too: on a self-sustaining farm. And if one of the things we are put on this planet to do is to find connection, then surely these two families, who exist in the same space but should be worlds apart, show us that maybe there is something divine happening here.

*　*　*

It's our second week at Rose Creek and we're getting to know everyone by their first name. I have slowly built a history of the group cobbled together from the family dinners we've had, the golf cart rides with Nathaniel and the time spent with Chaya. The town hall is up ahead and in it is a visual history of the group, so it's the perfect place for me to show off what I have learned with Seb and Georgia.

We walk into the room that's normally stuffed to the seams with the community. The couple who moved here from Chicago because God spoke to them through their toilet. The woman who had five abusive husbands before making it to safety here, the young farmers who exist on a raw food diet because their little girl got cancer. All are welcome. But now the town hall is empty except for us and the thousands of photos on the wall that tell the story of Rose Creek.

'So, let's start here,' I say, pointing to a photograph of a prom king and queen; tanned and young, they're the classic American hot teen couple. They could be straight out of a TV show set in the Valley, where everyone drives soft-top Jeeps and says things like 'Ugh, *as if!*'

'Can you guess who this is?' I ask.

'No . . . no way!' Georgia says. 'Is that Rachel and Nathaniel?'

'Yup,' I say.

'Jesus! They were seriously hot, so . . .' she says, looking closer at the photo, 'that's marked 1988.'

'And then this is them in 1993.' I point to another photograph of a man wearing a long mantel and headdress, a woman standing next to him in a headscarf and tabard.

'Unrecognisable,' Seb says.

*   *   *

You couldn't get much further from *Beverly Hills, 90210* than the New Israel. It's such a stretch visually, such a leap to take from America in the 1980s – a decade of excess, cocaine, yuppies and phones as big as toasters. It's nothing like the seventies groups that seem to share similar ideas about the anti-establishment, anti-Vietnam and the cries of Revolution. The eighties was the decade when the hippies became (in Nathaniel's words, not mine) 'Hippie-crites'. When they gave up and got into capitalism. The eighties when prom kings and queens joined a travelling band of people proclaiming to be the New Israelites? It's such a stretch, especially for people *this* beautiful.

'This is where it all started, a place called Mashum Inn,' I say, pointing to a photograph of a rural farm.

The first leader of Rose Creek was Noah Taylor, who started an offbeat congregation in Florida. He wanted more than church on a Sunday, he wanted to live by the Lord. One of the current residents, Jeremiah, told me, 'Noah Taylor had a burden for the Church, the *real* Church that you read about in the Book of Acts – which describes how they took care of each other and how they helped those in need. Noah wanted to see that happen and had a tremendous amount of fervour to bring it to life. We knew that's where we wanted to go, but we really didn't have a clue how to get there.'

Noah had a best friend who lived in the Twelve Tribes – he had visited them many times and at one point almost joined them. But instead he decided to lead his own group. He gleaned what he liked from their beliefs, including the outfits, and started up the fellowship that would later be called Rose Creek.

Nathaniel told me about that time period: 'At that point we really didn't know what we were doing. All we knew was that we wanted more out of our relationship with God than what we were experiencing' and then he added, 'That was when we embarked on this journey and started learning.' He smiled as he said, 'Mostly by making mistakes.'

Mash'um Inn was a farm that a generous believer and friend gifted to Noah and his followers to live in. In the photos it looks scrappy, full of babies, men and women wearing the classic garb of the Twelve Tribes – headbands, long dresses, even the shofar is present in these pictures. Again, borrowed from the Twelve Tribes was the belief that the women should be covered so the men weren't distracted. As I look at the photos, I am instantly back with Sofi, wearing these exact same outfits – hotter than hell, itchy fabric, sweaty head coverings, picking kale in the Californian fields, breaking our backs and losing our minds.

Nathaniel told me, 'It's a little bit of a shock when you embark on a new journey, going in a different direction than the previous 25 or 30 years. Friends and family hear about the cults and Waco, etc. and they see us doing similar things and are genuinely concerned.' Waco is bound to be a big concern for people when it comes to groups like this, especially if you live in a compound in a part of the world where guns are so readily available.

'How did you explain it to them?' I ask.

'How could we when we really didn't even know ourselves?' he replied.

Nathaniel has a candour about him that I find extremely rare and really likeable. There is a humbleness to how he describes the group; there are even parts of their history he makes fun of.

So many of my interviews with people in groups feel like they are read off a script, entire conversations can feel that way too. I grew up with that feeling of living with people who have been programmed, where you never really get a glimpse of how they actually feel, what they're really thinking – you're always searching for that crack in the façade, looking for authenticity. But here, there is a humbleness, a willingness to admit when they think they fucked up, a desire to learn and grow from those mistakes. And that's refreshing – and rare.

* * *

'Why did they end up leaving Mash'um Inn?' Seb asks me in the town hall.

'Well, that's a bit of a mystery as I have heard a couple of versions of that story.' I lean in for this water-cooler moment. 'The story I heard from Nathaniel was that the guy who had let them stay in his house had visions of grandeur about being the Leader of the group and taking it over from Noah.'

A mutiny of sorts. This to me sounds perfectly logical: if you lend out your home, maybe you will get possessive or power dynamics come into play. I mean, haven't we all had tyrannical flatmates and landlords that take things too far?

'And what's the other story?' Georgia asks.

'Well, that I don't know much about, so it seems a bit salacious to even talk about. But one of the Teens told me that everyone had to leave because something happened with the guy's daughters, the one who had given them the land. The generous believer. Apparently, he demanded that everybody get off his land in the middle of the night after his wife ran barefoot into the woods with her two youngest children. But I don't know if it's based on any kind of truth.'

'God, that sounds quite dramatic,' Seb says.

I nod, then continue, 'And from there, they moved to Hadasha.'

Hadasha is the land that we stand on now.

Nathaniel had told me, 'What you see now is not what it looked like back then. It had been a cow pasture, it had been a pumpkin farm, it had been a lot of different things and so it was very sparse, there was no grass, there were no roads, it was pretty spartan. We were living in tents and buses and anything we could scrounge together.'

They lived like this for around three years and called it Camp Benjamin. At times, there were up to 500 people here.

Nathaniel told me, 'My kids still think it was the best time of their lives, they still talk about it. I would cook them meals over a fire outside and we'd sit out under the stars at night. It was freedom.'

It sounds kind of idyllic, but bonkers to think that this group, which by all accounts seems pretty 'normal' now, were living in tents on an old cow pasture with 100 kids in the nineties. Apparently, the local government and social services were none too keen on this set-up. Rose Creek was investigated by the Department of Child Services. Chaya had told me soberly, without prompting, 'Policemen came with vans with bars on the windows to take the children away.' They said there were issues with how the kids were being housed – it wasn't adequate, there was illegal electrical wiring, they didn't have any toilets, the food preparation areas were hazardous. And they wanted the documentation and immunisation of all the children. They gave the group 30 days to comply.

I point to a photograph of the tents and vans – it's labelled '*Living in the Benjamin Camp, we were falsely accused of child abuse by the system*'.

They moved out of Camp Benjamin and into the mobile homes they live in today. This is where Nathaniel tells me, 'I have to say, for a while we were focused on ourselves and our appearance to the community. Because of course everybody thought we were a cult, everybody thought we had two or three wives. There were all kinds of wild rumours going around.' So, they complied with the authorities' wants and the community's needs to become more 'normal'.

'The kids were interviewed and the policemen are now our friends,' Chaya told me, by way of summarising this time period.

Georgia points to a photograph labelled 'The Chosen' – 'What's this here?'

In the picture a group of teenagers are dressed in a modest dress code. The first decade of kids that were born into the group were called 'The Chosen'. In fact, they still are. When Nathaniel talks about his kids, we know exactly who he means as they are divided into 'The Chosen' and then the rest of them. Interestingly, it sounds like all the kids that were part of The Chosen, bar maybe two or three, are still a part of the group to this day. They are on missions or live in a commune splinter in another city, doing the work of 'The Lord' there. But the kids born just after The Chosen have all left except for two.

Are the oldest kids the ones more likely to toe the line?

Many believe that sibling hierarchy has a profound effect on our personalities and can influence everything from the career choices we make to the people we fall in love with. Older children, in Rose Creek's case, 'The Chosen', are typically responsible, confident and conscientious; they are more likely to mirror their parents' beliefs and attitudes. Apparently, eldest siblings pick every expectation their parents have and strive to please.

I think about my own family. Out of the 12 of us siblings, the only one who chose to follow in my parents' footsteps is my oldest sister, Ruth. She not only followed them, she surpassed them within the group, overtaking them in the rungs of leadership. Are these older kids following in their parents' footsteps because parents are more invested with their first children? More pumped about the idea of 'getting it right', full of piss and vinegar and the notion of doing something differently to how *they* were raised? I think about my dad. By the time he had his eleventh and twelfth kid, I barely recognised him as the same father. Like a deflated balloon, he just couldn't be bothered to bully or scream anymore. By then, he was a washed-out, tired-out version of himself.

A husk of the hard man we grew up with.

Seb, Georgia and I get to some photographs that are wildly elaborate, bursting with colour and activity. Now this next time period is when things started to feel surreal. For me at least, it looks like the community had joined forces with an overzealous amateur theatre producer. From an aesthetic perspective, it was full drama and over-the-top. They went from their Twelve Tribes-style outfits – bland and plain and modest – to the women abandoning their head coverings, to the mantles of Joseph, which became more and more extravagant. One of the Leaders, Jeremiah, showed me his own mantel; it was made of perhaps 20 different materials, long and heavy, brightly coloured and ornate.

'I would go to the fabric store and pick material that felt like "me",' he told me as I slipped it on. 'I guess I was a little more flamboyant back then,' he adds as I swing around camp-like in front of his full-length mirror.

I looked at this all-American burly man in front of me, wearing a shirt and khaki slacks, and tried to imagine him choosing the fabric for this fabulous, over-the-top coat. And why not? It's not the first time people have tried to distinguish their culture or beliefs through clothing. Look at the Buddhists, Sheiks and the outlandish outfits that Catholic priests wear. The Oshos wear red, the slightly drabber Mennonites wear blues, greys and browns, the Realian leader Real wore awesome bat-winged white shirts, medallions and pleated pants. The Scientologists have their seafaring naval-style uniforms. The Source family kept it simple and sexy in all-white. And no one seems to have taken it further from a fashion perspective than Ruth Norman, the leader of the cosmology group Unarius. The Bowie of the cult world, she wore rainbow capes with 3D planets sewn in, gold jumpsuits and platform shoes, primary coloured gowns and skull caps. If you're going to start a NRM or a cult, you are missing a trick if you don't get down the haberdashery store and 'see what feels like you'.

Nathaniel told me, 'This time period, we kind of can joke about it and laugh about it, but we don't look at it as a mistake. We look at it as a stepping stone to transition, a process of coming out of that phase to be able to see something different. And this was just one of those steps. But it was really a fun time.'

This is also when the more dramatic rituals started. Weddings would involve suits of armour and the new bride being 'captured' by her husband, thrown onto the back of a horse to signify the 'taking' of his wife. This ritual nearly went wrong 'only' once when the newlyweds were almost, but not quite, thrown from the horse.

They never did it again.

Then there was 'The Passage' – a march from one side of the land to the other, to signify a girl starting her period. Dressed at this point in medieval outfits and long, velvet dresses. A period drama, if you will. These photographs look like a LARPer's dream come true. I wonder what effect this might have on a girl; to have to have their entire community know that they have just started their period. There is a side of me that feels that

Western society's ways of dealing with it – in secret, with shame, whispering about 'tampons' – might not be the healthiest reaction. God knows, the way women are made to feel about all the insanely magical and irritating things our bodies go through is far from progressive even now. I just wonder how a 'Period Parade' would have made me feel at the age of 12. Would it be to celebrate the wonder of my body? Would it be to signify that my 'life's work' of having children was able to start? Would it make me feel like I was now sexually ripe for the taking, or would it be a moment of pride, a pure coming of age?

And then, in among all of this theatre, a fascinating change was brewing. This change might sound like it came from almost comical and maybe innocuous beginnings, but led to the rebellion and potential liberty of a lot of the teenagers who were living at Rose Creek. And it starts with Michael Flatley. Yes, *that one*. The Lord of the Dance. A man that I never imagined could be connected to a religious Tennessee compound.

Teens at this time were still in quite a strict regime. They weren't really allowed to mix with the opposite sex socially. There was a rigid, disciplinarian rule. But from my own experience, hoping that strictness ensures compliance and staves off rebellion doesn't always work. Whether you're in a religious community or not, it can be scary when teens start to kick against authority. It happens in most families. There will be rebellion. And rebellion came to Rose Creek too. In the form of the Riverdance.

Sitting in Nathaniel's house one night after dinner, he pulled out a VHS tape and asked, 'Do you want to see something quite profound?'

He turns the TV on and the screen fills with a dimly lit gathering, the camera placed at the back of the room, giving us a wide angle of the crowd sitting in a very large circle. They must have been told that *something* was happening, but I doubt they were prepared for *this*.

The room falls silent. And then ten boys file in; silhouetted, they stand with their shoulders tall, their heads proud. Then the sound of violins fills the room. Out of the two back corners of the frame, ten girls proudly walk in and take their places between the boys, perfectly lined up. The first beat comes in. One row stamps, the next stamps. A loud, defiant rally cry. Then the music swells in earnest and all 20 of these teens start to move in perfect – and I mean *perfect* – synchronicity. They are absolutely flawless. There is a steeliness to it and such pride in their movement. The thing about this moment, regardless of what you think of *Riverdance*, or cannot fathom how it made its way to a religious segregated commune that wasn't even allowed a TV at the time, is that it's not about the dance, it's about the rebellion.

It was the moment that each of these kids stood up and said, 'This is me.'

In the video, the teens were still wearing their modest outfits. While the image jars with the traditional Irish dance, it spoke volumes to me. It tells me the story of how many hours went into practising this dance in secret, it shows me how much bravery it would have taken to pull this out in public for the first time, knowing that it could have backfired. Watching this display of them showing their parents who they are, who they want to be, moved me. And the beautiful thing is, it also moved their parents. They were so overwhelmed by their children that this was the day that Nathaniel says things started to change for the teenagers in the group, from how they were disciplined to what they wore and the separation of the sexes.

By 2007, the photographs in the town hall depict a version of what we see today: kids are in trainers and T-shirts, working the land and being schooled at home. The group had relaxed. The Chosen had gone on to their own missions and the next set of young adults started to leave to join secular society. I can imagine that a lot of parents who raise their kids in segregated environments feel that they have failed if their children leave. And perhaps by God's tough standards, of raising a righteous new bride for him, or a generation that are pure, with one purpose, they *have* failed. But for me, if children have enough free will to leave, this might fail God, but it doesn't fail them – it doesn't fail free will.

And it makes me ask, is the parent's loyalty to God first and then to their children? For my parents, the order went like this: the group came first, then God and then us. The human truth is that this isn't an issue that exists solely within the confines of cults or religions, it's everywhere. To some degree, it's an issue for every parent who raises their child to 'be something' rather than to just 'be'. It's an issue for every kid that is held to expectations rather than just guided, for every predetermined fate, every kid that's labelled, or categorised.

But the big test is the second chance a parent gets, when they *choose* how to react when their kid finds their own path. When their 12-year-old comes out, when their 16-year-old chooses to skip university, join a band, stop going to mosque. When they choose not to have an arranged marriage. When their child becomes less than they expected. Do you hold on to them, or do you shun? Do you let love lead the way and decide that if God gave you this child, maybe your one job is to love them unconditionally?

When my sister Kate got pregnant was when she *knew* that she would get out. She swore she would not raise a child in that environment. How terrifying and fiercely brave for a 16-year-old to start to plan her own escape and new life for her unborn baby. She was shunned by not only her own parents, but her whole community.

But her mothering did not stop there: she became the mom of our family. Every time one of my brothers and sisters would be shown the door by my parents, Kate would take them in. Looking after her siblings as if they were her own with her now-teen children. The sacrifices she made will always astound and humble me. It's not easy to take in kids from a cult. You think they will be grateful and well behaved, but they are damaged, difficult and rebellious. *And* angry. I hear the same thing can happen with kids from foster homes and the like, where your expectation is the kids will be full of gratitude. But what you should expect is what you actually get – damaged kids with trust issues, who are filled with rage and rebellion.

It wasn't easy. Some of it was *proper* shit. But with Kate as guidance, they got there. And she helped raise some of the finest people I know. When my parents failed to give unconditional love, she took up the mantle.

Rose Creek experienced both. They had children who left that they shunned, but they later realised this was not the way that Jesus would act. Now, I am told, all the kids who have left are welcome here. That doesn't mean they all come back, but they know they are welcome – and that does mean something.

I asked Nathaniel what he would say to someone who wanted to start their own commune. What's the most important thing he's learned?

'So, the first thing to understand about a community is, you really don't know what you're doing and you'll probably feel like that most of the time. But if God's with you, everything will be fine.'

It's a pretty relaxed and humble reaction to building a commune.

We finish our history lesson just as magic hour hits Rose Creek, bathing it in golds and pinks. We walk through a farm so beautifully lit, it's otherworldly. The place comes alive with children. There are kids squealing with delight on the swings, turtles crossing the road in slow motion, teenagers in the coops collecting eggs. The family of former Mennonites are rounding up the horses at the bottom of the hill. I feel like I'm walking through a film set. Cue turtle, cue the horses, cue the laughing children running by.

It's peaceful, beautiful and alive.

* * *

On my last day, I hang out with Chaya. She shows me the hurricane containers – 'This is where we come when there are big storms,' she says.

We climb inside the big metal cubes, our voices echoing off the corrugated walls. She takes a seat on an upturned box and, realising it hasn't come up yet, I ask, 'What do you want to be when you grow up?'

And it hits me as I sit across from this curious young girl that this is the question that I was asked, when I was around her age, that changed everything for me in an instant.

She says to me, 'Well, lots of things. I want to be a photographer, or an artist, or maybe a dance teacher, but I'm not sure yet.'

I smile as I remember my own answer when Walter asked me the same question, when I knew so little of the world or what was available to me: 'I want to be like you, I want to be a journalist.'

I feel a pang of love for her and an instant wave of nervousness, the need to make sure that she is OK here. But is it Chaya that I am protective of, or myself at her age? Is there anything that I have missed about this place? Have I been blinded and love-bombed by these people, like so many others were by the Children of God and countless other cults?

I take a deep breath and ask, 'Can you tell me if there is anything that you hate about living here, anything that worries you? Or maybe something that you're scared of?'

She looks up at me with her big green eyes, a sense of seriousness in them.

'Yeah,' she says, 'there are few things I *really* don't like here ... .'

'Go on,' I say, taking her hand.

'Well, there are snakes and coyotes and spiders. And the worst part is, we're way out in the countryside so we don't get cable.'

CHAPTER 16

Sex Cult Girl: 2 Years Before

The sun hits my face as I carry a load of laundry out to the garden. The day is crisp, the sky spotless. Hundreds of socks bob around, clumsily choreographed by the wind on the washing line. This garden is massive; manicured lawns, gravel paths, bushes and hedges that need to be constantly sheared. At the end is a vegetable plot – we don't use it, but gooseberries grow wildly without encouragement. And at the back, right down past all of this, are the woods.

I squint in the sun and I can almost see her, her figure backlit among the gooseberry bushes. She slumps, with a sad walk, constantly looking for her child. A broken mother, trapped between worlds. Destined to be here forever.

The Lady of the Manor.

Why she chooses to wander among the gooseberries rather than the woods I will never know, it's best not to question paranormal worlds that lie just on the surface of the world we live in. Like clingfilm, see-through and close enough to touch. Invisible yet wrapped around everything. I feel like I could press a finger onto the film and pop it straight through. This old house has seen so many lives, so much sadness.

Will she ever be free?

'Oi!'

The word boots me out of my daydream.

'Oi!'

An English accent. Where is that coming from?

'Over here, Sex cult Girl!'

It's the local kids again. It's been a while since I heard their taunts and I'm not surprised by what they shout over the gate, not now that I have seen in black and white what has been written about us in the papers.

I wonder if I am actually a sex cult girl, I mutter quietly to myself as I peg the final sweatshirt on the line.

'Over here, Sex cult Girl!'

Then, as if I'm sleep walking or being pulled with an invisible string, I find myself moving towards the voice instead of away from it. No thought to the consequences of this waking dream. I push through the trees and in a small clearing, four teenagers break into chants of 'Sex cult Girl!'

'What?' I say.

'Fuck!' They jump up from their trance-like mantra, clearly shocked that one of 'us' is standing in front of them. 'Wow, you're here!' I think they would be less shocked if I was the ghost of the Lady of the Manor. Dressed in baggy jeans and plaid shirts in different colours, bowl haircuts, bleached hair, their look is almost uniform. One of them even has a cigarette dangling from his mouth.

Very worldly.

My voice comes out calmer than I expect: 'Well, I thought I might as well say hello.'

Two years of persistent cat calling and finally, someone has answered.

'Ah-ha, brilliant!' one of them says, standing up, eyes smiling.

'My name is Bexy,' I say.

The cigarette-smoking guy grabs my hand firmly and mutters from the side of his mouth, 'I'm Raffa!'

* * *

A few weeks have gone by and this is the third time I've met up with Raffa. It's afternoon and I have snuck out again. We sit in the front of his car, enveloped in the smell of petrol and rolling tobacco – it feels dangerous and grown-up at the same time.

'So, why do you all have American accents?' Raffa looks me dead in the eye as he asks me this.

I pause, just about to spew out a learned response. I stop and think.

What is the real answer?

It takes longer than I want to sift through the answers rolling through my head to get to the truth.

I hope I don't seem stupid.

'I don't know,' I say. 'I guess because the group started in America, all the adults are pretty much American.' I feel like I'm learning this as he is. He picks up on absolutely everything, everything that I see as normal, but when Raffa picks it up and looks at it, it's not normal anymore.

'But did you grow up there?' he persists.

'I grew up in India, Mauritius, Africa . . .' As I say it, it feels like every word coming out of my mouth is in a foreign language, one he has never heard before. Like every syllable needs explaining, like I'm speaking in tongues.

'I suppose it sounds complicated?' I offer.

'It's interesting!' he says enthusiastically.

'Is it weird?' I ask.

'Yeah, it's weird.' There is a kindness in his eyes as he laughs. 'But you're not . . . OK, maybe a little.'

I join in the laughter with him, but a prickle of shame runs through me.

* * *

Raffa is 18 and is a mechanic's apprentice. The car we are in is 'a Ford Escort' he told me. The sides of his head are shaved, a mop of long hair on the top. When he talks, he fiddles with his earring in his left ear. Raffa has all the tell-tale signs of a Systemite. But he seems kind, speaks softly. And cracks a lot of jokes, jokes often aimed at himself.

But the reason I have made this trip three times, even though I know it is reckless and dangerous, is because being around him makes all the hard edges of home soften. When I talk, it feels like I am the only person he wants to listen to. I sink into his front seat and every minute is an escape from them. When I am in this car, even though it's never for long, I feel like I might be worth something.

'Listen, I better go,' I say.

'You just got here,' he says.

'No, I have been here for 35 minutes. That's about my max before someone notices,' I say.

'Is there any way that you could get out for longer, or ever at night?' he asks.

'I'll think about it, I just don't want to get found out. Then I'd be truly *fucked*.'

As I say the word, it feels unnatural on my lips. Raffa laughs – maybe it sounded as weird as it felt to say it.

'See you,' I say as I slip out of his car.

* * *

Once a week, the adults have a meeting. Usually one to two hours long, it's where everyone over the age of 18 prays about new decisions, where they read the 'adults-only' Mo Letters and where they vote on stuff from the week. 'Should we buy a new car?', 'When should Auntie Lilly ask her mother for money?' . . . every decision has to be made by the collective. These meetings have existed for years. Because it's mandatory, it's the perfect chance for me to try sneaking out at night for the first time. Of course, because it's at night, the stakes are higher if I get caught. There can be no logical excuse for me being missing at night: no 'just taking out the laundry', no 'just recording songs for the family music tapes', no 'just putting some food in the outdoor freezer'.

My job during these meetings is to watch the sleeping kids. That's how I'm accounted for. I check on the kids – little mounds in their beds, snuffling under their covers. Sometimes their breathing falls into a rhythm as they sleep. I do the rounds: one room, then the next. They are all deeply asleep. I slip on my shoes and run through the route in my head for the seventh time. The meeting happens in the front room of the house and the road that leads to the outside runs exactly parallel to this room. It's pitch-black at this point; I know the route well enough, there is no way I can take a torch with me.

Far too dangerous.

Here goes . . .

Ten minutes later, I pull open the passenger door to safety.

'You made it!' Raffa says, his wide smile full of large, straight white teeth, illuminated by the light on the car door. That alone makes the run feel worth it. I can't say anything, I need to catch my breath, so I just smile.

'I almost gave up,' he adds, putting his hand on my knee.

'Well, it's quite . . . it's quite a run, to be honest,' I say, breathing heavily.

'I can tell! How long do you think you've got?'

'About 45 minutes.'

This time with Raffa will be gone in a heartbeat and soon I'll be running back through the dark and I'll pretend that the only part of the day that I really care about didn't happen.

'What are they doing in there now?' he asks.

'Ah, I wish I had something interesting to tell you about that, but they're just making decisions.'

'Ah, so no exorcisms or anything?' he murmurs sarcastically.

I laugh, but it's a short laugh as memories of hands all over me come back, the smell of that carpet, the crushing feeling in my chest.

'Do you want some of this?' he asks, holding out a cigarette, bringing me back to the front of his car, back into his smile.

'Sure,' I say.

He touches my hand as he passes it to me, the tips of his fingers hot against my skin. Then he grabs my other hand in his and says, 'Are you safe in there?'

There's not a whisper of a smile on his face.

'Safer than it's been in there for a long time,' I reassure him.

'What do you mean?'

I feel like he's not satisfied by this answer.

'I mean it's much easier than it was before and comparatively safe. Anyways, we don't have a lot of time and I don't want to talk about what's going on in there . . . it's boring,' I say.

'Ha! Bex, you live in a cult, how boring is that?' He laughs.

'It's boring for ME!' I say, fiddling with the edge of the car seat.

'So, what music can we listen to?' I ask clumsily, changing the subject.

Raffa has been giving me a guided tour of music. I wonder if he's more excited about showing me music than I am about listening to it. He'll play me something and watch my face as I hear it for the first time. It's like he's watching a baby trying solid food – confused, delighted and maybe a little hungry for more.

He leans into the glove compartment to get some music out and as he does so, his hair touches my face. He turns and looks me in the eye and then kisses me.

He tastes of cigarettes and chewing gum.

*   *   *

I am living a double life.

Slipping out. Being deceitful. On edge.

I ache for my minutes away from this house. The freedom that just 45 minutes with Raffa gives me. It's like nothing really happens or even exists until I have told him about it. I save up every thought, idea or feeling till the moment that I climb in through his passenger door.

And today, I have something HUGE to tell him.

For my entire life, our leader, 'Father David'/'Grandpa'/'Dad'/ 'Moses David' has been in hiding. Him, his wife Mama-Maria and his inner circle, they've been underground our entire lives. He is an enigma. I have never known where he lived, nor what he looks like. We have books that he's in, we have children's stories featuring him, we have the adult 'Mo Letters' with him on the cover. But while he's the star of every show, he is always illustrated – drawn – a cartoon. Even the photographs of him have drawn faces on them. Like a sticker stuck on his face while the rest of him is regular, a photograph, real hands, real clothes, real shoes, but always a cartoon face. He is depicted as a man with a long white beard and white hair, kind eyes. Usually he's wearing something like a bathrobe, sometimes it's see-through. If he does have his top off in an illustration, he has quite a muscular physique. Sometimes he is fully cartoon, other times he is drawn as a lion. But I have never, ever seen a real photograph of him.

I have never once laid eyes on the man whose words we read, worship and follow every day. He has written hundreds of books, thousands of 'Mo Letters'. He has dictated every single moment of our lives: how we should marry, how we should have sex – with Jesus, outside of marriage, with children. It's his words that proclaim how we discipline the children, how we should eat, how we schedule our lives, the education we are allowed, the books we are not allowed to read, the music we can listen to. He has retold us the history of the world, what the evil Jews are responsible for, how black people are cursed and also, how to support ourselves through our mothers trading their bodies for money. He has told us what to do with wayward Teens, about his dreams on a daily basis. He has told us about his bowel movements, when to flee from the authorities and when to fight back. He gave us our codes that protect us from 'them', he invented new languages for us, he foretold our future – that we would die as teenagers, that we would have superpowers, that we were the chosen ones.

There has not been a single day in my life when I haven't heard about what this cartoon white-haired man wants, demands or decrees. And every day, his words change our lives in some way. Sometimes dramatically, sometimes more insidiously, but always, we live on the wind of his whim. But today, I will see for the very first time, a photo of what he, our leader, looks like.

Because today, Moses David is dead.

It's my mom who delivers the news: 'Last night, I received a phone call from Mama-Maria . . .' her voice cracks. 'And she told me that Grandpa has passed on.'

Gasps reverberate around the room, one of the Aunties starts to wail. Visibly moved, my mom clears her throat and continues, 'We are one of the first homes to know about this. While the others will be told over the next few days, our job is to prep for the Press.'

As the room sits in prayer and gives thanks for our leader's life and work, I remember how Grandpa once wrote, 'I wouldn't be surprised if you would want to commit suicide when I die. In fact, the Lord would forgive you for it, if you wanted to be up in heaven with your papa.'

He felt that this day would be *that* devastating, that we would all want to take our own lives.

But today doesn't feel like a day for mass suicide. No guns, no plastic bags on heads to be with Papa, like the other group they told us about who had committed suicide. Instead it just feels like a day of quiet mourning for the home.

My mom finishes on, 'Our job is to prepare our statement and expect another Press onslaught.'

My day is set out for me: faxing the statement about David Berg's death.

Mom's voice gives out orders and then fades into nothingness when I see it. On the table, next to the press release.

'Mom, is this him?'

'Yes, that's our Father David,' she says, wiping her face as another tear falls from relentless ducts.

Under the photo it says, '*David Berg*'.

'Is that his real name?' I ask.

'Not his *real* name, his legal name.' She smiles.

I hold the photo in my hand. He is not a lion, he is not a muscular man with a full beard and kind eyes – he doesn't even have a full head of hair. His eyes are sunken. I mean, really sunken, like they're moving into the back of his head. He has no eyebrows, he is balding – in fact, you can only see his hair coming back behind his ears. He has liver spots all over his face, a missing tooth. And he is smiling. But there is something about his smile and when I think about all the things that we have done and endured in his name, that smile makes me feel sick.

*   *   *

'Raffa!'

I'm out of breath, as always.

'What?' he says, looking worried.

'You're not going to believe this! Moses David is dead!' I almost shout.

'What?' he says.

'You know, Moses David.'

'Yes, I know his fucking name, Bexy! What does this mean? Does this mean you're free, that you can get out?'

As he says this, I realise that perhaps he wants me out of there as much as I want to leave.

'I saw a photo of him today,' I say.

'You've never seen him before?' I feel disbelief in his eyes.

'Never,' I say, shaking my head.

'What does he look like? I bet I can guess,' he says.

'Honestly, I had a vision of him and what he looked like my whole life, but when I saw him today, you know, he looked wrong,' I say.

'I'm not being funny, Bex, but if half the stuff that I have read is true, he was a fucking creep! More than that, he was an insane perverted paedophile who should have had his nuts sawn off years ago.'

I look up from my lap to his face – he's not saying this to be funny, he means it. Then I feel shame run through me as I think of the news clippings.

'How much have you read?' I ask, looking back down into my lap.

'Enough. My parents have kept every article,' he says.

'Oh.' I think of all the energy I've put into underplaying everything to him, trying to look normal.

'Look, nothing has *ever* happened here before. Can you blame them?' he says.

I wonder if he feels my humiliation. As I remember the effect the articles had on me, my cheeks burn as I imagine Raffa's parents reading them.

'You know, some of it is exaggerated,' I say, trying to claw back from the embarrassment I feel.

'Did the moms have to be prostitutes?' he asks kindly.

'Well, when you say it like that, yes,' I say.

'Did he believe that it was OK to molest kids?'

Again, there is no bite in his question and yet still I feel like I'm on trial. A trial that is happening in a parked car, 100 metres away from the scene of the crime, *my home*.

'Bexy, you know you are the victim in this,' he says.

'It's complicated,' I say back – because it is.

'It seems pretty black and white to me. I'm *glad* that piece of shit is dead, Bexy. I'm fucking glad!'

He grabs me and pulls me into his arms. I feel strangely rigid, my voice almost mechanical as I say, 'I need a plan.'

'What, babe?' he says.

'I'm going to leave. But I don't want to be stupid about it. I can't just run away or not have money or not have a plan. I need to get out, but I want to be smart.'

He looks at me and smiles as he says, 'Now we're talking! How can I help?'

* * *

A few weeks later, Raffa says he has a surprise for me.

It's Saturday morning. A beautiful hot day in May, it smells of summer, the kind of warm, itchy breeze that gets in your nose and makes it twitch. I sit in the passenger seat of Raffa's car, breathing in the familiar smell of petrol and cigarettes. A smell that I have grown to love.

Even years later, I will still love it.

'Put this on,' he tells me as he hands me a motorcycle helmet.

'Huh?' I say.

'It's either that or you can get in the footwell or on the back seat. I don't want you spotted by any "culties" in town.'

He laughs as he says this but I know he's serious.

I put it on and then start to wriggle out of baggy trousers into the shorts I have hidden underneath. The helmet turns me into a top-heavy lollipop and I smack my head on the dashboard loudly.

'Smooth!' he says, laughing.

My self-consciousness melts with his laughter.

'Where are we going?' I ask, my voice muffled inside the helmet.

'It's a surprise.'

He smiles again.

We drive through twisting country roads, past bright yellow fields and then pull up to the gate that says 'KEEP OUT' in big red letters. He pulls my helmet off and gives me a quick kiss.

'You excited?' he asks, smoothing my hair down for me.

'Uh-huh,' I say.

His eyebrows raise as he smiles – he clearly is.

We drive down an old dirt road with arms of underbrush and trees growing over it. A canopy of green so thick, I can see only slivers of the sky. It's like driving through a wooded tunnel across time, or maybe into another world. Then, I see it: a huge quarry surrounded by grey cliffs, dark like granite. Clear water reflects the vivid sky and broken-up clouds magically mirror on its surface, like the heavens are bursting through a hole in the ground.

'Shall we?' says Raffa. He seems pleased, his hand pushes my mouth shut.

We take off our shoes and walk down a thin path to a piece of rock that juts out into the sun. He pulls out a blanket, some sandwiches and two beers – it feels like a banquet.

'Let's get in,' he says.

'I didn't bring a swimsuit,' I say (I don't even own one).

'Who cares about that? Just do it in your pants,' he tells me.

'How do we get in?' I ask.

'We jump,' he says.

'From here?' I ask.

'Yeah, it's not that far down,' he says.

He must feel my fear. I look over the side of the rock – it's about a 30-foot drop. I see a path that goes down to the water.

He notices my eyeline and says, 'Come on, this will be more fun.'

'OK,' I say.

I strip off, very aware of how pale I am in this sun, almost reflective, and how skinny I must look to him. He is in his boxers, baggy with hotdogs printed on them. They look silly, but he doesn't care – he seems so comfortable in his brown skin. He takes my hand.

'Don't be afraid.'

'I'm not.'

(OK, I am.)

'Ready? One, two, three . . .' he says and we leap off the side of the rock.

We take flight.

Suspended between two worlds, it's just for a few seconds, but in that moment, in that suspension, it's like only the two of us exist. There is nothing else: no group to go back to, no scary plans to leave. My past, my parents and my future disappear in that leap, in those few seconds of nothingness and everythingness. My body, brain and soul are alive, not confined or muted.

I am free.

We slam into the water, my body descends a few feet into the icy quarry. Liberated by the lake's healing baptism. Through the bubbles, I see Raffa's face underwater. He smiles, then grabs me and pulls me to the surface.

'You OK?' he asks.

'FUCK! YEAAAAHHHHHH!' I scream.

We lie in the sun, my head in his lap. He tells me about coming here as a kid and how it used to be, that it's a secret now, we can stay all day. I look up at the clouds – I feel safe, I feel loved. I mouth the words: *I feel free.*

He wipes a tear from my cheek with his thumb and asks, 'Are you OK?'

'Yes.'

The word comes out in a low whisper.

'I think this might be the best day of my whole life.'

And I mean it.

CHAPTER 17

The Towers: 18 Years After

Sometimes I ache for the city.

This journey has taken me through both the East and West Coasts of America. From the deserts of Arizona to the forests of Alabama, the Red Rocks of California to the Rivers of Mississippi. And while my truck window has framed the landscapes of more than ten states, it rarely sees the lights of cities: religious communes almost never choose urban set-ups.

Almost never.

Georgia, Seb and I are en route to the Jesus People USA, who live right smack in the middle of Uptown Chicago. We have exchanged miles of trees for thousands of feet of skyscrapers. This alien environment sends a tingle of excitement through me. Dusk falls as we drive towards Uptown, gold lights create filmic silhouettes in the bars, the streets swap commuters for revellers and warm air invites people to drink on the sidewalks.

'I could murder a pint!' I say longingly.

But the thought is fleeting, I am eager to get to the JPUSA. Their commune is housed in a 500-room art deco hotel called The Friendly Towers that others have named 'The Towers of Hell'.

I glance at my watch: it's nearly 6pm.

'They cool with us coming tonight?'

Georgia, who looks as captivated by the street scenes as I am, doesn't break her gaze as she says, 'Yeah, they've invited us to dinner – BBQ.'

The JPUSA have physical and historical connections to the Children of God. Both groups were born out of the Jesus Movement, the American phenomenon that started in the late sixties and lasted until the mid-seventies. This was a time when a lot of young people truly believed that they would be the last generation on the planet and many felt that drugs, sex and alternative ideologies weren't working so the kids were turning back to Christ.

The Jesus People scene took root in Southern California, with over 100 churches, coffeehouses and communal homes as part of the movement. The children of the establishment, who were mostly white and from well-to-do families, rejected everything their parents had worked for, from the pay checks to the personal hygiene, and were now rebranding Jesus as a hippie.

For the Press, this was *gold*.

By June 1971, the Jesus Movement was on the cover of *Time* magazine. It's a brilliant cover – in fact, I have it framed on my wall. It could be a psychedelic band poster. Jesus is created pop art style: in shades of purple set against a red background, the words 'Jesus Revolution' make up his halo. And inside the magazine, it just gets better.

'Fresh-faced, wide-eyed young girls and earnest young men,' the *Time* reporters wrote, 'badger businessmen and shoppers on Hollywood Boulevard, near the Lincoln Memorial, in

Dallas, in Detroit and in Wichita, "witnessing" for Christ with breathless exhortations. Christian coffeehouses have opened in many cities . . . a strip joint has been converted to a "Christian nightclub" in San Antonio. Communal "Christian houses" are multiplying like loaves and fishes . . . Bibles abound.'

This injection of press exposure helped the scene explode across the United States. Even pop stars started converting, from Johnny Cash, Jeremy Spencer and Eric Clapton to Paul Stookey. But one of the most interesting parts of JPUSA's history to me is *who* started the group. Among new religious movements, it's rare for a woman to be the leader. Not just rare. It's almost unheard of.

'Out of thousands of different groups, Sheela Osho is the most famous woman at the wheel of a New Religious Movement: The Oshos of "Wild Wild Country" fame. Known for wearing red, and cathartically tripping out on dance and meditation. While Rajneesh was undoubtedly the messianic leader of that group, Sheela led the group with a powerful hand. She was the Maggie Thatcher of cult leaders, a strong, powerful matriarch.'

I feel that our understanding of cultic leadership overlaps heavily with toxic masculinity: the objectification and commodification of women, control over reproductive freedom, women being 'second rate' citizens, reduced to a workforce. However, there's frequently a kind of Girl Friday behind male cult leaders. They are the matriarchs, sympathisers, lovers and silent lieutenants.

Who are the lovers and lieutenants? Moses David had Mama-Maria (Karen Zerby), who took over leadership when he died in 1994. Bonnie Nettles co-founded Heaven's Gate. Jim Jones had Carolyn Layton, his lover for a decade and a woman

who was instrumental in the massacre at Jonestown. Hak Ja
Han married Sun Myung Moon, the founder of the Unification
Church, who still runs it now. Warren Jeffs had Naomi Jessop,
his 'favourite' wife, who stuck by him during his sentencing for
child abuse. Still, the stories of women in religious leadership
are often downplayed, disregarded or retold to the extent that
their power isn't even perceived as such. When I think back to
my own childhood, I saw my mom as a passive entity, feeling
the constant need to protect her, and that she was perhaps 'one
of us' rather than 'one of them'.

*Was I stripping her of her own agency, or was she as complicit
as my dad? Was she his Girl Friday?*

So, against all odds, here we are en route to the Jesus People
USA, which started out as the Jesus People Army and was led
by Linda Meissner, a female evangelist and spiritual leader in
her own right.

Linda's history is quite an interesting ride. Born on a small
farm in Iowa, she started her mission for Jesus in New York
City, where she traded idyllic fields for litter-strewn streets and
dilapidated squat houses. Brooklyn was dangerous, murder was
rife and Linda's targets were young people in gangs. A pretty
punchy and brave mission for a 19-year-old. Linda was not
immune to danger; she was attacked at knifepoint many times
and one night, a gang even tried to blow her up by planting
bombs on her preaching spot.

Then she went from evangeliser to evangelist.

Linda had a vision that would change the course of her life:
Jesus standing over the skyline of Seattle as she heard the words,
'There He stands with healing in His wings.' She had a new mis-
sion and the beginnings of a movement started to sizzle.

Immediately, she started to look for a base in Seattle and found a spot on North 45th Street that she called 'The Ark'. Before too long, she had a 60-person strong 'witnessing' team that invaded the parks, beaches, projects and university district to preach to the youth.

She called them the 'Jesus People Army'.

They were mobile and they were fresh. The Jesus People Army preached at music festivals, wearing T-shirts with Jesus slogans printed on them. They had a radio show and a magazine called *Agape*; they were growing in numbers, strength and ingenuity using the same tactics that revolutionaries across the country used to spread the ideologies of radicals like Karl Marx. They went from 'The Ark' to a large warehouse called 'The Catacombs Coffeehouse'. From 60 followers, they were soon preaching to thousands a night. From handing out the *Agape* magazine to passers-by, they started flying planes over music festivals, dropping the publication on people from the sky.

Jesus bombing.

When Linda preached, she would demand dramatically that a barrel be brought up on stage. She would challenge her audience to throw their sins into the barrel to burn – and they did. They threw their drugs, occult magazines, nude pictures, booze and cigarettes into the fire. One night, $12,000 worth of drugs burned in this barrel and the story hit state and national press. CBS Television came to film, *Time* magazine published an article.

Linda Meissner wanted disciples, not just converts – a last days' army to spread the gospel across the world. Her intensity attracted people who were aching to commit to something real, total and lasting. At its peak, the JPA numbered an impressive 5,000 members.

I went back in time through the JPUSA footage on the nights leading up to our visit, to the early eighties and nineties. Back then, Uptown Chicago was no joke when it came to crime and addiction; thousands upon thousands of people were in need. The city was in the midst of a severe housing crisis and in response, JPUSA started a mission to help the homeless. They wanted to do what they thought Jesus would if he lived in Chicago – not shy away from the darkness and need, but plummet into the depths to bring light.

By 1989, JPUSA's mission was fully realised. They bought 'The Friendly Towers', a 500-room, art deco hotel, which gave housing to single men and women, mothers and their children. But this introduction into the JPUSA and their mission, the old hotel they bought and Uptown Chicago, really doesn't give a full idea of their vibrant essence.

The JPUSA that the footage shows are scrappy, messy, alternative misfits, like the love child of a Janis Joplin and Iggy Pop. 'Right on', but with dreadlocks, blue hair, piercings and way more attitude. A young brunette talks about how she'd been suicidal since she was 12 years old before she found her place here; a ponytailed, beefy man tells how he has 'done time for burglary, stabbing, drug-related crime' before joining and a fresh-faced young girl talks about being heavily into hard drugs as a pre-teen, but now she is clean and in Jesus' service.

In the nineties, The Friendly Towers had queues of homeless and addicts snaking around the block, all hoping to be fed. Drunks would sleep on their front lawn and people who had driven hundreds of miles to see them would camp out overnight in their cars, up and down the street. The Jesus People got their hands dirty and in fact, they looked dirty – greasy, unwashed, with an attitude that radiated, 'Fuck it, we're doing the Lord's work!'

There is a part of me that respects that. The fact that they modelled themselves on a radicalised version of Jesus, unafraid, living in an area where shootings literally happened on their front doorstep. They didn't hide in the countryside, preaching, 'We must be pure, raise pure children and prepare for Jesus to return' or hole up in the woods, proclaiming, 'We shall be separate and not be influenced by the world.' They said, 'Jesus hung out with prostitutes, sinners and, *worst* of all, a reformed tax collector,' and they wanted to do the same.

Which, for a commune, is pretty radical.

And at the same time as these queues snaked around the front, around the back of the hotel are the children of the JPUSA: kids playing basketball, teenagers looking after babies and children flying about on roller skates. And physically dividing and uniting these two scenes is the hotel itself: home to the mission, the homeless *and* these kids.

And tonight, we pull up to The Friendly Towers, with all this history behind it, to stay in the hotel with the JPUSA.

*   *   *

I walk in to echoes of conversation bouncing through the marbled reception – bright, light and with an old-school grandness to it. It's said Al Capone used to stay here and there are secret tunnels he used to shuffle Marilyn Monroe in and out. I imagine the aroma of his cigars, the clacking of her heels sashaying around in this art deco building. But today, under a beautiful skylight, senior citizens roam, kids cycle through on bikes and teenagers cram themselves into the ancient lifts to get up into the Towers.

'Hey there, how y'all doing?' a woman dressed all in black behind the reception asks.

'Good, thank you. We're the film crew that are going to be staying with . . .'

'Yeah, I guessed that.' She laughs huskily, pointing to our kit before looking us up and down, all the while playing with her septum ring. 'We're all out back. Come along, hope you're hungry.'

Following her through to the courtyard is like stepping inside the JPUSA footage: a parallel universe. The smell of burgers hits me, mustard and smoke, laughter and conversations overlapping each other. Kids fly about on roller skates, basketballs pound on concrete.

We are really here.

We walk past clusters of pierced rocker-style hipsters with wide-brimmed hats, wearing all black. I can imagine interviewing these guys backstage at a festival. We stand in the queue for food amid blue hair, pink hair, dreadlocks, tattoos and big chains. As I pile bread and coleslaw onto a paper plate, I notice two girls, about 14, sitting by themselves, drawing quietly.

A weird, out-of-place, calm moment.

'See them?' I say, nudging Georgia.

'Ya huh,' she says, without looking up.

One of the girls has braces, thick, long black hair and a sereneness radiating from her.

'I want to meet her,' I say.

We are then swept up by Neil Taylor, one of the leaders of JPUSA and the head of public relations. Grey-haired, smooth-talking, slick, his words trickle out of a semi-smile. A talent for TV presenters and the media trained.

I'd *love* to be able to talk through a semi-smile.

My face betrays every emotion I am feeling and some I am not. Right now, I just have to make sure it doesn't reveal *shutdown* from being 'shown' around by the head of PR – first-hand experience of this makes it hard for me to engage. As Neil gives us the 'official' tour, I lose myself in the pockets of realness we move through: clusters of people roaming the hallways, girls playing guitar in the atrium, people on clean-up duty, banging pots and pans in the kitchen, and moms dragging laundry down into the basement. In the main dining hall, across the walls are thousands upon thousands of photographs. Children, bands, festivals, parents, road trips, even stuff dating back to when they were starting out in Linda Meissner's time, when they had the 'Jesus People' bus – it looks just like the one my parents went to Amsterdam on.

And as we finish the tour, Neil opens a door to a woody-smelling dorm crammed with bunk beds.

'You don't mind all staying together, do you?' he asks.

At this point we have shared everything from toothbrushes to pants so this dorm is the least of our worries. We make a promise to meet first thing in the morning for the rest of our tour.

The close sounds of sleep mix with the noise of the city: horns in the distance, voices on the street. I lie in bed, lost in the pine slats that hold Georgia suspended above me. Pieces of wood that meld together the bed and my memories of a childhood in countless dorms, my bottom bunk in the Twelve Tribes and now here.

*   *   *

We start the next day in JPUSA's coffee house. Chipper and bright, Neil talks us through the different beans and types of coffee. I might just be on a barista's tour rather than a religious commune. Neil walks us through their offices and the printing shop, where the magazine *Cornerstone* is produced. He takes us into the kids' schoolroom. Light streams into a now-empty study space, with different-size chairs and work that seems to belong to all ages hanging on the walls.

Neil wants us to meet Jon, who he describes as an archivist and historian, saying we'll get 'an excellent history of JPUSA from him'. I steel myself for what I'm sure is going to be more whitewashed PR, prepping my face with that contagious semi-smile.

'The Jesus Movement is bigger than is usually advertised. It's bigger than the borders set by a lot of scholars. It was a culture-wide spiritual awakening.' Jon seems quite excited to have an audience, his words come out with genuine passion. 'And it ended up going in different directions. It was also quite complicated. There were overlaps with other movements, charismatic movements, with social activists' movements.'

'Yes, I know,' I say, nodding.

'I was told you grew up in a group; which one was it?' asks Jon.

Even though I had told the JPUSA my history before we got here, this question surprises me.

'The Children of God,' I say.

He inhales sharply. 'You're kidding?'

I'm even more surprised by his reaction.

'Nope, deadly serious.'

'Do you know about *our* history with the Children of God?' he asks.

I shake my head.

'Well, they are kind of considered like locusts or termites here, one of the darkest groups that has existed.'

His voice becomes almost a whisper as he tells us that when things were at their most powerful for Linda Meissner and the Jesus People Army, right at the start, when they had the barrel for burning narcotics, when they had articles about them in *Time* magazine and were featured on CBS, things took a dramatic dark turn.

Linda herself says, 'This was a true revival and I wish I could say that my part in it continued until this day, from glory to glory. Alas, now we reach a sad, but equally important part of my story. I share this so that you, the next generation, will avoid making the same mistakes that I did.'

Jon looks at me soberly and says, 'And at the heart of this was the Children of God.'

At the time, CBS made a documentary – 'The Children of God' – which aired on *60 Minutes*. They presented a positive picture of the group living on their Texas ranch. It was so popular, the network showed it twice. Linda watched it and felt that they had exceptional music, were well organised and just another 'on fire' group of young people for Jesus. She invited them to play at the Catacombs café, which wasn't unusual – they had a different musical group play there every night.

Jon tells us, 'When the Children of God arrived, we thought they had come to perform on the stage. In reality, they had another agenda in mind: a hostile takeover of the JPA.'

Allegedly, Moses David had told his daughter, Deborah, to introduce herself as the Leader of the Children of God to Linda. Deborah was a young, charismatic and seemingly terrific leader. Linda was excited to talk with her and totally unprepared for what happened next.

The team from the Children of God divided the Leaders of the Jesus People Army and spent the entire night convincing them that the only *real* group that would make change and start a revolution was the Children of God, saying they should join immediately – and it worked. Almost all the leadership from Seattle and Tacoma walked out at the end of a 12-hour meeting with the Children of God. As if the Children of God was a Venus fly trap, swallowing the entire JPUSA whole, the Children of God didn't just want their leaders, they wanted to dissolve the entire group into their own.

Retrospectively, Linda felt that Deborah, who presented herself as an angel of light, was actually brainwashing her.

The drama surrounding the split in the Jesus People Army caught the attention of the mass media, who reported that Linda had joined the Children of God. The story went national on the Associated Press. There were apparently even fights on the steps of the Catacombs when some of the Jesus People Army were denied entry by the Children of God, who were now claiming the venue as theirs.

Sounds more like a mafia takeover than a religious experience.

I feel like Jon is almost apologising for this story as he tells it, as if he is sorry to be the one bearing the news, as if this might be the first time I hear of the damage my group has done.

Linda was sent to Europe, where she preached in the Children of God's name up until David Berg's letters about 'free sex' came out. That was her wake-up call and she left that very week. But she had abandoned her followers in the Jesus People Army and was now left with nothing.

'So, did Linda re-join the Jesus People Army when she left the COG?' I ask.

Jon shakes his head – 'She started her own mission in Denmark.'

Maybe she was too ashamed to come back.

I feel for Linda in that moment. She started with such brilliance and with pure intentions, zeal and a mission. And she was completely annihilated by the Children of God, wolves in sheep's clothing. She was also betrayed by a woman – Deborah – pretending to be the Leader. Someone who she possibly felt an affinity with, maybe had a strong connection to, both being female leaders of 'on fire' religious groups.

'Did Linda ever speak to anyone again from the COG?' I ask.

'Apparently, in 1988, she got a call from Deborah, weeping, saying she had lied and that if she had told her the truth about her father, Moses David, Linda would never have joined,' Jon tells me.

I know Deborah had defected from the Children of God by that time and in fact wrote a book and exposé on her father. I've read the book so I know that the other thing Deborah had been hiding at the time was not only had her father *already* come out with the new sexual practices for the leadership, but he was actively trying to take his own daughter on as his wife. He had been sexually abusing her for years, she says. This was at the time when my parents had joined, when Moses David was living in that cul-de-sac, already in hiding. The stark cruelness of family dynamics, power and abuse at play. Moses David managed to have his daughter under his control for so long, preaching in his name and even persuading other young people to follow him. All the while, he was violating her behind the scenes. I feel empathy for Linda and my heart breaks for Deborah too.

No one came out of this OK.

'And then, Deborah begged Linda for forgiveness on the phone,' Jon continues.

I hope it felt good for Linda to at least feel this sense of validation of her experience, even though it wouldn't change what had happened.

'And did she forgive her?' I ask.

'Of course she did,' he says.

* * *

It's late afternoon by the time that Neil takes us back up into the hotel. We walk down giant corridors, filled with yellowy tones, the smell of old hotel carpet. The long halls have what seem like hundreds of doors on each side, the sides of each decorated by the teens or kids that live within, signs with their names on, stickers everywhere – quotes from the Bible give a mark of personality.

Neil's voice is a little like pleasant background static as I slip into my imagination, which whips around the hotel and into the worlds that lie behind these doors.

'You know, the whole idea of living in community is unpleasant.' Neil's voice snaps me back into range.

Huh?

'I live here because of how much I love the people that I live with, even though everyone is terribly irritating and I'm included in that. But there are wonderful moments of connection and of transparency, and there's always support when you're going through a difficult time.'

I know what he's saying is true, even though I experience the spin of PR on the sentiment. There is something surprisingly wonderful about people living together and supporting each other.

As he continues down the hallway, he says, 'We used to have a floor for people in need, but now it's just us and then on the top floor, we run a home for senior citizens.'

'So why did you stop housing the homeless?' I ask.

'If you're trying to lead me into the topic that we agreed we wouldn't talk about, then let me just stop you right there.'

I shiver at the cold drop of his tone. The 'topic' he's referring to is a court case the JPUSA are in with some former members. In our negotiations before we arrived, it was agreed we were not allowed to ask about the court case or any of the factors that might have led to it. The 'topic' is completely out of bounds.

'Apologies. I really wasn't trying to manipulate in that direction,' I say.

Have I accidentally stumbled on the reason for the court case? Perhaps mixing addicts, the homeless and the rest of the commune was the issue? Is that why he shut me down?

Is that why some people call this place 'The Towers of Hell'?

Then I spot her, the teenage girl with the dark hair and braces, way up ahead. She looks over her shoulder, smiles and then disappears through a door.

Later on, after Neil's guided tour comes to an end, I take the lift back up to the third floor, walk back down the hall of signs, kids' names and stickers and knock gently on her wooden door.

'Hey!' She smiles as she opens the door. 'You're from the film crew?'

'Yes,' I say. 'Sorry to just knock like this, it's just I wondered if I could see what a typical teenager's room looks like?'

As the words come out of my mouth, I hope they don't come across as creepy as they feel.

'Well, I wouldn't say that mine is a typical room,' she says with a chuckle. 'Not everyone keeps a reptile farm next to their bed.'

* * *

Her name is Savannah, she is 15 and was born here. She has lizards, tadpoles and is breeding two types of cricket, all housed in her small room in this hotel. Next to her bed, she keeps jars of spiders and tells me she wants to be a scientist or a biologist when she grows up. She pops open one of the jars and allows the spider to stretch its legs on a walk up her arm as she tells me that she doesn't go to school here, but in a secular establishment a couple of blocks away.

'What do you tell the kids you go to school with about this place?' I ask, helping her sort food (dead bugs) for her crickets.

She laughs and says, 'Well, I have to be careful how I describe this place because if I get it wrong, people think we are a cult, which we are not. I say we live in a hotel, we run homeless missions, there are 500 of us here, we are a church, we share our money with the group and that the group takes care of us.'

'I suppose it does sound a bit complicated. Because you don't sound like a church if you all live off one pot of money and under one roof,' I say, thinking about how complicated it was for me to explain my life when I first left, and so I didn't for years.

'Yeah, I'm getting better at it now, though,' she says.

She tells me familiar stories about how her parents joined in the late seventies, how they heard the call from God and were 'saved' – the exact same story of enlightenment that I hear about most adults who join groups so I ask her what's different for teenagers about this place.

'Well, for starters, we're the only ones who go up on the roof.'

I follow her up to the top of the building, where the roof touches the incredible skyline of Chicago, where the stars meet the skyscrapers and the air feels lighter, even though this is inner city.

It's magic – and it's their own.

She tells me what it was like to be a kid at school here and how hard she found 'that kind of learning'. Her grades slipped to the bottom of the pile. Then she did something she had never done before – she left the commune by herself and went for a walk with no destination in mind. On autopilot, she found herself standing at the gates of a local school, just staring in. A security guard noticed her and took her to the headmistress's office. Savannah told her that she wanted to go to school there – 'I kind of said it without thinking. I didn't know why I felt so depressed before, but then it all seemed to make sense.'

At sunset, we take a trip to Lake Michigan with Savannah. We meet up with kids from the Towers as the sand turns light blue. Laughter echoes from every direction as they bury each other in the soft beach sand and crack jokes about 'going to each other's houses' (across the hall). It's intimate and so familiar to me in some ways: coming of age in a commune, sharing space, hormones, food, everything. And it seems normal here, tonight, too. But perhaps *what you know* is what's *normal*. The water shimmers, reflecting Savannah as she plays volleyball, laughing, almost airborne. She seems happy here.

*   *   *

Later, I pull back the covers on my bunk bed, tired, and pleased that it's bedtime.

'I heard back from one of the guys suing the JPUSA,' Georgia says.

'Really?' I pull the sheets up. 'That's interesting – happy to talk?'

Again, I lie looking up at the planks of wood above me, imagining what the life of a child who grew up here years ago would have been like. Savannah seems so well-rounded. It gives me a sense of hope that she is going to school, that the group are willing to risk the influences that come with that.

But something isn't right, is it? Can I have even an ounce of objectivity?

I don't know if I'm making connections because they are real or my brain *wants* to see them. Am I especially susceptible? Am I searching for patterns, or could I perhaps be creating them? My subconscious wants to make sense of it all. I find connections that are emotional, that shoot me back to moments in my own past. I find the connections in beliefs, ideologies and sometimes even in faces. Like a weary TV detective, plotting coloured string between events, people, photographs, beliefs, making the links come to life.

Coloured strings that twist around each other as I drift off.

Red yarn, blue yarn, green yarn.

I fall upwards through the lift shaft in the Towers, shadowing the suspended string. Running down the corridors, my legs ache as if the air is made of thick jelly. I grab the corners of the walls to pull me through the hall. String stretches across the sticky hotel carpet. As I chase it, I begin to run out of air. Tiny air bubbles dribble upwards from my mouth, my fist punches the wooden bedroom door open.

I wake up choking.

* * *

The next morning, I sit with a cup of coffee, index fingers in my eyes, clumsily trying to rub the tiredness away. I am waiting for my Skype call with Jaimie, who lived here till he was 20 years old. My hands shake a little from both lack of sleep and caffeine, maybe nerves too. The sound of Skype snaps me back into the room and Jaimie's face appears. And with it, my nerves dissipate.

'I joined the Jesus People with my father and mother when I was two years old. I was born and raised there. I don't have any memories of being a child outside of that experience.' The words come from a handsome and open face.

He pauses and I feel as if the next thing he says needs to be taken seriously, as if he has had to defend this point before: 'Jesus People will always be my home, no matter what they think about me or what I think about them. But like every family, like every small town, Jesus People is full of dark and light, trials and triumphs.'

I am nodding, knowing all too well how complicated it is to grow up somewhere and love the people you were with, the pieces of joy that you carved out of the days, but in the same breath carry a darkness. Maybe that is just called growing up? Maybe every kid has that.

'I can see why you are protective,' I say.

I see nothing but earnestness in his eyes as he says, 'I have a knee-jerk, built-in need to protect them, I still have that in me. Like, OK, I'm going to talk about something that isn't so good, but I really love them.' His words feel conflicted with pain.

'In 2007, after coming out of the closet and kind of fig-uring out what I wanted to do with my life, I was living in a small town in Indiana. I didn't feel like it was going anywhere for me. I decided I was going to move to Chicago and do this documentary.'

Already his story feels so familiar, I feel connected to him and to it.

He goes on: 'I just wanted to have conversations with as many people as I could about growing up in the Jesus People and what that felt like, how we were processing that as adults now that we weren't living there, what we were dealing with in our emotional space, in our psychological space. It came from a deep sense of love of my experience of the Jesus People. Like, "I can a make movie that can promote reconciliation and healing". I wanted to find this commune that I loved again so much, that's where my heart was.'

I believe every word he is saying, I feel it in my core. And I feel it's not easy for him to take me where he wants to go.

'That's the film I *wanted* to make . . .'

'That's not how things turned out, I take it,' I say gently.

He takes a breath before saying, 'The film I ended up making was very hard to make, traumatising for me. It was a film that exposed some horrible darkness, the assault and abuse of children.'

If this was a film, a sharp ringing would fill the room, the air would be sucked out, you would see my fingernails pierce my own skin, you'd hear the beat of my heart thump over his words as they echo out. But, instead, the room stays the same, just filled with heartbreak.

It's just him and me and an earth-shattering lack of drama.

He softly tells me stories of kids within the hotel, who had been sexually abused – he was one of them.

'Out of the 120 kids that I interviewed, 76 had been sexually abused.'

He had thought that his experience was a one-off, that it had only happened to him. But it turned out to be a story that came up time and time again in his interviews.

'Fuck! Those numbers are very high.' I say this while thinking, one child would have been too high. The stories that he tells me are ones you can't shake off, you cannot unhear – kids, toddlers, teenagers, it seems that no one was out of reach.

I ask him where the abuse was coming from, was it the outsiders they let in, or was it members of the group?

'One of the leaders at the time was accused by three people in my documentary. He and his wife were the first to leave. Most of their leaders were accused of being complicit or active in sexual abuse allegations. And no one's done any articles about that. So, it's all silence, all of this is silent, so . . . They weren't going to get that from me.' But Jaimie wasn't going to remain quiet. I recognise both the need to speak out and the burden that comes with that. He goes on to tell me about a cover-up:

'At the time they were silencing these kids, sending them away to isolate them, putting them away and telling them it's their fault, questioning their motives, "What were you doing, why were your pants down, why were you in that room with this person?"'

This side of abuse can be so damaging, sometimes as damaging as the physical side, to tell children that they *might* be to blame. I think about how this is not confined to abuse in communes, or churches, how it can happen anywhere. The insidious cruelty of handing shame back to the victim. The cover-up job was so effective that Jaimie didn't know about the other kids until he made his film.

Off the back of these interviews, Jaimie decided that to speak out meant taking legal action. He tells me, 'Some friends of mine, who were involved in the film, talked to a lawyer and I became a part of this legal case against them.'

So, now Jaimie and some of the other kids who grew up here are taking them to court (the case ended up being thrown out as there was an issue with a gagging order). That was the 'topic'.

The call leaves me stunned. I had told myself I wanted to know what had happened in these Towers and now I do. And it is beyond devastating.

*　　*　　*

I spend the day doing anything I can to avoid going back up into the Towers. I sit in our dorm, I watch footage from the trip, I clean our kit, I pace the room.

That evening, I walk back through the halls of the hotel. I *thought* I came back up to look for Savannah, but now that I'm here, I'm not sure what I'm doing. My boots tread the sticky carpet, the corridor feels like it's closing in; I feel a pain growing in my chest. I walk past doors that have the names of kids written on them, the drawings, maps and stickers, past the one that says, 'Savannah is going to change the world'. Anxiety rushes in, the tingling in my hands travels up my arms, towards my chest. I reach for my throat as if someone has pulled a plastic bag over my head as all the air is sucked out of me.

I take two steps at a time up the fire escape and hit the black of the roof on my hands and knees, just as the panic fully grips me. I come round shaking, my eyes blurry, my lungs exhausted, gulping in the night air, my arms still buzzing.

Fuck! I have to hold it together.

We can't talk about any of this. And even if we could, what's the point now? The damage has been done. The damage in these halls, done to the children that grew up here, who now carry this trauma of these corridors with them. If we could ask, would Neil Taylor admit the leaders' culpability? And it's so deeply frustrating, disappointing and painful to find that even a group that I can see is doing actual real good have this stain on them.

I wonder where this court case can go for Jaimie and the others who grew up here, if it can help heal, this many years on. I think about the court case in the UK, the day we were told, 'We have won,' and how it was only years later that I found out what that had meant. The judge had made the family renounce all the teachings of David Berg that pertained to sexual abuse, flirty fishing and the law of love and in a sense renounce him. They agreed to do this rather than have us kids taken away. And they could *only* do it because David Berg was dead. I read his judgment years after the fact:

> I am completely satisfied that David Berg was obsessed with sex, a perverted man who recklessly corrupted his flock and did many of them serious damage, which he made no attempt to redress and for which he never admitted any personal responsibility. Hypocritically, he did not practice what he preached, that confession and repentance are good for the soul. Now he is dead. May the Lord have mercy on his soul. There will be many who will not mourn his passing.

I couldn't believe that this was described to us as a 'win' – we had been told we should die rather than renounce his teachings.

When I left home I believed, or maybe hoped, the group I grew up in was a dark anomaly, that they were a nasty blip, it was 'us' and then everyone else on the planet. Then I started to realise that we were not unique, there were more of us than I could have imagined. Because groups like ours are born out of human need. I wanted to wrap the dark anomaly of *what they did to us* in the catch-all of 'madness'. Something inexplicable. Like looking at serial killers and defining them as plain 'evil'. *Other. Simple.* There is a comfort in that, rather than being able to see that the psychological and social environments that can create the 'evil' are often banal, simple and easy to replicate. How are we able to replicate the same pain and evil over and over again, even when the intentions start out as pure?

* * *

At breakfast the next day, Savannah's mom talks us through the application process for new recruits. How they are vetted and what proof they provide. I ask about the child abuse allegations and am warned again not to get into the 'topic'. But she tells us in no uncertain terms that people with a history of sexual offences are not allowed here.

I am out on the fire escape, looking out onto the streets of Uptown Chicago with Savannah. She tells me about her dreams of Bernie Sanders becoming president, of the scholarship she has gained to one of the best schools in the country, of starting her own family one day; she makes me feel that some good can come of this place. I ask her if the kids are safe. She says, 'They know that things weren't *always* done right here, but they have been changed and now they are.' And I realise that's as close to this as I'm going to get. Unsatisfactory, without closure, but I feel a selfish relief that I can give myself permission to leave.

* * *

As we leave the JPUSA and Chicago, I call Jaimie again. I want to know what a good outcome for him would look like.

He tells me, 'The honest truth is that for a while I wished that I hadn't made the film, I wished that I hadn't been a part of it, that's how much I felt robbed by it. I felt robbed by the entire experience. I was just bitter, I was completely like, *why did I do this*?'

His words are like a fist to the belly. *Is this where I'm headed?* I think about my own journey – the adventure, the heartbreak, the process – and ask a question that I don't know if I want the answer to: 'So, you don't think that it was worth it?'

'Well, now I do. They're very different than they used to be, they're very different than they were five years ago, they're very different than they were ten years ago. The public conversations we're having about child sexual abuse have altered the course of their lives for good.'

I am nodding, praying he *really* feels this way, that he can take something from the harrowing route he has been forced down.

He then says, 'So I feel really good about that and I'm really proud of what I did.'

I tell him I'm proud of him too. This has taken him seven years of hard work, of looking at his life in ways he probably never wanted to, of having to listen to the abuse of others. That is deeply traumatising in itself; it takes bravery and it's not without its costs. How can you go through that unscathed? But there is a power to it too: facing this has meant the Jesus People USA have to make changes because he refused to be silent.

I ask him what he wants from the JPUSA now.

'I want them to say, "We hear you, we're listening, we validate what you've gone through, we validate that during your childhood, parts of it were just horribly destructive to who you are, we are so sorry on behalf of everyone who lives here, most of the leaders who were involved in that are gone and we wish you well, and this – we – are still your home and we *still* love you."'

I hang up in tears. It's so simple: to want and need validation of what's happened to you, to validate the pain, to turn off the gaslight. To let those kids know that they didn't imagine it and that it wasn't their fault, that they are loved.

And that they *will* be heard.

CHAPTER 18

The Exodus: Year 0

The plan feels dangerous. I feel exposed, but it's better than having no plan at all.

Raffa is in 'escape' strategy mode.

'What's the time of day that you won't be caught out? You are going to need more than 35 minutes to earn some money. Even shifts in pubs are four hours minimum.'

'Shifts?' I ask.

'Yeah, the period of time that you work is called a shift,' he says.

I nod and say, 'Well, I suppose, if I really think about it, the time when no one would notice is after "lights out".'

The plan is all about money.

Six hundred pounds is the figure that we have come up with.

It sounds like an impossible amount.

Six hundred pounds for a new life.

Six hundred pounds is the price of my freedom.

I have about nine months to make that. Nine months until I turn 16. Enough people have left now that I can see if you're not prepared, things can go really wrong. I sting from very real stories of girls I know who have left and have become sex workers and lap dancers. Without an education or money, it seems there is always one thing that you can sell and it's the thing that we have been told our whole lives can be traded.

'So, after 9pm,' he says – he knows my schedules.

We look through a newspaper and he shows me the section where all the jobs are.

'Ah! Here, there's a job at a nightclub in town, shift is 10 till 2am, no experience needed. Let's get you there for an interview,' he says.

'How old do you need to be for that?' I ask.

'Eighteen,' he says.

'I can do that,' I say, hoping I come across confidently.

'You're going to need to wear make-up and do yourself up a bit to pass for 18.' He looks at me and then adds, 'And you're going to have to lie.'

That shouldn't be too hard.

*　*　*

Two weeks later, we drive through streetlights of the city centre towards my first shift. I have a buzz in me: nerves and excitement and the fear of getting caught.

Too late to back out now.

'I'll be right here when you're done, OK?' he says reassuringly. 'You've got this, OK? Good luck.'

I push through the doors to Mosquito Coast into the smell of sour beer, cigarettes and tables that have been wiped with cloths that aren't clean. The club is empty, dark, with mini spotlights circling round in different colours. They jitter and swirl, replicating the nerves I feel in my stomach and heart. A girl with green stripes in her hair shows me the tills and how to pull a pint, and tells me what drinks are what. The most complicated part is memorising the names of alcohols I have never heard of, especially when drinks have code names like Slippery Nipple, B52, Sex on the Beach.

'Where are you from?' she asks.

'America,' I say.

'Obviously, but what part?'

I want to pick it up quickly, but I'm slow. As the club starts to fill, I feel a rush of adrenaline. I'm completely out of my depth. Being an American helps as I can say I don't know what 'the British' call anything. A rationale that also helps with me when I don't get the money right the first or second time. The shift is busy, sweaty and goes quickly.

* * *

'How was it?' Raffa asks as I get in the car.

'It was great. I mean, I think I got away with it.'

I can smell the beer and cigarette smoke on me.

''Course you did,' he says, proudly.

I pull my T-shirt off and grab the set of clothes I stowed in his car to change into – I can't go home with clothes that smell of smoke.

'I told them I was American,' I say, pulling a clean top over my head.

'Ha!' he says. 'That's fucking perfect.'

* * *

The phone rings in the home.

Two months later, eight shifts in.

We have a phone upstairs and one downstairs; if you're in the middle of the house the sound clashes between them. It's *just* the ring of a phone. But today it feels different. Loaded. Like when an ambulance drives by and the sound bends. It feels like the ring is happening in slow motion. The hairs on my body stand up. I get the sinking feeling that the ringing is a warning, a bell foretelling doom. The feeling is so intense, I'm so sure something is wrong that I sit waiting in the living room for the aftermath.

And it is.

My mom rushes in, her face hysterical. Angry. And hurt.

'Go upstairs and stay in your room until we call you!' she shrieks.

My heart falls through me.

This is it.

This is the moment when everything comes crashing down around me.

They have found out.

This is it, I will be locked in forever.

Forget Raffa. Forget the plan. Forget everything.

It's over.

I have been lying to them for so long, but I had managed to convince myself that I would never get found out. Nine months, that's all I needed to get through. *Nine months.* My brain is in overdrive. I start to play out every possible way they could have found out and every possible reason to excuse myself. Desperate to form my defence, I go over and over every last detail, every tiny mistake I might have made. Did one of the kids see me coming in at night and say something? Has one of the adults been following me? If so, for how long?

Do they know about Raffa?

I feel his rage before I hear him and I hear him before I see him. Thundering towards the door, the wood crashing as he punches his way into the room. It almost happens in slow motion, the sound distorted.

I feel his fingers on my arm; he drags me out, his grip painful. I know my dad well – I know the best thing is not to say a word, not to cry out in pain. I have to keep silent. As he drags me up a flight of stairs, my eyes sting, they burn like acid.

But I'm not afraid in this moment, I am fucking angry.

My dad – the well-put-together man with eloquent words, the man who talks to the cameras in a calm, collected voice – has fistfuls of my hair in one hand and is gripping my arm with enough force to keep me from falling off the building. He is raging. Angry. Ashamed. I can feel it in the root of every hair he rips from my skull, every vein in my body.

I feel cold. Stone. Cold.

He drags me through the office, into his room and throws me down on the bed. He pins my arms down and is suddenly on top of me. I can feel all of his weight as he shouts in my face, 'How the HELL could you do this to us? How could you make such a fool of me and your mother? How the HELL did you think that you could get away with this? You are an idiot, stupid, IDIOT! Did you think you were clever, IDIOT? I have never been so ashamed in my entire life.'

But his words don't pierce me, they don't even penetrate. All I feel in this moment is pure cold hatred, so cold it's numb. He wants an explanation. I thought I would be

343

defensive or apologetic, but I'm not afraid of him anymore – it's gone too far.

'Dad,' I say, 'you are spitting in my face.' I say this with the kind of calmness that I know will make him even angrier. He wants to see my fear and I will not let him have it.

Not today.

Then a blankness. A second of nothing. Silence. I come to on the floor. My face is thudding, I can feel my pulse in it, but there's no pain. My mother comes in manic, crying. She sees me on the floor and shouts through her tears, 'DO you have any idea what you have done to us?' She is shaking. 'You emotionally blackmailed us for pieces of freedom and now you have done this!'

I look up from the floor and still strangely calm, as if speaking to a child, I say, 'If what *I* did was emotional blackmail, what *you* do is emotional rape.'

They've never seen behind the façade that they taught me to create. They've never heard the truth that I keep inside while I offer up what they want to hear. Now, it's as if they're truly seeing me for the first time. And they're disgusted: they see a filthy creature who is not their daughter. Like I've been taken over by a demon. Possessed. Or worse, I haven't, and the demon was in there all along.

'Enough! I will not hear another word out of you. I will not subject myself or your mother to whatever it is you have become,' my dad says breathlessly. 'You will stay in this room until we have decided what to do with you.'

The door slams and it's only then that I start to cry red-hot, angry tears. *Why do I cry when I'm angry?* As I stand up, I shake. I stick my face under the tap in their bathroom and watch the blood, snot and tears mix with the water, making circles around the plug hole and then wash away. I pull myself up, look at myself in the mirror, wipe my nose with the back of my hand, then take in a breath quietly.

'Fuck 'em!'

*   *   *

The ceilings are high in this train station. I am dwarfed by the massive building. Big black chunks of steel hold up the arched roof, the sun comes through the glass panels, creating pockets of light on the tarmac. I pull down the edge of my dress, it keeps creeping up my leg; I hope that the blazer I have on makes me appear older than my 15 years. As I walk towards the exit, I grab the handle of the bag containing everything I own in this world.

It all happened very quickly. The adults got together, in that large room, the one where we did so many interviews, the one we all gathered in to hear about Moses David's death. The one where so many decisions were made. And they were told what I had done.

When the phone had rung that day, it was my boss at the Mosquito Coast, asking when I was going to come in and pick up my earnings. I made a mistake, such a stupid mistake. Of all the stupid, stupid things to do. I had written our home number on the form instead of Raffa's, which was the plan. One stupid, stupid thing and now, there I was.

I had wanted to leave, but not like this.

The group was summoned and asked, 'Do we keep her? Can she be saved, or is she too far gone? Will her being here affect the rest of the Teens and influence them?'

It was unanimous. I am not surprised that my parents voted against me. The way that they looked at me was as if I was not theirs anymore. *And I wasn't. Maybe I never really was.* They handed over my fate, yet again, to other people.

I rang Raffa and I told him I was being sent to another country. I told him this so he wouldn't try to come for me and couldn't argue with me. It was a lie, but I felt so horrible and grimy and ashamed, so fucking stupid, and I didn't want him to be a part of it at all. And I couldn't face him – I didn't want him to think that he needed to look after me; it was time for me to look after myself. And there was a part of me that had shut down, I felt hardened, catatonic; I almost felt nothing as I heard his heart break.

So here I am, in this train station, in a city centre, pay check in my hand, a total of £350. *Half of what I thought I needed to survive.*

'Are you lost?' The voice comes from a guy leaning out of his car window as he pulls into the station.

'I'm fine,' I say back.

'Well, you look lost,' he persists.

I keep looking down at my feet as I walk. He pulls the car in front of me, blocking my path.

'Look, here's my phone number. Call me if you need anything, OK?'

The look in his eyes feels so familiar.

'You look like you need a friend,' he says as he pushes a piece of paper into my hand.

CHAPTER 19

There is No Ranch: 18 Years After

I can still feel those words on my lips. 'This isn't finished, not by a long shot.' And I meant it.

It is time.

We've driven through the lakes of Indiana, we've crossed through the mountains and forests of Kentucky. And now, we've hit Tennessee on our way to the Twelve Tribes.

This is a side of the state that I haven't seen before: vast fields of corn and tobacco, men with sniper rifles in full camo, stalking around farmland, ominous burn piles, stark industrial estates with no life on them. My mind drifts as we drive. These highways transport me to cop shows – colour palettes of washed-out greens, sweaty men at tabernacle revivals, swamps, serial killers, naked women tied to ancient trees and endless fields that hide thousands of secrets.

The Twelve Tribes have had a heavy hold on me in the last few years, ever since Sofi and I left. At times, I wake up in the night in their grip. They burrowed under my skin, it prickles when I catch myself thinking about them. Was it because we stayed at the time of the raids? Should we, or could we, have done more? Was it our duty to 'save' those kids? Did we lose ourselves in there and lose perspective? Or is it because I need to validate the last trip, one that on the surface looks completely fruitless?

I can still taste the failure. And the guilt.

Or is there something deeper, darker or otherworldly that's pulling me back to them? Like a black hole that wrenches my mind into it, with pieces of me destroyed, splintered on the other side.

Whatever the reason, my business with them is incomplete.

In the cold light of day, I feel the truth about the Twelve Tribes lies somewhere in the middle of the 'dark' Sofi was experiencing and the 'light' that they were showing us. I'd seen the emotional distress and anxieties evolving. Were they listening? Did they go through our stuff? Were they recording us? Maybe the core of the darkness we were experiencing was an echo of the treatment of their kids. I felt reverberations of the psychological tactics used in my own childhood. The echoes were there, not just in how the adults acted, but in how the children behaved – the quietness, the obedience, the godliness or the oppression.

But now it's a new day, and this experience at the Twelve Tribes will be different: we are being accepted as a film crew. Paz has produced it. Georgia got the permission to film first and I am so excited to finally get the Twelve Tribes on film. This time there will be no surprises. There will be no need to wear the headscarves, or spend days planting kale in the fields, or get up at the crack of dawn for the gatherings.

We are safe.

I think about the night Sofi and I drove into the group – the dust, the trees, it was dark and I was scared, and . . . *God, I miss*

Sofi. I miss our twosome, our bonkers way of doing things. Our erratic friendship-love affair. It was wild, unsustainable and brilliant.

Georgia interrupts my thoughts: 'I almost can't believe how easy it was to get permission. Considering everything . . .'

'Maybe that's why they're giving us permission. Even my group *had* to let the Press in at one point.'

My mind goes back to those nights as a child, being shoved into vans, grabbing our 'flea bags', on the run again.

'We just couldn't keep running away,' I say.

'Do you think they're dangerous?' Seb asks.

'Dangerous to whom? Us? No. To the kids? I think so,' I say.

*   *   *

We arrive in the town of Pulaski. I thought The Ridge was a hotbed of cultural weirdness, but this town is in a league of its own. Only 7,000 people, but a history that is staggering and full of darkness. Pulaski is not only home to the Twelve Tribes, it's got a massive Amish population and a cosmic commune called 'The Farm' – the oldest surviving community in the US. And on the dark side, Pulaski has two routes of the Trail of Tears running through it *and* it's the birthplace of the KKK.

Driving through this town is like going back in time. We pass the building where, on Christmas Eve in 1865, six Tennessee veterans established the rules for a new white supremist society, the KKK. It was a law office then and still is. We get out of the truck to read a plaque on the wall outside.

The plaque is turned around so it can't be read; now it's just a black piece of metal.

It's ominous. And empty.

'Ugh, it feels creepy here!' Georgia says.

She's not wrong. How could so much hate and inhumanity start from an innocuous office? As we drive out of the parking lot, a horse and cart driven by 'Abraham Lincoln' pulls out in front of us.

'Oh, wow, Amish!' Georgia says. 'It's like we are on the set of a film . . .'

'It's ridiculous,' I say.

With their straw hats, dark shirts, braces, bonnets, modest dresses and horse-drawn carriages, the Amish are so easy to spot. The town is weirdly ordinary – I keep expecting there to be *more*, something that validates the sheer number of events, communities and crimes against humanity that happened on this plot of the planet. The town is simple, boring, pedestrian, beige. All the buildings in the main square look 2D – it's like a set, paper cut-outs of buildings rather than real ones. Everything you see tells you that the things you've heard just *couldn't* have happened somewhere as plain and unassuming as this.

How could a town so nondescript have two routes from the Trail of Tears running through it? I imagine Native Americans walking through this place just over 100 years ago, in shackles, as they trekked through over 5,000 miles and nine states on foot.

On. Fucking. Foot.

I had heard of the Trail of Tears, but being in its wake is something else. The trail that killed 4,000. Their unmarked graves must be all around us. I expect to see the damage of this trail on the land – I want trenches, scorched earth, I want to see the pain on the trees. But again, this town is a cover job.

We pull up outside the Yellow Deli, the café run by the Twelve Tribes. I look around the truck.

'Right, everyone ready?' I say.

This should be easy, they are expecting us.

'They're going to offer us lunch, just be polite and eat. It's actually good food, so no one's trying to poison you,' I joke weakly.

* * *

A woman wearing a long dress and tabard sits at the entrance, a pleasant expression on her face. I smile back.

'Hi, we're looking for Maliki,' I say.

Before she can answer, a voice comes from behind her.

'Greetings!' A man with white hair in a ponytail, a white beard and gold-rimmed glasses appears from around the corner. 'You must be the film crew, come on in.' He smiles as he leads us to a table. 'I hope you guys are hungry,' he says, handing us some menus in a half-friendly, half-skilful manner. He looks Seb in the eye and says, 'I'll be back in a second.'

I feel my face twitch as I am reminded that women are at the bottom of the chain here. I start to read things off the menu with a fake enthusiasm: 'Ooh, Bean Burger . . . Matcha Latte . . . Vegan chilli,' hoping the words veil the voices in my head warning, 'this is too easy' and 'something isn't right'.

Compose the face, slow the breath.

Maliki flips between host and waiter. He takes our order, then sits down with us. In front of him is an aggressively hot herbal tea in a large glass. The steam rises as he takes us in, silently and unnervingly; he is in no rush. He smiles. And again, addresses Seb:

'Have you had to travel far?'

Now I'm confused. Maliki knows we have – we have been speaking regularly over the last two weeks.

'Yes, three days,' I say, determined to catch his eye. 'But we were so excited when you said we could come and film The Ranch that . . . well . . . we thought it was well worth the long trip.'

He smiles, almost serenely. I feel like he's in on a joke that I'm not privy to. Lunch arrives and with it, we spoon in hollow, yet loaded conversation. Back and forth, empty words and meaningless chit-chat, when the real topic hangs over us like a storm cloud, waiting to erupt.

But no one wants to mention the weather. Not yet.

Our matcha lattes arrive. And then comes the rain. Maliki looks at Georgia for the first time since we sat down.

'So, Georgia, you're from Swindon, aren't you?' he says.

I scan our conversations – we wouldn't have told them that.

'Yes,' she says, taking a sip from her drink.

I feel the surprise in her voice.

'And Seb, you're from France originally, right?'

Seb nods. And then Maliki adds, 'And how long have you been working with the *Guardian* newspaper?'

Now he has our full attention. He shouldn't know anything about Seb, that's for certain. I shoot Georgia a look: *This isn't right, we need to get this back on track.*

I cut to the chase: 'So, when could we come out to The Ranch and get started? We've got all our kit here, so we could just go now if that works for you?'

He looks at me strangely: 'What ranch?' he says.

Are the corners of his mouth twitching?

'*The* Ranch,' I say firmly.

He smiles and shakes his head.

I feel ridiculous even having to say it: 'The Twelve Tribes Ranch on the edge of Pulaski, the one we came to film.'

'There is no ranch,' he says, as if performing a Jedi mind trick.

Maybe this would be funny if it didn't make me feel a bit sick.

'Sorry, we've been talking with you about filming The Ranch for a while now. You guys told us to come.' Sensing demands will get us nowhere, I sweeten my tone: 'That's why we're here, to meet the kids and film your way of life.'

'Oh, you can film, but this deli is it. We haven't got any children here and there is no ranch.' He smiles again. 'This is it,' he repeats and points around the deli, as if that proves everything.

'Hang on . . .' Georgia starts.

'Our mistake.' I cut her off. 'Let us have a think about the best way to film as we had different expectations.'

I want to wrap this up before we can't bring it back, keep schtum until we get back in the truck.

We drive around the block, the silence broken only by my fingertips tapping on the dashboard nervously. Why did they want us here? Why would they say yes and get us to travel all this way? Just to play with us? What's their agenda? Is it manageable? Solvable? Can we charm our way in? Am I sliding back into my blind need to succeed when we really shouldn't have come here in the first place? Maybe we never should have come back. It seemed too easy.

Far too easy.

'So, what in the name of fuck is going on?' Georgia says.

'There might be a way around this. Perhaps they're just trying to show us their authority, show us who's boss,' Seb offers.

'Or maybe they're just fucking with us,' I say. 'They want us to know that they know about "us", that they have done their own research, looked into you guys . . .'

'How would they have found that stuff out?' Georgia says.

'It's pretty sophisticated for a religious group that doesn't really believe in technology,' Seb says.

My brain buzzes noisily, trying to make sense of what's happening, while another voice in my head tells me to be confident, to lead, that there is a way out.

'I believe we have two options . . .' The words tumble out without much thought but I hope a little conviction. 'Number one: charm offensive. Do what they ask, film the adults in the deli, interview them and hope that in a few days they trust us enough to let us into The Ranch. Or two: we sack off all of the deli nonsense, go out to The Ranch regardless and wing it.'

'So, we are sure that The Ranch exists?' Seb asks.

How quickly deception works: within minutes, Maliki has made us doubt ourselves.

'Yes,' Georgia says emphatically.

'Did we ever get an address?' I ask.

'No, they said they would take us there from the deli,' she says.

Our energy is frenzied and wild. It's easy when you're worn out and on the road, with a mission to go from zero to a hundred. I put my hands over my eyes, dig my fingers into my forehead, trying to rub sense into this situation, and Sofi's face appears. I think of how we felt when we were in the Twelve Tribes, how they *made* us feel then.

It's happening again.

'What if we just stake them out tonight at the deli and then follow them home?' Seb suggests.

I had promised myself, and them, that this trip would be safe, secure and better handled than the last one, but a part of me *loves* the idea of a stake out.

'Well, it's time for our call with Paz anyway. Let's see what he thinks,' I say.

* * *

Paz has been in some pretty sticky situations on documentary shoots in his time, from Japanese earthquakes to the Arctic circle, cholera outbreaks to terrorist attacks. This, in comparison, is a walk in the park. I'm sure he's going to be as into this stake out as we are.

'ABSOLUTELY NOT!' His voice is firm. 'Are you listening to me?'

Ugh! I hate being told off, even by a friend who cares about me.

'I thought you would be up for this,' I whine.

His tone becomes even more serious as he says, 'Number one, you are in a state where the gun ownership rate is 40 per cent. Number two, you have just told me they know more about you than you thought – you are in uncharted territory.

Number three, they have tricked you into travelling for three days to get you to them. And you don't know why. Abort this idea, I am not fucking around!'

'Buzzkill,' I say as I hang up, half-smiling, but prickling from his words. 'Of course, he's fucking right!' I say, rolling my eyes.

We laugh, deflated, defeated. Tension broken or at least scolded out of us.

Now that the adrenaline has worn off, I realise that dressing up as Amish people (just one of our disguise ideas) and staking out a religious commune is 'old me' thinking. Not new me. There is a smarter way of doing this, there has to be.

We drive through the town with no real destination in mind, past the cardboard cut-outs, past the Yellow Deli and the courthouse.

'Hang on, is that a library? Pull over!'

I jump out, straighten my shirt and walk in.

* * *

Large, open and brightly lit, the library is the first place I have been to in this town that makes me feel even slightly at ease. An old lady behind the counter adjusts her glasses and says, 'Marning!' I switch to the American accent I grew up with, blend in – I do it without thinking.

'Hi there, how're you doing? I'm in town for a few days – I just can't believe the history of this place,' I say, already regretting the American accent.

'I know, it sure is interesting.' She smiles, which makes the skin around her eyes crinkle kindly.

'I'm hoping to see some of this stuff for myself.'

She nods, eager to help. I get the feeling that perhaps people never come in here. Ever.

I start strong: 'Do you know where in town the birthplace of the KKK is?' I ask.

'Well, that's kinda a myth,' she says as she pulls a map out. 'But they say it's right here.' She points to the street with the law office and an ominous plaque.

'Thank you. How about the Trail of Tears?' I ask.

'Yes, of course, everyone does, there are two spots, here and here.' Her chubby, liver-spotted fingers mark the map.

'Thank you, that's super helpful,' I say, then I hesitate for a second. 'And I heard there's a Twelve Tribes Ranch?'

'You mean the Deli, hun?' she asks, her eyes widening.

'No, I mean their big ranch they have, about 150 people live on it – my friend who came here visited it once,' I say, wondering if I might have gone too far.

'Oh, right! You mean Abraham's Ranch on the edge of town?'

My heart quickens as I try to feign nonchalance: 'Uh huh.'

'Now, that's right here.' She gets a pen out and marks a spot on the map.

BINGO! She writes the address down for me.

* * *

'Got them,' I say as I get back in the truck.

'You did? Just like that?' Georgia asks.

'Yep, the Oracle has spoken. A hundred-year-old granny beats Google.'

'Shall we go there now?' Seb asks.

'No, I needed the address so I know we aren't mad. For now, let's do what the Twelve Tribes want and film them in the café,' I say.

Georgia asks, 'Isn't that a waste of . . .'

'It may be, but we have the option. We are here, we might as well. Let's play it out, it won't hurt.'

But as I say it, I wonder how much time Sofi and I wasted with this type of hope.

*   *   *

In the deli, everything transports me back in time – the smell of the food, the instruments being played. At one point, I startle myself as I sing in time with the band, knowing the lyrics to their song. The melodies of these songs about Babylon, the End of Days and Yashua are burnt into my subconscious.

It feels so eerie when the interviews we do feel like they are being read off a script. Like everyone just came from a briefing titled, 'There is no Ranch'. As they tell me it's a fantasy, I keep fingering the folded piece of paper in my back pocket with their address on it – I need to feel the paper to stay locked into reality. One guy slips up and mentions their children up in the farm. 'Mr Slip-up' is immediately sent away, I imagine to his death but it's probably just to the kitchen.

Then the real reason we have been brought across the country becomes clear: 'Hey guys, wait!' We're halfway through the door when I hear Maliki's voice. 'I want to get a photo of you.'

It's such a harmless request, but from a group of Luddites with whom we are not on friendly enough terms to ask for a keepsake, it feels very strange. In fact, it feels like a demand. And I get that sense, when internal politeness *should* be turned off, when the switch *should* flip, when you *should* tell someone to *get lost*. The politeness that allows you to follow the serial killer into the basement because he tells you he has 'something you'll want to see'.

Fuck politeness. Don't follow him into the basement!

'That's OK, thanks, we're not very *into* photos,' I say.

'Oh, come on!' he whines as he pulls out a state-of-the-art DSLR camera, which is so out of place here. In his hands, it startles me. Like a granny wielding a chainsaw. Wildly, he starts to snap pictures. Instinct makes me swing my camera kit in front of my face.

'Stop hiding from me,' he says, smiling, but I feel menace in his bared teeth.

'We're done here,' I say firmly as I grab Georgia and Seb and head to the truck.

* * *

'FUCCCCCCKKKKKKKK!' says Georgia. 'What the fuck was that?'

'*That* was probably the reason why they got us here,' I say.

Everything snaps into place: Maliki's private joke is out in the open and it's a sick one.

'That did not feel right,' Seb says.

'No, it didn't. It felt really weird, it felt gross – I feel gross,' Georgia joins in.

There was something about the intent behind the photo that felt violating. The action itself was so simple, so 'normal', but the purpose behind it felt loaded. I keep quiet. I don't want to stir the situation up, but I want to get to the bottom of what's happening and why the Twelve Tribes seem to be toying with us.

I look out the window of the truck into the starry skies of Pulaski, hoping for clarity from the night. 'Seb, do you still have the numbers of the former members you were talking about? I think now is the time to speak to them.'

There is no need for us to stay in here in Pulaski with this strangeness going on. 'We might as well get ahead of the game,' I say, packing up my camera kit, preparing to drive first thing in the morning.

* * *

I can't sleep. I writhe with frustration at being tangled up with the Twelve Tribes again. *What am I doing here?* It's like falling back into bed with an bad ex, naïvely thinking everything is going to be so different and waking up next to the same asshole you remember from last time.

As soon as the sun's out, I head to the kitchen to make coffee. I want jugs of the stuff, even though I don't need it – my adrenaline hasn't waned in nearly 24 hours. The feeling pumps through my veins like a heady narcotic.

'The reason you are like this is because you spent a childhood in danger,' my psychiatrist told me the year before. 'High levels of adrenaline are normal for you. Others find it stressful. You almost crave it. Lots of kids who grow up in danger, they have this and many, as adults, put themselves into situations that replicate it.'

'I mean, I can't relate,' I said sarcastically, thinking about my last trip with Sofi.

My therapist looked at me with a no-nonsense-but-I-love-you face and said, 'I am not just talking about you joining cults, although that's clear. There are other things: workaholism, drugs, extreme sports, anything that replicates and creates the cortisol, dopamine and adrenaline ... even dangerous relationships.'

It was like a hammer to the gut to realise that my addiction to this feeling was so powerful, that I had tried all of those things, which might make it the most dangerous drug I have ever chased. And I remembered my 15-year-old self, coming out of a cult and landing straight into the arms of a 32-year-old abusive, violent, psychologically traumatising man. Standing in that train station, bag by my side, feeling that I was free for the first time in my life and the first person that offered me 'help' became my tormenter – a man who could smell the vulnerability on me as much perhaps as I was magnetised to the dark familiarity of being with him.

*　*　*

Seb walks into the kitchen and vaporises this memory, phone in hand: 'I got a message from one of the ex-members; he wants to talk,' he says.

'Amazing,' I say. 'Let's call him while we're on the road.'

We get in the car. Seb adjusts his seat and says, 'Chicago?'

'One stop en route first,' I say, as I pull out the folded piece of paper from my back pocket and plot the address for The Ranch into my phone. I feel a hesitance fill the truck.

'Really?' Georgia says.

'I just want to be *sure* that they are fucking with us. I just want to see it. I'm not going to do anything Paz wouldn't want us to. Promise.'

Our wheels crunch and chew the gravel as we slowly approach The Ranch. Trees on either side of us barely cast a shadow in this early-morning light. We pass by a solitary donkey and a combine harvester, which until last night's camera action would have seemed high-tech for them. We pull over close enough, but not too close to look at the building in front of us that 'doesn't exist'.

Why did you bring us here?

As I stand, looking at The Ranch, I am taken back to the night that I interviewed my parents two years ago, the night that sent me under, threw me into depression and darkness. Why had it affected me like that? Why did they have so much power over me? Because they, like Maliki, were my gaslighters, rewriting the past. Like a menacing growl in the ear, a rough grab of the arm, quiet threats, telling me things were not so. Dressed up in normalcy. Like this town. The eloquent parents sitting in front of me, telling me that things that were so, *weren't* so. That things that happened didn't happen. That it couldn't be how I remember. That the tough years 'weren't really years'. Even the way that they looked, talked, acted, the stories they told, all denied my reality.

Manipulating my history, sowing seeds of doubt in my mind. As a child, this type of revisioning made me unable to trust myself. How can I trust myself when the two people who are supposed to guide me through life are convincing me that what I'm seeing and feeling isn't real? How can I trust my judgement? Sometimes I wonder if this was worse than the physical abuse. Being denied my reality as a child has given me bigger scars than any beating ever did.

I take my camera out.

'What are you doing?' Georgia asks.

'Getting proof.' I am sick of being gaslighted, lied to, tired of being told things that aren't real. I need this so that the eraser time uses on my memory doesn't make me believe *them*.

'Gotcha!' I say. And then I turn back to the truck – we'll get no answers from this building. 'Let's go.'

* * *

We get out of range of Pulaski and Billy's southern drawl comes through the phone. He has been out of the Twelve Tribes for five years. There's an openness to him, but I also feel a thick and heavy anger at not only the group, but at himself for ever joining. He was part of the Twelve Tribes for 15 years before he managed to extricate himself, and during that time he saw enough of the behind-the-scenes to give us a picture of the TT that we would never have been shown by them.

As we finish talking, all I can think is, *I want to speak to Sofi, I have to speak to her.*

I can barely contain myself as her face pops up on Skype.

'Sofi, you were right,' I splutter.

'About what?' she asks.

Of course, she doesn't know what I'm on about.

'About the Twelve Tribes. You were fucking right,' I say.

I feel she needs to hear this. I hope she needs the truth too.

She leans into her screen, her eyes widening: 'They were recording us?' she asks.

'You were right about what they were capable of. I'm sorry I didn't believe it, it seemed too far-fetched,' I say, babbling.

'OK, I'm listening.' Her German accent doesn't betray her – she could be feeling vindicated, she might be worried, she could be thinking, 'told you so', but all I hear is calm, cool, Sofi.

God, I miss her.

'You name it, we've heard it all today . . .

'I know that the stuff I'm going to say sounds bonkers, but I've spoken to eight different people today, from psychologists who have cared for ex-members to kids who grew up there, to ex-leaders.'

I needed it confirmed, I needed it from more than one source.

We had heard from Billy that they have hidden paedophiles and criminals, giving them new identities within the group, no questions asked. We heard from teenagers who tell us that they were starved as children, shut in cupboards, beaten daily and oppressed. We heard stories of kidnappings when the group has taken children and hidden them in different states and countries from their parents. And most upsetting of all, we heard from mothers who tell us that they have buried their own children in the woods, because they couldn't take them to hospital – they were told God would heal them and they had died because of blind faith.

I had to let Sofi know that when she was being emotionally traumatised, when they made her feel like she might be losing her mind, she could have been the sanest one there.

I am reeling from the amount of painful stories we have heard today. Of course, there is a part of me that knows that if you want a true account of a man, 'the ex-wife' might not be the best place to get your information from. Maybe there are some things that we can discount, but there is so much crossover and so many patterns in their stories. The child discipline and isolation came up every time and we found at least one kidnapping story in the papers when the FBI got involved. We already knew about the corporal punishment, and the hiding of criminals and paedophiles is something that I don't know if you could ever prove. The truth is, a lot of groups where you shed your past and identity are rife for an abuse of this, whether because of naïvety, or by design.

We had explained to Billy what had happened the night before at the deli.

'Oh yeah, I'm not surprised. They took a camera out and took your photo? Yep. Well, I can tell you now, that photo has been sent to their internal affairs group and to every commune they have all over the world. You are now on their radar.'

'Internal affairs?' I'm finding this hard to consolidate with the farmers we have met at the Twelve Tribes.

'Yes, they have a group called "The Watchers". They will have been researching you, finding out everything they can about you. They'll have a file on each of you now.'

I look around at Seb and Georgia, everything clicking into place as Billy finishes, calmly, but eerily with, 'The Watchers are watching you now.'

The car fills with thick silence, the kind you can choke on. Then Georgia breaks it with, 'What does this mean for us from now on?'

We have heard about the different groups that harass people; the Scientologists and their practice called 'fair game' where people who are judged to be a threat to the Church can be punished and harassed using any and all means possible. I have heard rumours of people's trash being rifled through, streets covered in slanderous posters and being followed for years.

This just doesn't seem possible, does it? What have I got us into?

* * *

We stop overnight in a small town.

The fresh sheets of the Airbnb envelop me in the scent of lavender, my body tired against the crisp, clean cotton. I have my own room tonight, for which I am grateful as my body and brain are buzzing like a electricity pylon in a storm – the slightest night-noise will feel like thunder. But then I fall asleep almost instantly, backwards into black.

At 2:45am, I hear a noise by my bedroom door. I open my eyes with a start. Out of the corner of my eye, I see a shadow standing by the doorframe. I can't sit up, my whole body is paralysed. I can't make out who it is. I try to call out, 'Who's there?' but my jaw is cemented shut. The shadow moves towards me. I still can't move, my head made of lead, like I have been anaesthetised badly and my mind woke up, but my body is not mine to control. I try to cry out, 'Seb, Georgia!' but their names are stuck in my throat.

The shadow walks through a slice of moonlight, showing grey hair, ponytail, gold glasses. I see him: Maliki. His face is above me now, his hands around my throat.

Sitting up straight in bed, I gasp like I've had my head held underwater. I leap towards the door, check the corners of the room, but it's empty. Then I move into the living room with my duvet to see out the rest of the night.

The sun rises in suburbia; the smell of coffee and toast float in from the kitchen. My stomach murmurs.

I can't remember what the last thing I ate was.

I walk out onto the front lawn, cup of coffee in one hand and my phone dialling Paz's number in the other. Every car looks newly washed, every garden newly mowed in this little suburban safety net.

Paz's face appears on my screen: 'Go on,' he says.

I get into the last 24 hours – the photograph, going out to The Ranch, the calls with the former members and I finish up on The Watchers.

'Well, I'm fucking glad you didn't put on a bonnet and try and follow them.' As he says this I get a rush of really, really missing him.

'So, how dangerous are we talking with these guys? How worried should I be? You only have a few days before your flight home, right?' he asks.

'Yes. We've moved the flights; there is no reason not to come home.' As I say this, I am not sure if I really believe it.

Paz interrupts my thoughts with, 'Do me a favour, can you show me around where you're staying?'

'What do you mean?' I ask.

'I mean, just walk around with your screen and give me a 360 of the street.'

Can he feel something 'off' even though he is thousands of miles away?

'Sure.'

I start to show him round this quiet, simple cul-de-sac of classic American homes – inoffensive suburbia, the American Dream.

'Hang on,' Paz says. 'What's that decorating truck doing across the street? The one with the giant aerial on the top?'

I spot it, a white van on the corner: 'Probably just a local business,' I say. But I'm unsure as I say it.

'Do me a favour, Bexy. Go and bang on the window and see who is in there – I don't want to freak you out, but that's a surveillance van.'

It's not, it can't be.

'Paz, if that's a surveillance van, the last thing I want to do is knock on the window and let them know that we know. I don't want a confrontation, I think we should just get out of here.'

I run into the kitchen as I say, 'Guys, we're getting out of here!' And before I have a chance to tell them about the van, Georgia says, 'Bexy, look at the Wi-Fi.' I look at the names her computer is picking up. One reads 'TT Surveillance van'. *What the fuck?* Why would they *tell* us they're there? How could they be *that* sophisticated, yet that dumb?

Then I realise: they want to be seen. This isn't about them spying on us, it's about us knowing they are there, feeling their presence.

They want us to know.

'Pack up, let's get the hell out of here!'

* * *

We drive through five states with the feeling of the Twelve Tribes constantly behind us, like an ominous drone that you can sense but not see. Like a shadow chasing you, just in the fringe. Always on our back. The effect that they wanted to have on us, it is effective.

We call Billy again. I want to know how much danger we are actually in: are they recording us?

'You know, the thing I would be more worried about is in the last five years, there have been a number of people who have come out and spoken against the TT, who had accidental deaths.'

'What? You can't be serious?' Seb says over the steering wheel.

'Look into it – car accidents, you name it.'

We drive down endless highways, through forests that seem to go out of focus, into sunsets that blur into the fluorescent street lights. And around every corner is another question: *Why are we here? Has it all been worth it?* We drive through fields as I think back to how I started out believing I was in a place of forgiveness with my parents, that I could be objective. And then realising I was not objective, that I couldn't be, that my lens was coloured by my experience, in both good and bad ways. And then the interview with my parents and realising I hadn't forgiven them – and that maybe I never would.

The roads seem to be in hyper-lapse – in and out of focus, streams of light flying past, painting neon trails – as my thoughts keep hooking onto a single night from last year. A night when I was searching for the same answers I am now – at an ayahuasca ceremony in a farmhouse in the countryside.

The road in front of me goes black, the lights fade, as I am transported back into that night.

I am wrapped in a sleeping bag, wearing all-white. I feel the air in the room shift. The sound of the ceremony changes pitch, like the atmosphere is being played like an instrument with the power to change key at any time.

I have spent six months in therapy, did time at a grief retreat and days, weeks and months trying to unpick my way through my bullshit, my defence mechanisms and the army of false selves I have created. Now I'm at a slightly more left-field ayahuasca ceremony.

Fuck it, might as well throw the kitchen sink at this one.

The therapy has been invaluable – given me strategies and daily practices that I didn't know I needed to stay sane. The grief counselling has given me opportunity to really feel things that I told myself I didn't need or want to feel. And the ayahuasca, what harm could it do at this point? Altered states of consciousness can be useful when it comes to understanding our human story. Sometimes psychedelics are ignored, sometimes abused, but they can be valuable for a new perspective. If the depth of the human experience is intellectual, physical, emotional and sometimes outside of the things we can feel and see, I might as well dive into all parts of it.

I am at an all-woman ceremony led by female shaman – a fierce, tiny woman from Sierra Leone and a gentle giant from Nigeria. I feel like I'm in safe hands. I have some of my most powerful female friends with me. I've left my cynicism at the door and have flung myself into this candle-lit room, filled with heavy fragrant burned wood and intentions to journey inwards.

I feel my eyes twitch and my jaw judder, the plant medicine fills me. Like having an anaesthetic, where it floods in from all corners at once. It's in me, but it's also me: it's my blood, it's my bones, it's my being.

It takes over.

My head feels like it falls six feet through the floor, but it lands in the most comfortable position, so comfortable I say to myself that I must remember how I landed so I can replicate it later. I worry for a second: *will I ever be this comfortable again?*

There is a hatch in front of me. I pull it open and go into a world made out of iridescent snakeskin. It ripples and glows, it's beautiful. It's like my breath is the atmosphere that makes it undulate and twitch. I exhale loudly and watch it quiver. *Why am I here?* I ask, thinking that I should be shown the dark parts of my soul so I can bludgeon my way through them.

It should be a struggle, shouldn't it?

A voice says, 'I thought you might want to see where your "spiritual self" lives. She lives here.'

Well, she's got great taste! Clever girl. I chuckle as I glance around the 'living' disco. Vines sprout into the edges of the iridescence. They grow fast until the scene is green and black. I am thrust deep into a forest, travelling through it while it is growing into itself, becoming thicker and deeper. Everything is simultaneously in motion, faster and faster, then all of a sudden, it stops. The leaves rustle. Then, as if they are made of two backgrounds in a play, they are pulled apart. Behind stands an owl-like creature made of the forest: big eyes, surrounded by leaves.

'Would you like me to help you make your film?' he asks.

The question surprises me: *I am not here for that.*

'Yes,' I say, without thinking about it.

'First, you must do something,' he says.

And in an instant, that world, the forest, the creature, disappears. Everything fades to black. I am replaced with a feeling – no, a reality – that is breathtakingly familiar. I am replaced with my ten-year-old brain. My adult self is gone. All my ambitions, my needs, wants, fears, vanish. And I go back to being *her*.

I recognise the fear, the fight in me, the not knowing what my future holds, the being invisible, the loneliness, the feelings of going mad. The tiny granule of hope, that if there was a way out, if there was a life for me beyond this, that I would tell people about what is happening.

I will tell people what is happening here.

Because it is not OK.

It's like I have never been anything but *her* in this moment. As if the last 20 years haven't happened. It's cold, I am afraid. It's too familiar: *she* is me.

I hear a dripping sound; I open my eyes as the water echoes around a cell made of concrete. I wrap my arms around my legs, bunched up into my chest, the tiny legs of a ten-year-old. Green mould crawls across the walls, water stagnates on the floor. There is a shaft of grey light coming through a tiny window, but too high up for me to look out of. The room glitches and it turns into the dorm I slept in at this age, glitches again and it's a concrete cell.

I feel a roar inside me, a deep animalistic painful roar, but it's trapped too. Beating and throbbing and aching. Then it ruptures, and it floods, pouring out fear, betrayal and loneliness. Then, just as I feel I can't take any more and that this is my reality from now on, I am back. I am in my own brain, my identity, experiences and 20 years of healing rush in. And I am so grateful. So grateful to be where I am now, to know what I know now and feel how I do.

It's a gift to be me; I breathe it in.

My relief is brief as I realise that I left *her* there. I am safe now, I am an adult, in this room with women all around me all on their own paths, but I have left her, in her darkest hour in that cell.

I can't leave her there.

I have to go back to save her.

And as those words come out, a hole rips in the room. It starts small, like a cigarette being stubbed out onto the fabric of this reality, then it burns bigger, the edges glowing, scorching a tear into the dorm where I lay, as a ten-year-old, crying in my bunk bed, asking God to break and release me. Watching her go through what I can now feel, with a stronger clarity than ever, is the worst night of my life.

I poke my hand through the burn hole, I stroke her face as she cries, I comfort her; I tell her it's going to be OK, that she will grow up and she will be safe, and she will be able to speak again, she will not be invisible. She will love and be loved. And that there is a life outside of these walls. The room starts to glow with a golden warmth. I don't want to leave her, but the porthole between our worlds closes up.

*   *   *

I hear the words, 'She is why you are doing *this*, never forget that.' I nod. In tears, knowing more than ever that '*this*' isn't over, not by a long shot.

'Give her the voice she wasn't allowed to have.'

I promise I will.

And as the highway in front of me comes back into focus, I know that *everything* that I have done, all the groups that I have lived in, the moments of madness, of danger, have been leading me back to here.

Back to her.

I have been looking for answers and every place that I have visited has given me something, has taught me more about myself, about why my parents did what they did. Every single experience has added to my understanding. And yet I wonder, have I given this little girl the voice that she needed? That girl who went through so much. I know that a part of my promise was to tell the world for her. It's why I am on this journey. But a bigger piece and a scarier one is facing my parents. Not giving them a platform to gaslight me like before, but talking to them on *her* behalf – no revisioning, just my truth.

After joining ten groups, travelling through thousands upon thousands of miles of American roads, challenging myself and cult leaders, I realise I have to go back to the thing that I am perhaps most afraid of.

My parents.

CHAPTER 20

Everything: 19 Years After

And suddenly, they appear: with the power of a magnetic pull, my parents come to me: *'It's your dad, we are in the UK.'*

My world around the text message goes out of focus.

We haven't spoken in nearly three years – since the night of 'the interview'.

Is it the laws of attraction? Some cosmic force? When you 'think a thing' it happens? I have only been back home for a few weeks. I thought I would have more time to settle into 'normal life' before facing them.

I am not ready yet, not this quickly.

I am back in my flat in London. The first week home, I wake up confused, my sheets and room unfamiliar, quietly startled that I am not in the middle of a religious commune, a farmhouse or the Towers in Chicago. I take long walks in my local park, thinking about the friends I made, the things that I have learned and the kids that I left behind. I have been doing wonderful, ordinary things since I've been back: boiled eggs and buttery toast for breakfast, paid work, drinking endless cups of tea, watching movies on my laptop in bed with my cat Grayson until the early hours of the morning.

Seeing people that I love and have missed: Kate, my brothers Josh and Sam. I spend my Sundays in pubs, telling tales of my trip – and failing – because I can't do it justice. I look in the mirror often: can I see the miles I have travelled on my skin? The same shapes create the familiar outline of me, but so much has changed.

Patting my belly, I wonder if I can be bothered to shift the pounds I mysteriously put on while we were on the road. My eye falls to the bad tattoos I got on my fingers before we boarded the flight home. Inked into my skin as a memento of the trip, as if I could ever forget, these smudged shapes are as permanent as the memories will be.

And then this text from my parents shakes everything: all things, all moments, leading up to now. The message burrows its way into the pit of my stomach. Sometimes I can go a whole month feeling disconnected from the blood, guts and flesh that carry me around, then something happens that pokes a finger to remind me that we are one, my soul is linked to my belly, my emotions linked to the tremor in my fingers, my thoughts linked to the tightening of my throat.

My phone goes again.

Christ! Them again?

But it's Paz.

'You around later? I've got something for you,' he says.

Paz has been filming in Africa and I haven't seen him since I got back. Again, my stomach twists, but this time for different reasons.

'I'm in . . . Come over anytime.'

*   *   *

I flick my phone onto 'Silent' and toss it across the room.

I need everything back in focus.

I *know* I need to see my parents. I know that it's the logical, maybe even the spiritual, next step. But there is also a part of me that just doesn't want to, that would love to delete this message and idea with a bottle of strong liquid.

And then there is the little girl in me, who is still terrified of her dad.

I want to be prepped – I want to plan it, to write out what I want to say. But I need what I say to come from the heart. I run scenarios through my head, all the ways it could go wrong. It's difficult for me to keep it real when it comes to speaking the truth; when the stakes are high in a conversation, my tendency to freeze, go into a 'story' or become someone else becomes high too.

When the stakes are high is when I can lose myself.

I pace around my kitchen, rubbing my arms trying to get warm, but the chill comes from the inside: What is it that I want to say? What do I *really* want to say to them?

I pick up my pen and I write:

This journey has been about seeking truth and freedom.

It has wrenched me from myself, pulled me out of the corners I hid in, torn me away from my bullshit. It's ripped off the false selves I created, and even though I want to claw them back, put them back on for comfort and warmth.

I need to be able to do this – speak the truth – in front of the two people that have hurt me more than anyone else in the world.

I write in handwriting so agitated, I know I will never be able to read it.

I don't expect closure, I don't even know what 'closure' looks like, but I have to keep my promise to myself. If I can walk away from them, knowing I did what I needed to do for myself, then maybe that will be enough.

I write till my fingers feel like claws, disconnected; I write till the ink flowing out of my pen feels like the bile in my throat. And as I write, I realise that this might be the last time that I ever speak to my parents.

An unexpected sadness fills me. Maybe the little girl in me is still hanging on to the idea of parental love. Maybe there's a part of me that still, even now, wants them to be proud of me. But, if telling my parents how I feel makes this the last time we see each other, I realise that will have to be OK.

And with that realisation comes a quiet peace.

* * *

It's 11pm when the doorbell rings. Paz's familiar silhouette is traced by light coming through the glass of my front door from the street. An almost embarrassing keenness pushes me off the sofa as I run to let him in.

There is always a change in the energy when Paz enters a room. He fills every space with a high frequency, joy, positivity and sometimes loud noises. Tonight, he walks in and the whole house seems to glow, maybe even pulse. He pulls me in for a hug, long and deep. I resist for a second and then sink into it, losing myself in the clean fresh smell he wears around his neck.

'Beer?' I pull away.

'Sure,' he says.

We sit on the bench in the kitchen. My cat Grayson jumps on his lap and starts rubbing himself shamelessly all over him.

'Cheers.' He winks, half saying it to Grayson, who is splayed out like a rotisserie chicken across his knees.

'So, how was Africa?' I ask.

'Clammy,' he says.

I laugh.

'Every day was a rumble punch,' he adds.

He tells me about his adventures in Kenya, Cameroon, Nigeria and Ghana. Blind footballers, abject poverty, hot, wet nights, the negotiations, the bribery, the bodyguard who went everywhere with him, an ancient revolver stuffed in her purse, the food that gave him dysentery – 'Well, whatever you caught, you look fucking great!' I laugh.

He does look great, though.

We talk about the trip across America. It's comforting that I don't need to explain things. While he might not have *physically* been there, he was with me on the ride into Tennessee, he was by my side in Alabama, he was my guardian across the Atlantic. He spotted the surveillance van from thousands of miles away, he held me through the journey.

His voice goes a little quiet as he says, 'There was a point at the end that I was a bit worried about you.' I feel his warm hand on top of mine.

'And . . .' I slip my hand out to take a pull of my beer. 'It's not over.'

'Go on,' he says.

'My parents are in town.'

He shoots me a look loaded with concern.

'I know, I know, but it will be different this time . . . things are different,' I say.

My body shudders as I'm transported back to the night where he fed me whisky as I sat catatonic, destroyed at seeing my parents. The night he told me that it was clear that I hadn't forgiven them.

Maybe he is remembering that night too.

Then he sits up straight, almost business-like: 'When's the showdown?' His expression has changed. Perhaps it's the look of a person who is weary of trying to protect someone they care about.

'Tomorrow, in Margate,' I say.

He inhales sharply. I try to read his face: does he want to come with me? Does he feel like he *should* offer to? I feel a need to have him by my side but I sense that he can't hold me through this next part. He pulls out his bag: 'Well, you will be needing this then,' he says as he places a red checked blanket in my lap.

'It's a women's Masai warrior blanket.'

The blanket is heavier than it looks, blue threads run through its rough texture. I trace the squares as I hold it.

'I got it for you because, well, I thought you would like it, but now maybe it's for your protection . . . or maybe because you are a warrior.'

He smiles, but his eyes are serious.

My eyes mist.

Don't say a word.

I don't want to reveal the slab of emotion stuck in my throat at both the kindness of this gift and the thought of the battle ahead.

'It's getting late, I'm going leave you to it,' he says.

As he gets up to go, Paz turns and hugs me: 'You're going to be OK. You know that, right?'

I nod.

'You got this,' he says into my hair.

I look up at him for reassurance. And then, he kisses me.

*   *   *

The drive to Margate snakes through the countryside. It's early in the morning, grey and wet. There is a slight chill in the air, something that was rare on the American road. The blanket Paz gave me sits on my lap and I keep touching its rough edge. My breath clouds the window as I give in, wrapping the mantle round my shoulders against the cold air. Although the vista is wildly different, being back on the road feels like I never left the highway.

Maybe this is just another mile of the same journey.

Maybe this was always where I was headed. I don't feel nervous anymore, it feels right.

I love that moment on a trip when the sea suddenly appears in the distance, floating above the land, licking the sky. I crack the window, taste the salt in the air – it wakes me up as it whips in. I pass by the spot where the Vikings invaded, the beach is right near where my dad was born. I remember him telling us that we were descended from the Norse warriors when we were kids. I don't know if it's true, but it led to a whole year of us playing Vikings in secret, bashing the crap out of each other and speaking in bizarre accents. I try to imagine him growing up on these shores, in this clear, salty air.

Did he play on these beaches pretending to be a Viking as a child? Would he escape here when things got too hard with his own violent father?

I pull up to the spot we said we would meet at, right on the seafront. I wait, watching the skies. A clap of lightning cracks across the sea. Thunder rumbles. The clouds have moved in quickly, heavily pregnant and ready to burst. The storm is rapid, there are explosions across the sky. Big raindrops hit the windscreen like angry punches that are trying to break the glass, trying to get inside. Then, abruptly, it stops.

I get out of the car, feeling strong and ready.

I scan the road waiting for *them.*

This is it, this is the time.

We are not fucking around now.

I see my mom first and when I see her, I am shaken up. Her hair is wet from the rain, her fringe sticks to her forehead. She looks yellow, her eyes are wet – like she's been crying – but I realise they are bulbous, murky with illness.

She makes her way towards me.

'Hello, Bexy,' she says.

I don't recognise her voice. It's a cracked, raw, difficult whisper. A surge of emotion, that old, deep need and desire to protect her, to look after her, fills me again.

I am completely unprepared for this.

When I see him, I wake up from my empathetic haze. They are both wrapped up in too many clothes for this temperature: scarves, pullovers, coats. Their tanned faces give them away as outsiders – leathery textured and liver spots where the African sun has marked its stay on their skin.

'How are you?' I say as I touch my mom's dehydrated hand. The question is directed at her.

'I'm not sure . . . we can't figure out what's wrong with me,' she whispers. 'It's one of the reasons we are here so I can get tested.' She seems defeated, wearing her illness with resignation. Like it may now just be a part of her. The memory of the dreams she told me about a few months back flood into focus: *she died and none of her children went to her funeral.*

My dad talks over her, his loud voice booming: 'There are a number of things that this could be linked to . . . It could be her liver, an infection . . .' He fades into the background of my thoughts.

We walk together on the seafront. I want to be close to the sea – I need its power, the magnetic pull of the tide gives me strength.

Come on, Cameron, you can do this.

It's now or never.

We sit on the seafront, facing the clouds that now drift apart. I wait for a breath and then say, 'So, the last time we met, I wanted to talk to you about our group and how I grew up . . .'

'I know you were making a documentary,' my dad says, throwing me off for a moment.

'Well, I want to talk to you again . . .' I continue.

'Well, as you know, we have been interviewed by the BBC and hundreds of newspapers and channels, so of course we can be interviewed . . .'

My dad seems to be playing a part again. It feels like a trap that I cannot afford to fall into.

Not this time.

I interrupt him: 'Well, seeing you last time left me pretty messed up for a while. I realised that it's because I never actually told you how I really felt. I realised that if I couldn't stand in front of you two and be honest, then maybe I can never really be free of all the . . . stuff . . . that growing up in the group left me with. If I can't tell you, maybe I can never *really* forgive you.'

My dad looks at me, maybe with defensiveness, maybe cynicism. Mom leans in as if she hasn't heard me right, or is she trying to show me I have her attention?

Dad takes in a breath, about to say something. 'I would like it—'

But I cut him off: 'I would appreciate it if you would just let me speak and you two just listen . . . Is that OK?'

My dad shifts back.

Is this a defence move or is he ready to attack?

I go on: 'I don't want to get into arguments about what did or didn't happen. Or for you to feel like you need to defend, yourselves, or *them.*'

They sit together. There's barely any distance between us – I could reach out and touch them if I wanted.

'Because my experience is exactly that: *mine.* And it cannot be argued with.'

They nod obediently.

I look out at the sea for a second, take a breath and start.

'Growing up, I feel like I split into two little girls. One acted how I needed to on the outside to survive, the other one was who I really was on the inside, in a battle to stay sane and safe. I felt completely controlled, unable to be myself, unable to say what I thought, what I needed.'

I picture that girl now – her brave efforts to keep herself safe, the tactics she used to stop herself from going mad. Small, resilient, without a voice.

Now is the time to give it to her.

'The group forced me to betray the other children, my friends, daily. I felt that, at times, you allowed *them* to tear up the thing that I held most precious and desperately needed: my family, isolating me from my brothers and sisters, my life.'

My dad is completely still, like he's been cast in stone. Mom holds his hand.

I see the little girl I was in full focus, full colour. Frizzy hair waving in the wind. She is willing me to go on, giving me some of the strength that she had as a ten-year-old to get through *that* year.

'And the worst year of my life was the year that I was on Silence Restriction. I felt completely invisible. And I felt like I was losing my mind, unravelling and going mad. I would lie on the bed, desperately trying to hold on to my sanity and I was just a kid. And the fact that you don't seem to believe me that this went on for 11 months just makes me feel that you knew very little about what was going on with your daughter, me. But I lived every day of that.'

This seafront is still empty, cleared by the storm, but out of the corner of my eye, I can see the teenage me. The girl that ended up in that train station, alone with a suitcase, who desperately wanted to be an adult but was clearly still a child.

'I want you to know how deeply damaging and scary it was for me as a kid to think that I would never grow up because I would die in the Armageddon, that I would not have a future.

That I would never get to grow up into the adult that you see here now.'

I have often feared the vision of myself as a teenager. She was angry and at times I didn't feel she was as worthy of love as me as a child. I haven't carried the same compassion for her as the ten-year-old I have grown to love. But she, in her awkwardness, her defiance and deep insecurity, is here now too, waiting to be heard.

'It was so terrifying and confusing to then *actually* grow up as a teenager and have to deal with, and survive, in a world that I was completely unprepared for.'

She stands here, the girl who battled for survival, who yearned for love and connection. The one who lied, stole and clawed her way into a new existence.

'I didn't know how to deal with that and some really bad things happened after I left because of it.'

We are all here now, together; all the versions of me that need to be heard standing together in my parents' presence.

'As an adult, one of the biggest things I struggle with is how you defended a group that we know abused children.'

I feel the power of all of us now, of me at every age, of every bit of strength I have ever had. I am so grateful to that kid who got through that time, I am grateful for what that teenager had to deal with, grateful for the resilience she had to get through it.

'What I needed from you, but never got was the freedom to be myself. I needed to feel that you were on my side. I needed to feel protection from the group and the other abusive adults within it. I needed you to put me first. Even if it was just once. I needed you to admit the truth about our group, instead of protecting it. It goes so much further than me and my siblings. That is something that you owe to a generation of kids from the Children of God, whose voices were never heard.'

The air has been cleansed; the storm cleared it out. I look my mom directly in the eye and my gaze doesn't waver as I say, 'What I *want* to forgive you for some day is the lies, the betrayal, the lack of protection. For not leaving the group when the leader was unstable and dangerous. For being the public face and protectors of the group. For raising my brothers and sisters in a toxic and dangerous environment.'

I look at my dad, who still hasn't moved, and I say, 'I want you to know that I now have a life that I never, ever dreamed was possible as a kid. I have happiness and joy beyond my wildest imaginations. And I have all that, in this world which you raised me to be separate from and to fear. I have the real connections that I craved so much as a child. I have my brothers and sisters that you gave me and they are my world.'

The other versions of me fade. Now, it's just the three of us: me, my mom and my dad.

My mom cried. My dad still hasn't moved, he's barely blinked. The stillness between us is filled only by the sound of the ocean.

Mom whispers, 'What can we do? How can we heal our family? We want to be a family again.'

'The sad thing is, seeing you two is a reminder of everything we want to forget.'

'We are sorry,' she says.

*　　*　　*

As I walk away, the air is light as it fills my chest. I feel a sense of euphoria, a real rush of the stuff. A very real, clean high – the kind of feeling I had hoped for when I first tried to forgive them, years ago.

I have been told by religion, therapy, society, films, God Himself that forgiveness is the only way to find peace and that it's a gift. But really the gift I needed was one I had to give myself: standing here today, honouring the truth.

My journey to finding peace with my past has had less to do with forgiveness and more to do with going from being the victim of my childhood to parenting myself, holding my own hand and spending my life with people who really love me. It lies in processing the anger within me with the ferocity of a lioness and creating something meaningful from the childhood I was given.

So, I could let go.

I am now grateful for my childhood, because I am free of it – I can love it, I can laugh about it, I can share it, I can learn from it. My identity is not about what was 'done to me'. Who I am did not start, nor end, with being born into a cult. I respect what I withstood, at every age, when I was in that world. But I will be damned if I would let another child go through that.

And while I can let go, for myself, when it comes to the injustices that are done to other children, I know that it's *not* my place to let go, forgive or forget. It might be my place, my responsibility to shine a light, to demand that it does not happen again; that the violation of children's human rights are not a part of any parent's *right* to freedom of religion.

Because, we, the children of yesterday, are the guardians of today's kids.

*　　*　　*

I walk away from the spot where my parents sit, so far away that they become dots in the distance, and then disappear completely. My parents who pay for their decisions every day, whether they realise it or not, by missing out on the children that they created. In their longing for connection with a religious group, they will never experience the connection that we have with each other. In their need for purpose, they have lost the purpose of being parents. In their spiritual quest, they lost the love of family.

I walk, and I think of my family, my pack, the ones they gave me, and the ones I chose. My brother Josh, who is one of the funniest and most loving men I know. My brother Sam, who is generous, kind and mischievous. The strength of my little sisters. The older ones who became parents, the ones who have struggled (we all have) and the ones who have flourished. The family that I chose: my friends Sofi, Maria and the other incredible, fierce women that I have surrounding me. I walk past a spot on this seafront in Margate that in a few years will be where Maria makes a home, where Paz and I will celebrate getting engaged, where this book will be written and where Maria and I fulfil the promise we made on the day they sent Maria away.

That 'one day we will live together'.

I stand and I look out onto the beautiful, unpredictable sea, knowing the reasons behind this journey have been as changeable as these waters: sometimes calm and collected as if it was research, sometimes wild and dangerous, as if I was seeking out trauma. Sometimes the driving force was deep and dark and angry, with a vicious undercurrent that I couldn't control. Sometimes it has shone with perspective because I was on the journey to understanding. Sometimes it dragged me under and I nearly drowned.

Today, it's grey and glistens.

Today, it's calm and peaceful.

And today, I can rest, because I have told you just *about* everything.

Acknowledgements

Nike thank you for being adventurous, and mad enough, to journey around the states with me, WWFIO forever my shuuuzen. To Seb and Georgia, for the (almost) wholesome journey that was to follow.

Thank you to every kid on this journey who showed me how to gut fish, milk goats, herd sheep and ride horses. To the ones who showed me their hiding places and the spots they played; told me their dreams, fears and stories; and spent their time with me, thank you. I will be forever changed by you.

Paz, for producing me, encouraging me, feeding me. This would be a pipe dream without you. You, me and the stars.

Maria, from that first 'whisper in the dark', to being my soul-mate, to collaborating on covers, taglines, visual memories, to being brave enough to wade back into the murk of our child-hood with me (I know that wasn't easy). My blood is your blood.

To my sisters: Kate you read every page, advised me and sharpened my memory; Checca you brutally and brilliantly, edited my words, and to all three of you girls for lifting me when this all got a bit too much. I thank you. To my broth-ers, thank you for your support and ridiculousness, you have my heart.

Toby Jones, who would have thought a pissed-up conversation waiting for a night bus in Soho would (eventually) lead me to Marilia Savvides who coaxed, pushed, and encouraged this book out of me? Marilia you got me through some pretty shady bits, and constantly told my 'dark side' that I could write – without you my words never would have made it to the page.

To Susannah Otter, my editor, thank you for seeing something in that rough first draft and getting this book to where it is today. It's A THING! And to the whole of Bonnier Books for believing in me enough to put your fantastic team and your time into the words on these pages.

Dakota Johnson, Ro Donelly and Riley Keogh, from our first conversation which felt like group therapy because there was no-fucking-around-with-niceties-straight-to-the-deep-stuff magic, thank you for believing in this story enough to pull it into your creative world.

Annabel Jones – my beautiful guinea pig, your advice, encouragement, and being on the end of the phone during this process was a godsend. Julia Nightingale – the Patsy to my Edwina, for writing, rewriting, collaborating with me. Selina Barker – my constant cheerleader, everyone deserves one of you (but you are mine). To the 'Celebration-Sisters' – my Sheros, a constant source of divine-badass-shitkicking feminine power. To Cliff Taylor – for our Tucson adventure, you are one a bajillion. To Jaimie Prater – for sharing your time and story with me, I am humbled. I hope I did you proud. I am forever grateful to every child, teenager, and in-between that shared their story with me in every group I stayed with on this journey.

Eternal gratitude to Walter Schwartz (RIP). Who knows what would have happened without that 'one simple question'.